Gene Daly

OLD VIRGINIA HOUSES

THE MOBJACK BAY COUNTRY

& ALONG THE JAMES

COMBINED EDITION—TWO VOLUMES IN ONE

OLD VIRGINIA HOUSES

THE MOBJACK BAY COUNTRY
& ALONG THE JAMES

COMBINED EDITION—TWO VOLUMES IN ONE

BY

EMMIE FERGUSON FARRAR

ILLUSTRATED WITH PHOTOGRAPHS BY

HARRY BAGBY & OTHERS

AMERICAN LEGACY PRESS
NEW YORK

Old Virginia Houses

THE MOBJACK BAY COUNTRY

BY

EMMIE FERGUSON FARRAR

ILLUSTRATED WITH PHOTOGRAPHS BY
HARRY BAGBY & OTHERS

CONTENTS

ILLUSTRATIONS

ILLUSTRATIONS

FOREWORD

WITH the reawakening throughout the country in Colonial Architecture, thousands of tourists each year make pilgrimages to the old homes of Virginia. Nowhere in America is there to be seen a greater exhibition of Colonial Architecture, of English origin, than in Tidewater Virginia.

Tidewater Virginia is just what the term implies. It is all that territory of Virginia contiguous to the Chesapeake Bay and its estuaries. In it the English made their first permanent settlement in America. Here, from the crudest pioneer conditions flowered a civilization that assembled the first representative legislative body on the American Continent. It was in that cradle of democracy that trial by jury was first instituted, on the narrow peninsula between the James and York Rivers.

British dominion in the United States had its beginning at Jamestown only twelve miles from where it ended at Yorktown. Physically this region is little changed since the "Golden Age," or half-century preceding the American Revolution. It has continued consistently pastoral, a haven from hurry and standardization of twentieth century life. There is still Arcadian simplicity in this land of water.

The old houses dealt with in this book are located in Gloucester and Mathews Counties, in the heart of Tidewater Virginia. These counties are not matched elsewhere in number and variety of old houses in various stages of survival or restoration.

The very isolation of this region where communication was once almost solely by water has spared many of its fine old houses the destruction that progress would have brought them.

Among the glories of Gloucester and Mathews today, are numerous surviving mansions that were owned and occupied by celebrated personages, or were the scenes of historic events which greatly influenced our national character and institutions.

This region affords the student of Colonial Architecture a great opportunity to study the development of the early house, from the medieval cottage of one room and loft, to the great Georgian mansion, symbol of eighteenth-century living.

Time and again attempts have been made to simplify the subject of old houses for the benefit of the layman, with disastrous results. Where romance and tradition are concerned many people respond to their emotions rather than their intellect.

The pioneer student of Colonial Architecture, of a generation ago, assumed that when the seventeenth century was over, the colonists graduated suddenly from the straw thatched huts of Jamestown and Henrico City to the great plantation manors of Westover and Rosewell. These great houses were developed, not invented.

Only in the last quarter of a century has any patient or prolonged study been given to the transitional examples that form a missing link between the medieval and classical styles.

It might be said that the medieval period in Virginia architecture began with the landing of the first settlers at Jamestown in 1607, and ended with the building of the Governor's Palace at Williamsburg in 1706. The building of the Governor's Palace in 1706 marked the beginning of Georgian Architecture in Virginia, which is divided into three periods: Early Georgian 1706 to 1750, Mid-Georgian 1750 to 1765, Late Georgian 1765 to 1776.

It is true that most of the houses built during the Seventeenth Century have disappeared, taken in the toll of time, fire and the elements. Nevertheless, traces and documents and credible tradition make possible a good general idea of the evolution of the early house.

Under the Civil Works Administration in 1933, a great number of unemployed architects and draftsmen supplied a highly trained personnel, fitted by antiquarian interest and architectural experience to make a survey of Historic American Buildings.

When several hundred photographs and floor plans of many kinds of structures were gathered together over a period of years, we came unexpectedly and very much by accident upon the subject of the transition which comprises a new chapter in the history of American Architecture.

The transition is a development in architecture which may be summed up as follows: A step toward the Georgian goal of more space, more balance and more formality; a period of experimental stepping stones toward more elegance and gracious living which marked the eighteenth century.

xiv

FOREWORD

In attempting to establish the age of any old house, one has to discover what changes have been made in the course of the years in its structure, and when. This is often difficult to do, in many instances almost impossible, and therefore we have to rely on analogy and deduction. All houses cannot be dated from the fact that they have the same features as houses of known dates, even in the same general locality, as there were "carry overs" (so to speak) where styles persisted long after they were supposed to have ended.

The author has made no attempt to establish the date of origin on the old houses in this book by their structural features, but only through surviving documents and credible tradition. It is well written in simple everyday language from the viewpoint of the layman, and contains much information not available elsewhere. It is copiously illustrated with rare photographs whose subjects in many instances disappeared more than a half-century ago.

JOHN FRANCIS SPEIGHT

APPRECIATION

IN the preparation of the manuscript for this book, I wish to express appreciation, first of all to Nina Taliaferro Sanders, (Mrs. H. O. Sanders), who knows and loves the "Mobjack Bay Country" as no one else does, and who gives so freely, with love and enthusiasm:

To the late Dr. Douglas Southall Freeman, who encouraged me in my work for almost a quarter of a century.

To Dr. Gertrude R. B. Richards, who is experienced in research, possibly more thoroughly, than any scholar now living, and who has given of that knowledge so freely;

To Mr. and Mrs. Webster S. Rhoads, Jr., of Elmington, for lending unpublished manuscripts and pictures, and for bringing me in contact with Mrs. Sanders;

To Mr. and Mrs. William Ingles, of White Marsh, who gave much information;

To Dr. and Mrs. H. Page Mauck, of Richmond and Gloucester, who so kindly checked much data, and gave much information;

To Miss Dahlia Callis, of the Mathews Public Library, who gave much information;

To Mr. and Mrs. Wesley C. Morck, of Belleville;

To Mr. and Mrs. Theodore Pratt, of Little England;

To Mr. and Mrs. Gordon Bolitho, of Toddsbury;

To Major and Mrs. Jeffrey Montague, of Lowland Cottage;

To Mr. and Mrs. F. Higginson Cabot, of Green Plains;

To Mr. and Mrs. A. P. Blood, of Auburn;

To Mr. and Mrs. Hope Norton, of Hopemont;

To Mr. and Mrs. E. Stewart James, of Cappahosic House;

To Mr. and Mrs. Chandler Bates, of Airville;

To General and Mrs. R. E. Starr, of Starr Lynn;

To Mr. and Mrs. E. Wright Noble, of Church Hill;

To Mr. and Mrs. George Kirkmeyer, of Kingston Hall;

To Miss Eleanor Perrin, of Goshen;

To Mrs. George Upton, of Poplar Grove;

To Mr. and Mrs. Matthew Fontaine Werth, of Dunham Massie;

To Colonel and Mrs. John Holcombe, of Newstead;

To Mr. and Mrs. William Ashby Jones III, of Ditchly;

To Mr. and Mrs. Stanley Crockett, of Warner Hall;

To Mr. and Mrs. John Maxwell, of Hesse;

To Mr. and Mrs. J. W. C. Cattlett, of Timberneck;

To Dr. George Carneal, of Eagle Point;

To Mr. and Mrs. James Ervin, of Sherwood;

To Mr. and Mrs. George Cunningham, of White Hall;

To The Wellfords, of Glen Roy;

To The Masons, of Wareham;

To The Dabneys, of Exchange;

To The Janneys, of Roaring Springs;

To The Pages, of Shelly;

To Dr. and Mrs. H. E. Thomas, of Gloucester;

To Mrs. Alfred Bell, of Gloucester;

To The Moormans, of Midlothian;

To The Hutchesons, of Fiddler's Green;

To The Kings, of Pig Hill;

To Major and Mrs. W. Milner Gibson, of Colraine;

To Mr. and Mrs. John Warren Cooke, of Mathews;

To Mary K. Spotswood, (Mrs. J. B. Spotswood), of Wicomico, Gloucester County.

Also:

To Mr. Paul Titlow, Editor of the Gloucester-Mathews Gazette Journal;

To the staff of Richmond Newspapers, Inc., especially Mrs. Marjorie Burrell Gratiot and Mr. Earl Jones;

To the staff of the Virginia State Library, especially Eudora Elizabeth Thomas, Bertie Craig Smith, (Mrs. Pinckney A. Smith), Milton C. Russell, and Martha Winfrey;

APPRECIATION

To the staff of the Richmond Public Library, especially Katherine Throckmorton Taylor, (Mrs. Lewis Taylor), Mary Meacham Gilliam, and Margaret Beauchamp;

To the staff of the Library of Congress, in Washington;

To the staff of the Virginia Historical Society;

To the staff of the Virginia State Chamber of Commerce;

To the staff of the Chamber of Commerce of Charleston, South Carolina;

To Nell Carneal Drew, of Lansdowne;

To The Frary Brothers, who own the Shelter;

To Lloyd N. Emory, of Waverly;

To Mr. and Mrs. John L. Lewis, Jr., of Williamsburg, Mrs. F. Snowden Hopkins, of Gloucester, Mr. and Mrs. Catesby G. Jones, of Gloucester, and Miss Mary Kemp, of Richmond;

To the staff of the Book Shop at Miller and Rhoads, Inc., especially Miss Elizabeth O'Neill;

To Miss Lucy Throckmorton, Librarian at the University of Richmond.

Also:

To Ruth Nelson Robins Gordon, (Mrs. Thomas C. Gordon); Janie Schoen Venable, (Mrs. A. Reid Venable); Parke Rouse; John Francis Speight; P. Franklin Tuck; Cornelia Scott Tuck; Franklin Farrar; Virginius Dabney; George Scheer; Marie Sowers; Emma Craddock; Grace Branch; Jane Spence; Bessie Crumpler; Elizabeth Crone Pitts; Mary Cabell Crenshaw; Mr. and Mrs. Lee Hines, Jr.; Mr. and Mrs. Harry Fleshman; Mr. and Mrs. Nimrod Ferguson; Mr. and Mrs. John J. Farrar; Mrs. Huestis Cook; Mr. and Mrs. Theodore R. Martin; Mr. and Mrs. Ellis Berry; Mr. and Mrs. Thomas Hubbard; Clifford Dowdey; Miss Etta Munford; William E. Ellyson, Jr.; Mrs. Fred Brown; Emily Major; Miss Hardy; Susan Seddon Taliaferro Wellford Marshall (Mrs. Thomas R. Marshall); Mr. and Mrs. Beverley Randolph Wellford Marshall; Mr. and Mrs. Laurel Barnett Boyd; Francis Edward Jarvis; Clara Sharpe; Marian Canfield; Annie Hayes O'Neil; The Lane Studio; Harry and Marie Bagby (who take such beautiful photographs), and especially to Teddy Martin, Jr., Franklin Martin, and Martha Lynn Berry.

INTRODUCTION

IN the new Rand-McNally Atlas, the Map of Virginia shows the entire area of the Mobjack Bay country as covering a space about an inch square. In our treatment of "Old Virginia Houses," which in its entirety will cover the state, we are devoting one-sixth of our time, work and space to this square inch. This is because as an area of early homes, there is no other vicinity that surpasses this section in the number of old houses, or in the continuity of years of occupancy. Here we find history and legend. And it was from here that the frontiers of the state and nation were rolled back.

The Mobjack Bay country consists of the counties of Gloucester and Mathews, whose shores are deeply indented with that arm of the Chesapeake known as the Mobjack Bay, and its four estuaries, the Severn, the Ware, the North and the East Rivers. On the south the borders of the land are washed by the waters of the York, and on the east the vista of vision is lost in distance over the blue Chesapeake itself.

It is certain that in tradition, beauty and glamour, there is no part of the Old Dominion that surpasses this area.

It was here that the ancestors of "The Father of His Country" lived, died and lie buried. It was here, also, that the ancestors of a good percentage of that great company, known as Mr. and Mrs. America, lived and died—or went west.

Many authorities agree that there is not a state in the Union, hardly a city, town or county, that does not have some inhabitant who can truthfully say, "One of my ancestors came from Gloucester County in Virginia." (Mathews was originally a part of Gloucester). No wonder tourists come every year, from all over the country. It is simply a case of returning to the land of their fathers.

Hospitality is a grace that has not been forgotten. Most of the porticoed old mansions have two fronts, so they seem to extend a welcome to the traveler, whether he approaches by water or by land.

The old churches stand open, so the wayfarer may enter and kneel, if he feels so inclined.

This is truly the "Magnolia-Honeysuckle South," a land of roses, of moonlight on the water; of sunny gardens, shady lawns, enormous box; of "noble bays, broad rivers and tall trees;" a "Land of Life Worth Living."

In the halls of the old houses, one hears in fancy the soft strains of violins, the swish of silks, the staccato rhythm of military boots accentuating the flutter of tiny slippers.

With all the romantic beauty and traditional charm of this part of the state, there is one sad thing, one grim thing, that impresses us, grieves us, and tears our hearts, as we go from family burying-ground to quiet church-yard. On almost all the old tombs, there is so little span, too little span, between dates of birth and death. A girl "of greatest beauty, gentlest spirit, and quiet demeanor" would have lived, loved, been married, have borne several children, died and been buried, all before she had passed her early twenties.

Many little children, sometimes several in one family, would have died at tender ages. Men would have served in His Majesty's Council, or the House of Burgesses; built homes, married two wives, raised large families, built houses for their sons, yet died before fifty.

All this tells the tragic story of the lack of medical care, of pestilence, or other misfortunes, which harried the early settlers.

Destiny, however, keeps an even balance, or sometimes presses down a measure for posterity. So, perhaps to compensate for her grim record of early deaths shown by the dates on the old tombstones, Gloucester has evened up matters by giving the world a man whose work has saved thousands of lives, Walter Reed, who discovered the cause of yellow fever. His birthplace is now a shrine not far from Belroi.

HISTORY

WHEN the three little boats, the Sarah Constant, the Goodspeed, and the Discovery tied up to the trees at Jamestown that day in May, 1607, and the first English settlers of the new world stepped ashore, to fall on their knees in thanks to God, already the gardens and fields of what is now Gloucester County were planted with the food crops that would sustain these settlers, and prevent their starvation.

At Werowocomoco, north of the York, about twenty-five miles from the confluence of the Mattaponi and the Pamunkey, and in all probability on the site of Shelly, was the seat of the great King Powhatan, who became the ancestor of many prominent Virginians of the white race through the marriage of his daughter, the Princess Pocahontas, to John Rolfe.

It was to Werowocomoco that John Smith was taken as a prisoner, and where he was about to be killed, when, in one of the most dramatic episodes of history, his life was saved by Pocahontas. It was to this place that Smith sent the Dutch to build the wooden house with the marl chimney for Powhatan.

Here Powhatan was crowned by the English, this being the only occasion of the crowning of a king in Virginia, or in the United States, for that matter.

John Ratcliff and a party of thirty went to Werowocomoco in 1609, to negotiate for food. He was not as fortunate as Smith. He and all but two of the party were killed. One was saved by Pocahontas, and the other escaped into the forest.

Sir Thomas Dale burned Werowocomoco in 1612.

There have been many conjectures as to the name of Mobjack. There is a story that, when the sailors called out over the waters of the Bay, the echo would come back from the thick forests along the shore. They said the Bay would mock Jack (the sailor). Then "Mobjack" probably was a corruption of "Mock Jack."

It is not easy to get a continuity of history in Gloucester, for the records have been destroyed three times: first, at the time of Bacon's Rebellion, and the burning of Jamestown in 1676; second, when the Clerk's Office burned in 1820; and third, on the occasion of the evacuation and burning of Richmond in 1865, where the records had been sent for safe-keeping.

In 1634 Virginia was divided into eight shires, the Pamaunkee Shire including the Mobjack Bay country. Then in 1652, the shires were divided into counties, Charles River County including Mobjack.

Owing to the danger from Indians, witness the terrible massacres of 1622 and 1644, there had not been during this early period a great deal of expansion of settlement, but after a treaty with the beloved Necotowance, who had succeeded the cruel Opecancanough, there was never any more widespread trouble with the Indians in Tidewater Virginia. This treaty was made on the fifth of October, 1646, and permitted the Indians to live and hunt on the north side of the York. While there had been many hunting expeditions and temporary camps made by the whites in the Mobjack Bay area, and land grants had been made to some, it was not until 1649 that Gloucester was really opened to the public for settlement. It is probable that the parish churches were organized very soon after this.

From the records in Richmond which were copied from the English Public Record Office, we find that the earliest land grant was in 1635, to Augustine Warner. In 1642 Thomas Curtis, John Jones, Hugh Gwynne and Richard Wyatt took up tracts; James Whiting, in 1643; John Robins, in 1645; Thomas Seawell in 1646; Lewis Burwell and George Reade in 1648; Richard Kemp and Francis Willis in 1649; John Smith, Henry Singleton and William Armistead in 1650; John Page and Thomas Todd in 1653.

Later on came James Rowe, John Thomas, Robert Taliaferro, William Wyatt, William Haywood, Henry Corbell, Anne Bernard, John Lewis, Thomas Graves, Lawrence Smith, John Chapman, George Billups, Charles Roane, William Thornton, Thomas Walker, John Buckner, Philip Lightfoot, William Humphrey, John Tompkins, Robert Peyton, John Fox, Ben Clements, Symond Stubblefield, Robert Pryor, Peter Beverley, John Stubbs, Mordecai Cooke, Humphrey Tabb.

A little later came Thrustons, Roots, Throckmortons, Nicolsons, Vanbibbers, Pages, Byrds, Corbins, Ennises, Dickens, Roys and Smarts.

Home building along the rivers, (for there were no roads), began in earnest, and it was then that the beginnings of houses now standing, or their predecessors on the same sites, were erected. Small houses were built, and later additions made. Still later, alterations, reconstructions and restorations have been undertaken. The houses of Gloucester of the 1950's have evolved through a period of three hundred years, and that evolution is a fascinating study.

Tyndall's Point, where Argoll Yeardley patented 4000 acres of land in 1640, began to be a town, which later was called Gloucester Towne (now Gloucester Point). As early as 1667 there was a fort there.

In 1676 Augustine Warner was Speaker of the House of Burgesses. It was also in 1676 that Bacon's Rebellion extended to the shores of this area, and the body of the leader now enriches the soil of Gloucester, or, perhaps, rests beneath the waters of the York.

Mr. Paul Titlow, Editor of the *Gloucester-Mathews Gazette-Journal* says of Gloucester, "Three wars have been fought on its lawns and fed from its fields." But the sons of Gloucester have fought in nine wars—if one includes the Korean engagement.

From 1607 to 1624 Virginia was ruled by Council (appointed by the London Company), with the House of Burgesses, and a Governor. From 1624 to 1776 Virginia was a Royal Province, ruled by the King's Council (the members of which were appointed by the King, after being recommended by the Governor), with the House of Burgesses and Governor. Many prominent members of the King's Council were from Gloucester. A large number of men from this county also served in the House of Burgesses.

Gloucester men who served on the King's Council were:

George Reade, 1657;
Augustine Warner, I, 1660;
John Pate, 1670;
Augustine Warner, II, of Warner Hall, 1677;
Matthew Kemp, 1681;
John Armistead, 1688;
Henry Whiting, 1690;
Matthew Page, of Timberneck, 1699;
Lewis Burwell, of Carter's Creek, 1702;
John Smith, 1704;
John Lewis, I, of Warner Hall, 1704;
Robert Porteus, of Newbottle, 1713;
Mann Page, of Rosewell, 1714;
Peter Beverley, 1719;
Lewis Burwell, of Carter's Creek, 1744;
John Lewis, II, of Warner Hall, 1748;
John Page, of North End, 1768;

John Page, II, of Rosewell, 1773.

Members of the House of Burgesses from Gloucester were:

Hugh Gwynne,		Nathaniel Burwell,	
Francis Willis,	1652	Ambrose Dudley,	1710;
Abraham Iversonn,		Peter Beverley,	
Richard Pate,	1653;	Ambrose Cooke,	1714;
Thomas Bremen,		Henry Willis,	
Wingfield Webb,	1654;	Thomas Buckner,	1718;
Thomas Ramsey,	1655-56;	Henry Willis,	
Lt. Col. Anthony Elliott,		Nathaniel Burwell,	1720-22;
Capt. Thomas Ramsey,	1657-58;	Giles Cook,	1722;
Capt. Francis Willis,		Giles Cook,	
Capt. Augustine Warner,	1658-59;	Henry Willis,	1723-26;
Capt. Francis Willis,		Francis Willis,	
Capt. Peter Jennings,		Lawrence Smith,	1727-36;
Peter Knight,		Beverley Whiting,	
David Cant,	1659-60;	Francis Willis,	1740;
Capt. Peter Jennings,		Beverley Whiting,	
Capt. Thomas Walker,	1663;	Lewis Burwell,	1742;
Ajt. Gen. Peter Jenyngs,		Beverley Whiting,	
Capt. Thomas Walker,	1666;	Samuel Buckner,	1744;
Col. John Armistead,	1685;	Beverley Whiting,	
Capt. James Ransom,		Francis Willis,	1745-49;
John Baylor,	1693;	Beverley Whiting,	
James Ransone,		John Page,	1752-54;
Mordecai Cooke,	1696-97;	John Page,	
Peter Beverley, Speaker,		Thomas Whiting,	1755-68;
Mordecai Cooke,	1702;	Thomas Whiting,	
Peter Beverley, Speaker,	1706;	Lewis Burwell,	1759-75;
Peter Beverley,			

The Delegates of the Conventions of 1775, 1776, were Thomas Whiting and Lewis Burwell.

After the outrages at Williamsburg, the gunpowder plot, and other incidents that led Virginia to join in the rebellion against Britain, Lord Dunmore began his ravaging depredations along the Bay Coast. He landed on Gwynn's Island—with the British fleet near by. The Virginian forces under General Andrew Lewis attacked the fleet, forcing it to withdraw, taking Dunmore along; he never returned. This was the end of Royal government in Virginia and happened July 9, 1776.

Towards the end of the Revolution the scene of activity shifted again

xxvi

to Gloucester. Cornwallis had troops all around Yorktown and in Gloucester. Virginia militia with French forces under Choisy assisted by the cavalry of the Duke de Lauzun had an active engagement with Tarleton's cavalry forces, which ended in British withdrawal. A few days later when Cornwallis found himself bottled up at Yorktown, he planned to cross the York into Gloucester, hoping thus to escape, but a storm prevented his doing so, and he had to surrender on October 19, 1781.

The militia of the county during the Revolution were under Colonel Sir John Peyton, with Lt. Colonel Thomas Whiting, Major Thomas Boswell and Lt. Warner Lewis on his staff. Other officers who served in the Revolution were:

Captains:

John Billups, Richard Billups, George Booth, William Buckner, John Camp, Jasper Clayton, Gibson Cheverius, John Dixon, John Hubard, Richard Matthews, Robert Matthews, Benjamin Shackelford, William Smith, John Whiting and John Willis.

Lieutenants were:

Churchill Armistead, James Baytop, James Bentley, John Billups, Thomas Buckner, Dudley Cary, Samuel Cary, John Foster, Robert Gayle, George Green, Richard Hall, Hugh Hayes, Edward Matthews, William Sears, Phillip Tabb.

Ensigns:

Thomas Baytop, William Bentley, Peter Bernard, Richard Davis, William Davis, Samuel Eddins, Josiah Foster, John Fox, John Gale, Christopher Garland, John Hayes, William Haywood, James Laughlin, George Plummer, Henry Stevens, Thomas Tabb.

Major General William Boothe Taliaferro tells in an article in the *William and Mary Quarterly Review* of remembering that his father told of watching the British fleet in the York River, during the War of 1812, when his father (Warner Taliaferro) was a young boy. He said his father watched the fleet from the porch at Airville. It is a matter of record that the fleet committed unpleasant incursions from time to time along the coast. The militia were called up for defense, and were under the command of Colonel William Jones. His staff consisted of Capt. Catesly Jones, Capt. Baytop, and Capt. Richard Jones of The Cottage.

Colonel Scaife Whiting had command of the Gloucester Horse, and served outside of the county.

In the Clerk's Office at Gloucester there is a complete roster of the officers and men of the county who served in the Confederacy. Reading these names is like reading the rolls of the old parishes. They are the same names, the same families.

During the Civil War the women did their part, too.

After the Civil War, as Sally Nelson Robins so neatly puts it, "The pride which the sons of the old land-owners took in being scions of Cavaliers, and fathers of the Union is changed into this glory, 'My father was a Confederate Soldier.'"

From then on Gloucester has lifted up her head, and in spite of the struggles and losses she had just endured she kept pressing forward. Progress has continued. Northern money, and, yes, Southern money too, have combined with aristocratic blood and patriotic courage, to make this area one of culture and prosperity. Since the turn of this century the cultivation of tobacco has gradually given place to the cultivation of flowers and the raising of beef cattle.

The public libraries of both counties are kept up-to-date, and privately owned libraries are becoming larger and of wider scope in subject matter than of yore.

Never in the history of the Mobjack Bay country have the homes been more beautifully kept, more artistically and tastefully furnished, nor more comfortable to live in than now, in the 1950's. Up-to-date utilities and modern gadgets; late model cars and excellent roads; motor boats, daily papers, television, radio, telephones and airplanes all combine to make the Mobjack Bay country as convenient a place to live in as any part of the country. The excellent gardens, the nearby rivers, quick transportation and the innovation of the "deep freeze" unite to provide even more sumptuous tables than those so famous in the good old days. In fact, the residents of Gloucester and Mathews no longer need to reminisce about the "grandeur that was;" they may freely revel in the grandeur that is again.

THE OLD HOMES
IN THE 1950's

IN *Old Churches, Ministers and Families of Virginia*, Bishop Meade wrote of the homes of the Gloucester-Mathews area during the 1850's. Almost fifty years later, Mrs. Sally Nelson Robins gave some account of these same houses in her delightful little book, *History of Gloucester County, Virginia, and Its Families*. Then in 1915, Mr. Robert Lancaster gave an even fuller account of the homes in this section, naming owners, and showing illustrations in his extensive work, *Historic Virginia Homes and Churches*.

All these books are out of print. Edith Tunis Sale's books are also out of print. The demand of the public for descriptions, pictures, information as to the lives of owners, in fact any information available concerning these old houses, has been so great, that I feel impelled to present to the best of my ability a picture of the old houses as they are now, in the 1950's, together with the history, the various reconstructions, restorations and remodelings of these houses, as well as legend and tradition about them. Some have changed hands many times—others not so often. Some of the houses have vanished, but because they are so intertwined with the early life of this section, mention is made of them.

Although this work is presented more or less from the viewpoint of these charming old houses as homes, their architecture has been a fascinating study too. It has its own characteristic style which has, of course, been subjected to many influences that inevitably have given direction to its evolution. In many cases it is difficult to say just where the "old" part of the house ends and the "new" begins. The most definite influences represented are Georgian, Dutch Colonial, Palladian and Greek Revival.

Little England land front. Wing to right is older part.

PART ONE
ON THE YORK

THE natural eminence of the terrain along the banks of the York provided desirable homesites and led to the building of many beautiful mansions overlooking the broad blue waters of the York river. In the July 1894 issue of the *William and Mary Quarterly*, the Editor, in some notes, remarks that down the York from Porteus Mansion there had been well-built brick houses about every mile, and at the time he wrote, some few still survived. He mentions the families which lived along the river in years gone by, and used it as a travel route to visit back and forth. Those included in his list were the Smiths, of Purton; the family of Capt. John Stubbs, of Cappahosic; the Burwells, of Carter's Creek; the Warners, of Warner Hall; the Pages, of Rosewell; the Manns, of Timberneck, and the Perrins, of Sarah's Creek.

LITTLE ENGLAND

THE mansion nearest the mouth of the river, and situated on Sarah's Creek, is Little England, formerly called Sarah's Creek House.

From "Observations in Several Voyages and Travels in America in the Year 1736" from the *London Magazine* of July 1746, in a discussion of excellent harbors on the Eastern Coast of Virginia, we find mention made of the "Harbor of Men of War, in which is Sarah's Creek."

John Perrin, aged twenty-one, sailed from London in 1635 (Hotten's "Emigrants"). Entered in the Court proceedings of the York records for 1648 was found an undated letter from his mother to John Perrin, the immigrant. It reads:

"Son John: My love to yo', and I was very glad to heare of yo' health, but very sorry to heare of ye' accident wch befell yo' by fire. I have sent yo a boy wch I desire that you would have as much care of as if he was yo owne alsoe. I have sent yo some things, so much as I am able at this tyme, and if God shall enable me to live another yeare I shall send yo more. Ye father hath departed this life, and hath left you a little house in ye south-gate streete in burg worth the matter of 40 lb., there is a note in ye barrell it lieth at ye topp in ye new blankett, and I have sent you by Tho; a small piece of gould for your wife alsoe I have pd for ye boy his passage, his name is Backer Yo' Uncle Christopher lives at Ascamack at Cheryston Creeke,

As yo desire my blessing have a care of ye boy, and learn him his trade, and not to pt from him. . . . my love to you an yo' wife desiring of God to keepe. . . .

Your loveing mother Susan Perrin"

This letter would indicate that the Perrin family was one of integrity as well as ability, and certainly this mother-in-law displayed a high degree of tact in sending her daughter-in-law a "small piece of gould."

The grant for the land was dated April 1651 and embraced 400 acres. It was deeded to John Perrin by Governor Berkeley, for transportation into the colony. (Evidently John Perrin brought over several immigrants with him.)

There are several graves at Sarah's Creek. The inscription on one tomb is

Here Lyeth Ye Body of
Mrs. Mary Perrin Daughter
of Mr. John and Mrs. Mary
Perrin died Sep^br Ye 18th
1738 Aged three years
One month and five days.

This must have been the great grand-daughter of John the immigrant. There is another tombstone the inscription of which reads

Here lies the Body of
John Perrin Son of Thomas
and Elizabeth Perrin

2

Little England from corner of the garden.

Little England river front. Home of Mr. and Mrs. Theodore Pratt.

> Who departed this life
> Nov^{br} 2d 1752
> Aged 63 Years 1 Month
> and 2 Days.

Thomas, son of the original John, and Elizabeth raised their family of six during the last fifteen years of the seventeenth century:

> Elizabeth baptized in February 25, 1686.
> Mary baptized April last 1688.
> John, September 21, 1690 (Capt. John Perrin of Sarah's Creek).
> Susannah baptized March 2, 1698.

Little England showing new bath house and swimming pool.

Catherine Xber 30, 1700.
Isaac baptized February 26, 1702 (buried September 2, 1733).

Their descendants married into many old families.

Sarah's Creek was named for Sarah the Duchess of Marlborough.

On July 16, 1781 in a communication from Capt. Samuel Eddins to Governor Nelson is this message:

"A Pilot Boat from Gloucester Town seized some time ago by order of the Baron, belonging to a gentleman in Maryland is sunk in Sarah's Creek, and might be sold advantageously."

5

Staircase in great hall at Little England.

In 1781 Brigadier-General Weeden mentions the Perrin House in a letter to Washington. In this letter he reported: "I have a lay of Horsemen from Perrin's House to Camp. The House stands at the mouth of Sarah's Creek and commands a full view of Gloster and York and all their shipping." This "lay of horsemen" were experienced French hussars from the legion of Lauzun which had arrived in America with the army of Rochambeau. Lauzun, popular at the Court of Versailles, and believed to be a lover of Marie Antoinette, was the first to announce the surrender of Cornwallis to Louis XVI.

Lookouts in the Perrin House kept the commanders advised of enemy operations in the York River.

During the War of 1812 Little England became a hospital for wounded soldiers. In the *Virginia Historical Magazine* in a discussion of the Perrin

6

Living room at Little England.

family, there is a description of Little England as it was early this century. It reads:

"In Gloucester County, at the mouth of the York River, opposite Yorktown, the old Perrin Mansion is still standing in good condition. It is in the style of architecture so usual in Virginia during the reigns of the Georges, a large brick building two stories high, and four rooms on each floor, wainscoted and panelled. The house is in full view of Yorktown, at the mouth of Sarah's Creek, on the east side of Gloucester Point."

Little England was built in 1716 by Capt. John Perrin, (son of Thomas and

Dining room at Little England.

8

Dining room mantel, at Little England.

9

Elizabeth Perrin). The plans were said to have been made by Sir Christopher Wren. There is a frame wing (early Colonial), with gables, which was built before 1690. It was in this building that Thomas and Elizabeth raised their family. In the main building there is a grand central hall with one huge room on each side. The large windows in these rooms open to both fronts. The brasses on the doors of both fronts are original, and the superb staircase leads to the second floor, where the floor plan of the first floor is repeated.

The paneling in the hall and the great rooms is beautiful, the color tone being a delightful pale green. Williamsburg Restoration representatives have conferred with Mr. and Mrs. Theodore Pratt, the present owners of Little England, concerning this color tone which has been declared the truest of the colonial decorative colors.

Inside the mansion, which Mr. and Mrs. Pratt have restored to its original beauty, one finds exquisite antiques and priceless paintings. There is a Rembrandt Peale over the mantel in the dining room. It is of General George Washington. Here we also find a Daubigny, a Bonheur, and a Monticelli, and other paintings.

In the living room there is a magnificent Waterford glass chandelier, and in the dining room the chandelier has a center of deep purple Bristol glass and gallery of gilt with tear-drop crystals.

The grounds spread out in great stretches of grass with enormous quantities of box, cedars, crepe myrtles, and trees of different varieties. Adjoining are flower and vegetable gardens, and beyond, endless fields of priceless daffodils. In the spring these blossoms turn the fields to stripes of green and gold.

Down where the lawn meets the river, Mr. and Mrs. Pratt have built a large swimming pool, and a modern bathhouse, complete with a big fireplace in the lounge, and showers in the wings.

TIMBERNECK

THE ample rambling old mansion known as Timberneck Hall stands on the York River, opposite Ringfield, and not far from Powhatan's Chimney, which was built for Powhatan by Capt. John Smith. The mansion was built by the first John Catlett in the county, probably in 1776, and is now the house of Mr. and Mrs. John W. C. Catlett, who are of the fifth generation descendants of the first John. This house of frame construction, in Georgian style, superseded an earlier house, also known as Timberneck Hall, which was on land granted to George Minifye. In the latter half of the seventeenth century it was the home of John Mann, the immigrant, and Mary, his wife. Their daughter, Mary, only child and heiress, was born at Timberneck in 1672. She was

10

Timberneck Hall front view.

married to Matthew Page, son of Sir John Page, of Williamsburg, and for some years they lived at Timberneck with her parents.

Practically all trace of the original Timberneck house is gone. Almost a hundred years ago Bishop Meade visited the scene. He refers to the place as "Mr. Catlett's farm." "In, or near the stable yard, in an open place," he found tombstones lying around, or piled on each other. According to one of these tombstones, Matthew and Mary Page buried a daughter, Elizabeth, aged three years, here. She died March 15, 1693.

John Mann, and Mary, his wife, were buried here. He died January 7,

11

Timberneck Hall side rear view.

1694—aged sixty-three. She died March 1703-4—aged fifty-six.

When John Mann died, his name died with him, but his daughter named her son Mann, and among his descendants, particularly the Pages, the name has been used every generation, for more than two hundred years.

Part of John Mann's vast acres passed to his daughter, and on to her descendants, the Pages. But part of the estate went to the Catletts, descendants of John Mann's wife's children by her first husband, Edmund Berkeley, of Gloucester County.

In a letter from Mr. John W. C. Catlett, of Timberneck Hall, to Mrs. H. O. Sanders under date of January 29, 1951, he says in part:

"I have before me a copy of the original 'Land Grant,' taken from Patent Book I, page 704 in the Land Office at Richmond.

" 'To all whom these presents shall come I, Sir Francis Wyatt Lt. Governor and Captain Generall of Virginia, etc., etc. By Instructions from the Kings Most Excellent Magestie directed me and the Councell of State etc., etc., Give and grant unto George Minifye Esq., Three thousand acres to start at the creeke upon the west side of the Indians feilds, opposite to Queene's Creeke and extends down the river to a creeke called by the name of Timber Necke Creeke Eastward.' "

Mr. Catlett continues by saying:

"This is by order of Court bearing date the Eleventh of October Anno 1639, and was given for 'transportation at his own ppr costs and charges of sixtie pons to the Colony.' Mr. Minifye was a member of the 'Councell of State'. . . .

"This three thousand acres is supposed to have included Rosewell. . . .

"I don't know anything about the original house. This house [the present home of the Catletts], we have been told, was built by the first John Catlett, who came here, according to Cousin Merriweather Jones, in 1776. . . .

"The present Timberneck house was originally 40 x 40 feet, a cellar, two stories and an attic. Three large chimneys, two of them running all the way from the cellar. The cellar, seven feet pitch; the rooms on the first floor, ten feet pitch, actual measure; and the second floor eight feet. The dining room sixteen by twenty-one feet—the parlor a little larger. The house is frame.

"There are two places an older house could have been. There is a very distinct old foundation we have plowed into, an hundred, twenty-five yards East of the house, and my wife thinks she has found one in the flower garden in front of the house.

"The original [present] Catlett house, had seven rooms. Grandpa added three and a hall in 1856. The original had a hall on the north end too.

"Some of the names Minifye brought to the colony were Pixlry, Greene, Chapman, Martin, Burgis, Ward, Prince, Sheers, Turner, Gauett, Sharples, Sherbourne Williams, William Jones, Wilkinson

13

Rosewell from an old photograph taken by H. P. Cook in the 1870's.

Kennon, Richards, Hawkins, Mason, Reed, Leech, Powell, Walker.
"The Assembly acted on this Grant January sixth, 1639 and it was sealed with the 'seale of the Colony at James Cittie the ninth of March 1639.'"

ROSEWELL

MATTHEW PAGE and his wife, Mary, daughter of John Mann, moved from Timberneck to a "simple wooden structure" on a high promontory on the York, not far from Timberneck. This was to be the site of Rosewell. The exact

14

date of their moving is not on record, but according to the tombstones at Rosewell, Matthew Page died the 9th of January, 1703, aged forty-five, and Mary died March 24, 1707 in her thirty-sixth year.

Before August, 1704, three of their young children, Matthew, Mary, and Ann were buried here.

Mann Page was the only child who survived his mother. With the inheritance from both parents, he was a very wealthy man. His first wife was Judith, daughter of Ralph Wormeley. After her death, he married Judith, daughter of Robert Carter. In 1725 he started building Rosewell.

Overlooking the York River, and Carter's Creek, this mansion (in the style of a Georgian town house), was four stories high, including the basement, and had two turrets on the roof, inside of which were little rooms. These had windows on the four sides, and made excellent look-outs.

Built of red brick, in Flemish bond, and with marble lintels, and other elaborate masonry trim, Rosewell was the finest house in America. The carved staircases, mantels and paneling were said to have been exquisite beyond description. The entrance hall had full-height pilasters. Sally Nelson Robins says eight people could ascend the great staircase abreast. The balustrade of the stairs was carved with designs of baskets of fruits and flowers. But Mann Page did not live to finish his work. In 1730 he died, and the magnificent home he was building for joyful celebrations became a house of sorrow and death.

Mr. Page's son, Mann Page II, completed the house, but there were many difficulties in the way, and he was compelled to ask to have certain entails on property left by his father lifted, before he could pay his father's debts and continue work on the mansion. It was about 1744 before it was finished.

Mann II married, first, Miss Alice Grymes, daughter of the Honorable John Grymes of Middlesex; and second, Miss Ann Corbin Tayloe. John Page, a son of the first marriage, became Governor of Virginia. He was a close friend of Thomas Jefferson. They were in college at William and Mary together. They both went courting in the Burwell family. Mr. Page was successful, and married Miss Fanny Burwell (a cousin of the Carter's Creek Burwells). Mr. Jefferson, however, was refused the hand of the lovely Miss Rebecca, of Carter's Creek, and his heart was temporarily broken.

Governor John Page was a brilliant man and a great leader. He was simple in his tastes, however, and entertained large numbers of friends with an ease and simplicity that made them feel an everyday at-homeness at Rosewell. Mr. Jefferson used to visit him for days, and it has been said that he wrote the draft for the Declaration of Independence in one of the turret rooms on the roof of Rosewell. It was on this roof that the first weather bureau in America was put in operation. John Page died in 1808.

15

In 1838 the vast Rosewell estate passed from the Page family. It was bought by a Mr. Booth, who paid $12,000 for it. He sold $35,000 worth of cedars, bricks, wainscoting, etc.—and received $22,000 for the place. Alterations and modernization took place, presumably during his ownership.

The deck-on-hip roof was changed to low hip, and pediments were added to the end pavilions. West and East dependencies were built, but were later removed.

(According to an insurance policy, a brick stable 24 by 120 feet had been built in 1802).

In 1855 Rosewell became the home of the Deans, who were charming gracious people. They made the mansion again a center of society. One of the Dean daughters was married to Judge Fielding Lewis Taylor and they made their home here.

In 1916 the mansion was burned.

Before the wings were removed, there were within the walls of Rosewell thirty-five rooms, three wide halls, and nine passageways.

Mr. Thomas Tileston Waterman, the distinguished architect, says that even in ruins the walls of Rosewell show a fineness in construction not equaled elsewhere in America.

SHELLY

SHELLY, long the home of the Pages, is near the York. It adjoins Rosewell, and was originally a part of it. The name was derived from the great quantities of shells all about the place. It is known to have been a center of great celebration among the Indians, and is probably the site of Werowocomoco, Powhatan's capital.

Elizabeth Nelson, daughter of General Thomas B. Nelson, married Mann Page and for a long time made her home at Shelly. In 1827 Julia Randolph was married to Thomas N. Page, of Shelly. They became the parents of the noted author, Thomas Nelson Page, of Oakland, Hanover County.

In her last days, Elizabeth Nelson Page (Mrs. Mann Page), wrote down many interesting memories of her earlier life at Shelly. In a letter to the Honorable H. A. Wise, of Washington, D. C., of December 1, 1837, she writes of the sacrifices made by her father of health, life and fortune. She says, "He never had a day's health after the siege at Yorktown."

Shelly is still in the Page family. Mr. Mann Page, the present owner, tells us that the original house, built in the eighteenth century, was burned some time after the Civil War. He says that it was a two-part frame building, with dormer windows, large chimneys and two outside entrances.

The present house is of frame construction, with center hall, and rooms

16

on each side. There are two stories; and before some of them were closed up, there were fireplaces in all rooms. The rooms are large, and the woodwork good. Most of the old garden is gone, but there remains some fine boxwood. This, the present house, was built in 1885.

CARTER'S CREEK

THE early home of the Burwell family, sometimes called Fairfield, was architecturally unique. The main building had two wings extending back at right angles. One of the wings was demolished or burned in early years. In the other was the ballroom.

The basement had a vault in the center, built of bricks, which probably was used to store valuables. The ceiling of the basement was supported by brick arches.

The chimneys were of interesting treatment, being somewhat similar to those at Bacon's Castle. Fairfield, or Carter's Creek, as it was later called, was near Rosewell.

Lewis Burwell, the immigrant, married Lucy Higginson, only child of Captain Robert Higginson, early commander in Indian wars. It was to this Lewis that 2350 acres of land were granted in 1648. He died in 1658, having lived in York County most of his married life. Some authorities say he may have built Fairfield, but dates and records seem to point to the son, Lewis II, as the builder, at least of the main part.

There was the date 1692 in iron figures, in one gable. The iron letters L A B were also built into the wall. Lewis Burwell II's wife was Abigail, niece and heiress of President of the Council, Nathaniel Bacon.

Their son, Nathaniel, inherited the estate at the death of his father in 1710. (Abigail had died in 1672.) Nathaniel married Elizabeth, daughter of Robert Carter. Their son was Lewis Burwell III (1710-1752).

He attended Cambridge University, and became President of the Council and Acting Governor of Virginia.

His daughter, Rebecca, after refusing the hand of Mr. Thomas Jefferson, became the wife of Mr. Jacqueline Ambler. They had several beautiful daughters, who were great belles. One of them, Mary Willis Ambler, became the wife of Chief Justice John Marshall, of Richmond.

Lewis Burwell IV was educated at Eton and Inns of Court, but when the Revolution came, his sympathies were with America. He married Judith, daughter of Mann Page II, and they had many descendants.

It was during his lifetime that Carter's Creek passed from the Burwell family.

For a good many years Carter's Creek was the home of the Thrustons.

Carter's Creek (Fairfield).

Thomas Waterman mentions in *Mansions of Virginia* an unusual urn at Timberneck Hall. He says the bowl of the urn was carved with baroque bas-relief ornament of leafage, and a grotesque monkey's head. This came from Fairfield (Carter's Creek), and was probably a central finial of the mantel—or one of a pair of crossettes.

Although the mansion burned many years ago, traces of the foundations of the house, and of the dependencies may still be found.

In 1930 the land on which the house stood was bought by J. W. Lambert, wealthy yachtsman, of St. Louis, who was a descendant of the Burwell family.

CAPPAHOSIC HOUSE

UP the river a mile from the mouth of Carter's Creek was the wharf of Cappa-

18

Cappahosic House.

hosack. The first time this name was found in American history was in 1608 when it was shown on a chart sent to England with Captain Smith's "News from Virginia." At least this chart was found in the Spanish Archives, and is generally conceded to be the one which was sent to England in 1608. At that time Cappahosack was an Indian village on the York, and Powhatan offered to make Captain Smith "King of Cappahosack" for the price of "two great guns and a grindstone."

There has been a great deal of discussion about the meaning of the name, variously spelled in the old days when spelling was subject to personal whimsey—Cappahosac, Capahowsick and Cappahosic. William Wallace Tooker, an authority on Indian names, says that it is the Natick Kuppoho-we-es-et,— "at, or near the place of shelter," "a haven," "covert," or "woods." The main stem means to stop or close up.

19

From the *Calendar of State Papers* we find transportation at the site by ferry, in 1706. "From Capt. Mathew's to Cappohofack—the price for a man fifteen pence, for a man and horse, two shillings and six pence, etc., etc."

Thomas Buckner kept the Ferry sometime in the eighteenth century.

From "Laws of Virginia under George II" we find that in October 1748 the price for crossing the Ferry was one shilling, three pence, each, for horse and man.

In the *Virginia Gazette* under date of March 28, 1751, we find:

"The subscriber, having undertaken to keep the Ferry at Capahosack, gives Notice, That the said Ferry for the future shall be kept in the best manner, having provided a good Boat, and a sufficient Number of Hands for that Purpose, and a very large Canoe for putting off Footmen, or such as don't choose to cross with the Horses. Also keeps a Public House at the said Ferry, where all Gentlemen may be well accommodated, and depend on meeting with all possible Dispatch in crossing the said Ferry and on making a Smoake on the other side of the River, The Boat will be immediately sent over.'

Signed

William Thornton."

Cappahosic House itself was built in 1712 by Captain John Stubbs, who had patented the land of the Cappahosic tract in 1652 and in 1702. The austere simplicity of the architecture makes for classical beauty in the finished product.

The house (early Georgian) is almost square, with a hall in the center; with four rooms downstairs, and four rooms upstairs. In each of these eight rooms there is a corner fireplace. The two huge chimneys, each with four flues, are built to the front of the ridge of the roof, for all four front rooms are smaller than those at the back. This arrangement resulted in very unusual roof treatment, inasmuch as the gable ends were clipped. The house is built of red brick which has been covered with white water-proofing cement paint. This not only keeps dampness out, but makes an excellent appearance.

Inside, the glistening of the wide pine floors is reflected in the fine old

ON FACING PAGE

(*Above*) Dining room at Cappahosic.

(*Below*) Fireplace in dining room at Cappahosic.

20

In the drawing room at Cappahosic.

hand-carved mahogany paneling, which in the dining room extends entirely to the ceiling, and in the other rooms to chair rail height. Above the living room mantel the paneling extends to the ceiling. The downstairs ceilings are twelve feet high, and those upstairs, ten. The staircase is unique in its simple beauty.

The Stubbs family lived at Cappahosic House for many years. Later on it was the home of the Baytops. During their residence here the place became known as "Baytop."

In 1947 Mr. and Mrs. E. Stewart James purchased the place, and set

22

Fireplace in the living room at Cappahosic.

about restoring it. This was a tremendous job, for the house had been closed up for several years. However, perseverance won out, and from attic to cellar the restoration is perfect.

At the back there is a later wing which has several bedrooms and a modern kitchen and bath, but the Jameses live in the old part, too. There is an old square grand piano, with a tone like a harpsichord; there are open fires; gleaming antique silver; a tester bed with a crocheted spread; Hogarth prints; and an ancient mariner's compass. The light fixtures are unique. They,

23

Bedroom at Cappahosic, notice the bed steps.

24

and the charm of the iron grill work, and the atmosphere of antiquity, lend the illusion that one is actually living back in the days when Cappahosic House was first built—two hundred and fifty years ago.

The gardens are being restored in the spirit of the age to which the house belonged.

PURTON

UP the river from Cappahosic, in an olden day, was the house known as "Portan," "Poetan" or "Purton." We find many references to this old place. A grant for 1665 acres, dated March 31, 1649, was made to William John Clarke. This land, commonly known as Portan, was bounded by Broad Creek, York River and Tanks Poropotank Creek, or Adams' Creek.

The home in its heyday consisted of two stories and basement with front stoop and back porch. The view to the river was excellent. There must have been a mill near the home, for mention is made of a mill dam.

It was near Purton that some servants who were former soldiers of Cromwell held a rendezvous in 1663 at which they planned a rebellion. One of their number, however, gave away the plot, so they were prevented from carrying it out by the Governor, Sir William Berkeley.

In studying the history of Purton we find references to the Berkeley family, the Bernard family, also the Whaley family; but it is the Smith family which is most frequently identified with Purton. And to be a descendant of the Smiths, of Purton, is almost like being descended from royalty.

Mrs. Stanley Lloyd now owns Purton. She has recently made some additions to the house, and is restoring and enlarging the gardens.

POROPOTANK

NEAR the mouth of Poropotank Creek, on the York, formerly stood a classically-simple, early Georgian old home called Poropotank (now long gone), later known as Violet Banks. This house was said to have been the counterpart of Cappahosic House, and was the home of Edward Porteus. Some say that he planned both houses. It was through his son, Robert Porteus, that Queen Elizabeth II, of England, is claimed to be related to George Washington, Robert E. Lee, and many other distinguished Americans.

There are references in early Virginia history to the Poropotank Warehouses; also to the meeting at John Pate's house, near Poropotank, of the Loyalists, about the time Governor Berkeley's friends rose in Middlesex, during Bacon's Rebellion.

In connection with Poropotank we find many references to the Porteus family, also to the Dudley family, and the Lewis family. Charles Roanes was granted land on Poropotank Creek, possibly adjoining the Porteus property. In his notes, *William and Mary Quarterly*, 1894, the Editor says:

"'Violet Banks' is the modern name of the house of Edward Porteus, the emigrant. It is an old square brick bldg., two stories and a half, with four rooms to the floor. Though abandoned, it still retains the fine panelling and interior carving of the long past. It fronts York River and on the West is Poropotank Creek. Rob't. Porteus, his son, lived at 'New Bottle' subsequently called 'Concord.' In 1693 Edward Porteus was recommended by the Governor of Virginia for appointment to the Council as a 'Gentleman of estate and standing suitable for appointment to Council,' (Sainsbury, Mss.). He was a vestryman of Petsworth Parish in 1681 (vestry book). He married 'The Relict of Robert Lee,' who left in his will 'seven pounds to the poor of Petsworth.'"

Edward Porteus's tomb is at Violet Banks at the mouth of Poropotank Creek.

26

PART TWO
ON THE SEVERN

WARNER HALL

THE land on which Warner Hall stands was patented by Augustine Warner I (1610-1674), very early in the history of Gloucester. He was Justice of York in 1650, and Justice of Gloucester in 1656. He was the great-great-grandfather of George Washington and through him Robert E. Lee, The Queen Mother of England (1955), and Queen Elizabeth II, are kin. His wife's name was Mary. They lie buried in the graveyard at Warner Hall.

Augustine Warner II (1642-1681) inherited Warner Hall at the death of his father in 1674. He married Mildred Reade, the daughter of George Reade, founder of Yorktown, and after her death, Elizabeth Martian. Augustine II was speaker of the House of Burgesses during Bacon's Rebellion in 1676, and also was a member of the Council.

After the burning of Jamestown, Bacon came over into Gloucester, making Warner Hall his headquarters. It was while here that he invited the "Oath of Fidelity" of his fellow countrymen.

When Augustine Warner II died he left three daughters (his sons having died young). Mary became the wife of John Smith, of Purton, on the York, and their son Augustine Smith was said to have been one of the Knights of the Golden Horseshoe—with Governor Spotswood, on his famous expedition across the Blue Ridge in 1716. Mildred, another daughter of Augustine Warner II, married Lawrence Washington (grandfather of George), of Westmoreland, and her second husband was George Gale. Her three Washington children were John, who built Highgate, Augustine, father of George Washington, and Mildred. Augustine Washington married Mary Ball, and named his son George for his great-grandfather, George Reade, who founded Yorktown.

Warner Hall river front. The home of Mr. and Mrs. Stanley Crockett.

28

The stables at Warner Hall.

Elizabeth, the third daughter of Augustine Warner II, became the wife of John Lewis and inherited Warner Hall. Their son, John Lewis II (1702-1754) was a member of His Majesty's Council, and was prominent in the county. For generations the Lewises lived here, and members of the family emigrated to all parts of the United States. Their descendants built Belle Farm, Eagle Point, Abingdon, and Severn Hall, all in Virginia. Elizabeth and John Lewis I's grandson, Colonel Fielding Lewis, of Belle Farm, married Catherine Washington, and after her death married Elizabeth Washington

29

(better known as Betty), sister of George. He built beautiful Kenmore for her, in Fredericksburg.

In the early part of the nineteenth century Mr. Colin Clarke purchased Warner Hall and continued the tradition of hospitality for which the Hall was so widely known.

Always pretentious and large, Warner Hall was of brick, connected by a brick covered way to the kitchen on the left. Another brick covered way connected the house with the office on the right.

In 1845 the center of the original building was burned, leaving only the two wings—each with a hall and one large room on the first floor, and a quaint platform stairway going up to a hall, and two nice size bedrooms upstairs.

The following is taken from a note written to Mrs. H. O. Sanders (who was Miss Nina Taliaferro), of Gloucester County, by her cousin, Mrs. Martha Page Vandegrift, who died in 1932 at the age of one hundred and two:

> "The old Warner Hall house was burned in 1845. Mr. Colin Clarke who then owned it added to one of the brick offices a brick bungalow in which he lived until his death in the early 60's. The original building had very large rooms—so large was the drawing room that I remember being at a large party there, when a child, and the Clarke boys and Bryan girls and my brother and I had our own cotillion in a corner of the room. In those days neighbor children were invited to the "grown up" parties. Mr. Cheney, when he built the present house, connected it with the brick offices. Warner Hall and Eagle Point were among the anti-bellum houses with many others far famed for their generous hospitality, as has been said, 'every house was a club for guests.'"

After much research we conclude that the main part of the first house on the site was built in 1674, although there may have been a house or a wing on this site earlier in the 17th century; a later house was certainly built about 1740. Several fires in the 18th and 19 centuries took their toll of this structure. But research establishes pretty conclusively that the restorations and additions that have been made have salvaged as much of the original as it was possible to salvage. Today Warner Hall with magnificent center of frame construction having columned fronts towards the land approach, and towards the Severn, and the two brick wings, stands as majestically as ever in its grove of century-old trees.

Its occupants still enjoy the use of some of the original dependencies.

It was sold by Paul T. O'Mally and Herbert I. Lewis in 1946 to I. S. Crockett. Beef cattle are grazed on the large rich fields which border the river.

An original outbuilding at Warner Hall.

Eagle Point in the river, from which the place gets its name.

32

The land of the Warner Hall estate joins that of Eagle Point, which also faces the Severn, and that of White Marsh, which extends to the shores of the Ware.

EAGLE POINT

EAGLE POINT, on the Severn River, was the house of John Randolph Bryan and his wife Elizabeth Tucker Coalter. Mr. Bryan was a namesake of John Randolph, of Roanoke, and was educated under his watchful care.

Elizabeth Coalter was a beloved niece, and the heiress of John Randolph, of Roanoke. When she and Mr. Bryan were married, it seems the combination of their fortunes enabled them to entertain lavishly. However, thirty-two years after their marriage, the gracious hospitality for which Eagle Point was famed, came to an end, due to the outbreak of the Civil War. In 1862 the estate passed from the Bryan family. It was part of the original Warner Hall Grant.

Many years later, the distinguished Mr. Joseph Bryan, publisher and philanthropist, of Richmond, who was born at Eagle Point, bought back the estate. He enlarged and beautified the house, improved the grounds, and re-established its reputation for hospitality. His portrait hangs at the Courthouse in Gloucester. It has the following inscription:

"C. S.A. 1862-65
Born at Eagle Point, Gloucester
County, Va. Aug. 13, 1845.
Died at Laburnum, Henrico
Co., Nov. 26, 1908."

Eagle Point is large and handsome, with many gables, columns, chimneys, and porches. The rooms are beautifully and comfortably furnished with a tasteful combination of the modern and the antique.

The name, Eagle Point, derives from a formation of land that juts out into the river. The house is now the home of Dr. George Carneal.

The old family graveyard is on a small island in the Severn River, near the house, and the dead rest in the shade of the pines.

SEVERNBY

SEVERNBY, sometimes called Severn Hall, was originally part of the Eagle Point estate. The present house was built by Mr. Alfred Withers, and is a pleasant home which overlooks the river.

LANSDOWNE

LANSDOWNE, also on the Severn, was long the home of the Thrustons, a prominent family of Gloucester. It was here that Miss Nelson, the charming young daughter of Dr. Wilmer Nelson, came as the bride of Edward Thruston. Lansdowne is now the property of Nell Carneal Drew.

Eagle Point land front.

Eagle Point river front.

A garden spot at White Marsh.

36

PART THREE

ON THE WARE

WHITE MARSH

BACK from the Ware, on the Tidewater Trail in Gloucester, on the original grant of land to the honorable Lewis Burwell, of Carter's Creek, stands White Marsh. The grant for the land was made in the very early days of Gloucester's history, which began in the 1640's. White Marsh was the early seat of the Whitings, and remained in the possession of that family over a period of years. They built the main part of the present mansion about 1750. It was then a simple Georgian Colonial house, without wings or pillars.

The distinguished lawyer, Thomas Reade Rootes, owned White Marsh for a time. We find a note saying that Martha Jacquelin Cary gave a fortune to her nephew Thomas Rootes, Esq., of White Marsh. At Mr. Rootes' death his estate passed to his widow, who had been his second wife. She, too, had been married before; she left the estate to her children, who were Prossers, offspring of her first marriage.

One of the daughters, Evalina Mathilda Prosser, became the wife of John Tabb, son of Phillip Tabb, of Toddsbury. John bought out the interest of his sister-in-law in White Marsh, and he and Mathilda made it their home. At that time, after adding his wife's fortune to his own, John Tabb was said to have been the wealthiest man in Gloucester. There were then three thousand acres of land in the White Marsh Plantation, and from three hundred to five hundred slaves were employed to operate it. (1500 slaves rest in the slave graveyard, near the peach orchard.)

Mrs. Tabb did not wish to continue living in the country, but insisted upon moving to Norfolk or Williamsburg, in order to enjoy a gayer social

White Marsh showing front portico, magnificent box, and the largest ginkgo tree in America.

life. Mr. Tabb promised that if she would make herself content, and remain in the country, he would lay out for her the finest garden in Virginia.

It was then that the terraced gardens were built, and many rare and fine species of trees were planted in the park. It was also about this time that the house was remodeled, and the wings and pillared portico built.

Phillip, son of John and Evalina Mathilda Tabb, inherited White Marsh, while another son, John Prosser Tabb, received Elmington, over on the North River (see Part IV).

The Tabbs were related to the Lees and General Robert E. Lee was a visitor at White Marsh. He is reported to have said of White Marsh, "It is the most beautiful place I have ever seen." It was here, when he made his

38

White Marsh, from the playhouse portico.

last visit in 1868, that he gave a piece of heartfelt advice to Virginians, which has been much quoted in histories and Lee biographies. After dinner, while visiting with the Tabb family and guests in the parlor, one of the ladies present asked him,

"General Lee, what does the future hold for us poor Virginians now?"

"We must work for Virginia, and we must teach our children to love and cherish Virginia, and work for Virginia, that she may become great again."

General Lee occupied the northeast bedroom during that last visit to White Marsh, after the war. His son, Captain Robert Lee, was his roommate on this occasion.

Front view of White Marsh with its magnificent box.

In later years, Mr. H. M. Baruch, of New York, owned White Marsh, having bought it from W. J. Burlee, now of Tree Hill Farm, Henrico County. It was Mr. Baruch who planted the great profusion of boxwood which, in the years that have followed, have grown to such enormous proportions. He made his home here until 1942, when he sold to Horace Gray, Jr., of Waverly. The estate was later bought by Mr. and Mrs. C. H. Lawson, of Williamsburg.

There are various legends, or ghost stories told of White Marsh. It is said that Evalina Mathilda Tabb has been seen ascending the stairs in rustling silks. She goes immediately to the nursery and opens the drawers of the chests where the children's clothes were kept. She folds the tiny garments and replaces them. The tombstones in the family burying ground on the knoll back of the apple orchard, and overlooking the lower fields, attest that

40

The playhouse at White Marsh.

Evalina Mathilda lost two of her children in infancy.

Another story is that subsequent owners of the house on returning home late at night have found all lights on and have heard music, as of a dance or party coming from the house. As they alighted from carriages or cars, the lights went out, the music ceased, and the house again stood dark and silent.

Today there are a little over two thousand acres in the White Marsh Plantation, and it is now owned by Mr. and Mrs. William Ingles; Mr. Ingles is a tenth generation direct descendant of Lewis Burwell, the original grantee of 1642.

Almost every visitor who goes to White Marsh involuntarily agrees with General Lee that, "It is the most beautiful place I have ever seen." And why not? There are magnificent porticoes on both fronts. The children's play-house

(Above) The old ice house, in the garden at White Marsh.

ON FACING PAGE

(Above) White Marsh, showing the circle and end steps.

(Below) The gate into White Marsh.

42

Detail of stair-case at Airville.

44

has miniature reproductions of these pillars. There are more than a hundred varieties of fine old trees growing in a park of twenty acres, and along the borders of the mile-long avenue. Among these trees, there is the famous ginkgo, said to be the largest ginkgo in this country. Then there are pecan trees, which the Forest Service people declare are the largest they have ever seen. There are huge elms, enormous crepe myrtles, arbor vitae, boxwood, magnolia grandiflora, dogwood, cypress, holly, tulip poplar, Irish yew, Italian yew, shellbark, and several other varieties of hickory, several of oaks, maple, beech, horsechestnut, broadnut, butternut, Chinese chestnut, locust, black walnut, English walnut, filbert, cedar, Oregon spruce and many other varieties of trees.

The great size to which many of these trees have grown is attributed to the stratum of marl which underlies the land here. The green grass of the park, caressed by the shade of these trees, is of a quality of beauty that once seen enriches a lifetime.

At the back, from the terraces, a great vista of space is felt. The peach orchards; the apple orchards; the vast meadow, with its herd of beef cattle; and beyond the far trees, the Ware River; all these emphasize the extent, the largeness of White Marsh Plantation.

And the old house, with its big rooms and wide halls, shady and cool, rich in polished woodwork, sweet with the odor of many flowers, gives a feeling of home—a sense of fulfillment.

White Marsh has been dubbed "Queen of the Tidewater."

AIRVILLE

SITUATED on a high hill with a lovely view of well-cultivated fields running down to the Ware River, is Airville, home of the Dixons.

In some old notations of Gloucester we find that "John Dixon, Sr., of Airville, Gloucester Co., Va., only son (born 1778, died Sept. 5, 1830, buried at Mt. Pleasant, his father's home), married Sarah, daughter of Warner and Julia (Langborne) Throckmorton, and had issue:

"(a) John Dixon M.D., born 1812, died 24 June 1835, unmarried. (He was also buried at Mt. Pleasant.)

"(b) Harriet Peyton married Jacob Sheldon, and lived for many years in Williamsburg, Va."

Mrs. Page, of Shelly, tells of her Aunt Sarah, her mother's eldest sister, being married to Mr. Dixon of Airville. John, Sr., of Airville, was a son of The Rev. John Dixon, a colonial minister of nearby Mt. Pleasant, and his wife, Elizabeth Peyton, of Isleham. (Mt. Pleasant house is long since gone, but traces are discernible.)

45

Beautiful old Airville, now the home of Mr. and Mrs. Chandler Bates.

General Taliaferro, in writing of Gloucester, says that Airville is one of the old residences of the county, and goes on to add that "—all the old seats have their histories and traditions full of suggestions to romantic and imaginative minds."

In writing of the War of 1812, General Taliaferro says, "Our seabound situation rendered us liable to maritime incursion, and my father has often told me how as a boy he watched from the portico at Airville the manoeuvres of the British Fleet." (His father was Warner Throckmorton Taliaferro.)

Airville, overlooking the Ware and the Bay beyond, is a charming old frame structure, the oldest part of which was built by John Dixon in 1756.

46

There is a beautiful hall with unusual hanging stairway, and the house contains the original fine old woodwork.

In Airville, as in a few other old Virginia houses, is a secret chamber. This, of course, adds a note of mysterious glamour. The main building consists of a full basement, and two stories and a half, the third floor having dormer windows. Wings have been added. The architecture is in the Georgian influence. There is a small front porch with high steps.

From the Dixons the Airville estate passed to the possession of Major Thomas Smith and later to the Harwoods. The grounds, of natural beauty, are well kept, and the gardens have been restored.

It is now the home of Mr. and Mrs. Chandler Bates.

STARR LYNN

PART of the Airville estate was cut off some years ago and called Clermont. During this time, it was the home of Marius Jones and his wife, Mary Armi-

Starr Lynn, the house of General and Mrs. R. E. Starr, formerly part of Airville.

(Above) The old kitchen of Airville incorporated in this dwelling.

ON FACING PAGE

(Above) The living room at Starr Lynn, showing some of the priceless antiques the
Starrs have collected and (below) the fine old oriental chest.

49

stead Cattlett. Later this property was sold to General and Mrs. R. E. Starr by Mr. Van Bibber Sanders, and a good deal of remodelling and restoring has been done and additions made. They have renamed the place Starr Lynn, incorporating the family name with Mrs. Starr's given name.

It is remarkable how General and Mrs. Starr have retained the beauty and tradition of the old place, yet have attained a thoroughly modern and comfortable home. The old quarters kitchen has become a modernized family kitchen—the only regrettable part being the removal of the huge old chimney.

Starr Lynn houses many priceless antiques. During General Starr's duty in the far East (or the far West!) Mrs. Starr made frequent trips into out-of-the-way places deep in the interior of the countries they visited, and from natives acquired valuable pieces of china, ivory, ebony, linens, and embroideries. Her furniture and rugs have been selected with infinite care, and the blending of decorations and furnishings have been effected with exquisite taste. The measure of age is not in American years, but Chinese and Japanese periods. One Chinese bowl Mrs. Starr has dates from a pre-Ming Period.

On the land belonging to Starr Lynn are the old slave graveyards of the Airville estate.

WILSON'S CREEK

GENERAL WILLIAM BOOTHE TALIAFERRO refers to Wilson's Creek (which has disappeared long ago) as a pre-Revolutionary home of Gloucester. In connection with the Throckmorton family we find that Thomas Throckmorton, of Wilson's Creek, son of Major Mordecai Throckmorton and grandson of Sir John Peyton, Baronet of Isleham, married Julia Lewis, daughter of Warner Lewis, of Warner Hall. The marriage took place April 29, 1815 at Severn House (*Richmond Enquirer*). He died without issue.

COLRAINE

ON Wilson's Creek, not far from the site of the old Wilson's Creek House, now stands Colraine, the modern home of Major and Mrs. W. Milner Gibson.

SHERWOOD

THIS attractive old place was a part of the Robins grant, and was for many years the home of the Seldens and Dimmocks, descendants of the Lewises of Warner Hall. It was originally called Shabby Hall.

With its Dutch type slate roof, its spacious piazzas, an excellent view

50

Colraine, the home of the Gibsons on Wilson's Creek. Not far from the old Wilson's Creek house site.

Sherwood, which faces the Ware. Notice the substantial chimneys!

52

of the river, in its setting of tree-studded grounds, this has been, and is still, an ideal country home.

Mrs. Robert Munford, a widow, went to live with her relatives at Belle Farm. Here she remained until her only surviving child grew up and was married to Mr. John Sinclair, of Shabby Hall. Mrs. Munford then went to live with her daughter, Margaret Ann, at Shabby Hall, later Sherwood. The Sinclairs left a number of descendants, who intermarried with the best Gloucester families.

Originally Sherwood was an L-shaped dwelling. When the house was remodeled, the original mantels and other beautifully carved woodwork were retained.

Sherwood is a large mansion, of Colonial style. Its third story dormers, and its tall chimneys can be seen from some distance. It was built in the eighteenth century.

Sherwood was purchased in 1830 by Mr. and Mrs. Robert Colgate Selden, and for many years remained in their family.

Mr. Selden's mother, Charlotte Colgate, of England, planned the garden. It was laid out in the shape of an H and was two hundred feet wide by four hundred feet long, flanked by crepe myrtles, and planted with many rare, beautiful and sweet flowers and shrubs. Mrs. Colgate copied an old English garden, and to this day many varieties of the plants she grew are still found at Sherwood. This garden was famed throughout the Tidewater and was resplendent with roses, lilacs, snowballs, pride of China, English bay, sweet bay, Cuban laurel, spirea, mock-orange, pomegranates, lilies, iris and Japonica.

The lawns were, and still are, dotted with large elms, magnolias, pecans, tulip poplars, and different varieties of maples.

The silver service of Abingdon was kept at Sherwood by Mrs. Selden.

Mrs. H. A. Williams, a grand-daughter of Mr. and Mrs. Robert Colgate Selden, and Mr. Williams were owners of Sherwood for many years, and they made their home here. It is now owned by Mr. and Mrs. James Ervin.

WHITE HALL

FRANCIS WILLIS, a native of Oxford, England, a member of the First Burgesses, member of the Council . . . died in London, leaving his Virginia property to his nephew, whose descendants long lived at White Hall.

Ann, the wife of Francis Willis, is buried under the chancel at Ware Church, and on her tombstone the arms of her own family are impaled on those of her husband. The old Willis home was known as Edge Ware. Just

White Hall, the home of Mr. and Mrs. George H. Cunningham.

when the name was changed is difficult to say. We do know there were several Francis Willises.

In 1751, Colonel Francis Willis (possibly the Third) gave "three pistoles" to Mr. Bacon's school in Talbot County, Maryland. Mrs. Willis gave a doubloon.

From *Education in Colonial Virginia* we learn that Francis Willis, of White Hall, in company with many other distinguished Virginians, attended the school in Gloucester County of Rev. William Yates, Minister of Abingdon Parish, in 1752. We think this must have been Francis IV.

We think it was this same Francis, (IV), who is spoken of as Francis Willis, the son of Francis Willis and Elizabeth Carter, and lived at White Hall. We have read a contract with "Nathan Jacobs, of the County of Frederick, distiller," which bargains for the making of good whiskey on the place at White Hall. This whiskey must be "merchantable; of sufficient proof." Mr. Willis allows Mr. Jacobs a holiday of twelve days, four times a year. Jacobs is to have "two able hands" to assist him, and Mr. Willis promises to lodge and board him.

This contract was dated September 19, 1793.

When this Francis Willis died, about December 4, 1797, he left a large fortune and nine children.

The *Virginia Gazette* says that he had warehouses and a bakery on Mobjack Bay. This must also have been the Francis Willis who rode horseback to Mount Vernon, to visit Washington for several days.

Miss Mary Willis, a descendant of Francis Willis, was married to Dr. Samuel Powell Byrd, who built the present White Hall in 1815. The estate descended to their son, Richard Corbin Byrd, who married a granddaughter of Chief Justice John Marshall.

White Hall has changed hands several times in the last fifty years. It was at one time owned by Harry E. R. Hall. His widow lived there for some years. She later became the Countess of Beatty, having married the Earl of Beatty, son of the hero of Jutland. At one time it was owned by Ernest C. Rollins, and later by John G. Hayes, Jr. Mr. Hayes sold the estate in 1947, to Mr. George H. Cunningham, a native of Culpeper, who came to White Hall from New Jersey.

Located on the Ware River near Zanoni Post Office, and about five miles from Gloucester Court House, White Hall is one of the very fine old Gloucester homes. It is a colonial type house with broad porches, many windows, huge chimneys, and large wings. The mansion stands three stories high, with the front facade having a large fanlight in the wide gable. The interior is beautifully decorated, and the mantels, staircases and window and door frames are in exquisite taste.

White Hall showing wing and chimney.

56

The estate consists of about two hundred and fifty acres. There is a huge, spreading lawn, and beautiful water front.

The crepe myrtles and boxwood here are magnificent. The old Willis graveyard is nearby.

GOSHEN

THE original seat of the Tompkies family (from which "Captain Sally," of Poplar Grove descended), Goshen on the Ware River, was built between 1750 and 1760.

The earliest unit of the house consisted of a central hall with a large square room on each side. Unusual features of this house were high mantels, and wainscote. There were also other details of the interior of an interesting and quaint character. About one hundred years after the house had been built, a section was added at the back, and still later, in 1926, a wing was added to each end.

The grounds take in a considerable acreage, with extensive gardens rebuilt around remaining crepe myrtles, and other shrubs.

Of the dependencies, one slave cabin and the original smokehouse have been preserved intact in the back.

In 1830 this property was brought by William Kennon Perrin, and for more than a hundred years remained in the Perrin family.

It is now owned by Mrs. George Mackubin, a descendant of the Perrins, and Mr. Mackubin.

A unique silver lard-oil lamp in the parlor belonged to Mrs. Mackubin's great-grandmother, of Alexandria.

The beautiful old silver service, inherited by the family, was originally owned by the mother of Matilda Prosser Tabb.

Family portraits by well-known artists adorn the walls, and the view across the lawns to the blue waters of the Ware enhance the beauty of a superb setting.

WAREHAM

THE original grant on which many generations of Cookes lived, was for 1174 acres in the Mobjack Bay region, to the first Mordecai Cooke, in 1650. The place was known as Wareham, and sometimes, also, as Warham. It was a very early seat of the Cooke family, on the Ware River, and in their house Governor Berkeley took refuge during Bacon's Rebellion. Berkeley occupied the old "Chamber," a room that he probably found convenient as a hiding place,

Land front of Goshen, the home of the Mackubins.

Another view of the land front of Goshen.

A substantial looking dependency at Goshen.

since there were some cubby-holes there in which he could take cover in case the rebels came looking for him.

We know there was a pre-Revolutionary mansion on the site, but we do not know whether it was the house in which Berkeley took refuge, or whether it was built later. In any event, there is no house now at Wareham.

Mordecai Cooke's son, John, married first Anne Todd, born 1682, died 1720, eldest daughter of Captain Thomas and Elizabeth Todd. Her tomb is at Wareham.

John's second wife was Mary Smith, born April 14, 1691, died March 15, 1724. Her tomb is also at Wareham. She was the eldest daughter of John and Elizabeth Smith.

A later Mordecai Cooke's tomb is at Wareham, as well. He was evidently the grandson of the first Mordecai, and was buried in 1751—aged forty-three. His wife, Elizabeth Whiting Cooke, born 1713, died 1762, is buried at Wareham, too.

The property now belongs to H. M. Mason and Brothers.

The dining room, in the oldest part of the house at Goshen.

Church Hill, the home of Mr. and Mrs. E. Wright Noble.

CHURCH HILL

THE original grant of 1174 acres of land to Mordecai Cooke was made in 1650. In 1658, a large brick house was built on the elevation just above the Ware River. This home was called Mordecai's Mount, and was one of the earlier "grand" homes of Gloucester County. The garden was laid out in four terraces, at the foot of which a long meadow extended to the Ware. The view from the windows and the terraces was said to have been very beautiful.

Mordecai Cooke was sheriff in Gloucester in 1698, and a member of the House of Burgesses in 1696. One of his daughters was Susan, who married Captain Henry Fitzhugh.

Another daughter, Frances, married Gabriel Throckmorton in 1690, and gave the land on which the present Ware Church was built soon after.

In the 1700's the main part of the house was burned, leaving a brick wing. To this a frame addition was made. Much later, the brick wing burned, after which the entire frame house was built on the old foundations, as an addition to the frame wing of earlier date.

The name, Mordecai's Mount, was changed pretty early to Church Hill.

The Cooke property passed in a direct line from the Cookes to their descendants, the Throckmortons. Then one of the two heiresses of the house of Throckmorton married Mr. William Taliaferro, and when she died, her sister and co-heiress married the widower. Thus the estate passed to the Taliaferros.

The Throckmortons had already been prominent in England before they migrated to America. They seem to have had some connection with royalty. They are spoken of during the reign of Henry the Eighth as "the ancient family of Throckmortons." And after their migration to Virginia, they became important both socially and politically in Gloucester. But today, although the name figures prominently elsewhere, it is no longer found in Gloucester. This, of course, is owing to the fact that the male members of the family moved away; but the women remained behind. Thus it is that those descendants of the Throckmortons still to be found in the county, no longer bear the Throckmorton name, because they trace their line back to female members of the clan.

From Mrs. Page's manuscripts we learn that her grandfather, Warner Throckmorton, married Mary Langborn (or Langbourne). Warner's brother, Mordecai, married Miss Peyton, of Isleham. Mrs. Page says her grandfather, Philip Throckmorton, married a Miss Smith.

A valuable genealogical brochure by Professor William Carter Stubbs, Ph. D., of Audubon Park, New Orleans, Louisiana, is very interesting. In this he traces the Cooke family from 1650, giving records of births, deaths, baptisms, college records, arms, etc. He includes an account of Mordecai Cooke and his descendants, also of other families, among them the Booths, Buckners, Baylors, Baytops, Burwells, Fauntleroys, Fitzhughs, Masons, Mallorys, Pauls, Thrustons, Taliaferros, Whitings and so forth.

Later, Dr. and Mrs. Stubbs enlarged this brochure into a book, (1923), called "Descendants of Mordecai Cooke."

Some of the distinguished descendants of the Cookes, Throckmortons and Taliaferros are General William Boothe Taliaferro, Major Thomas S. Taliaferro, Judge Beverley R. Wellford, Jr., Mrs. Nina Taliaferro Sanders, Judge Warner T. Jones.

The big chimney at Church Hill.

64

An interesting ghost story is told of Church Hill.

One of the owners of this estate, a Mr. Throckmorton, took his beautiful young daughter for a visit to London. There she met a handsome young English gentleman, with whom she fell deeply in love, and he with her. They both declared eternal faithfulness to each other, and arranged to complete plans for their marriage, by correspondence, after which he would follow her to Gloucester to claim her hand.

But the father would have none of it. He did not approve of the match, so all letters between the two were intercepted, and neither ever heard from the other.

The daughter fell ill and died. She was buried the afternoon after her death near sunset, in the family burying ground. That night the distraught father heard what he thought was a dog scratching at the door, but in his distress he paid no attention. The cook saw a pale face at the kitchen window, but in her fright, instead of informing the family, the terrified domestic fled to bed, not taking time to undress, but burying her face in the pillow and covering up her head.

The next morning, the manservant, whose duty it was to tidy up the front of the house, found the young girl's body on the front steps, covered with snow that had fallen during the night.

A manservant who had been unruly and rebellious, had been punished not long before the death of the daughter. To get his revenge, and because he knew she was buried with expensive jewelry, he had dug up the body, and cut off her finger to get her rings. The shock of this revived the girl from the coma which had been mistaken for death. She made her way to the house, but on account of her illness and inability to attract the attention of anyone to let her in, had died of exposure during the night. Ever after, the occupants of Church Hill on the first cold nights when snow is imminent, can hear the rustle of silken skirts passing from room to room, while the ghostly wearer is presumably making sure all the fires are replenished, so no one will suffer from the cold. There is a spot near the steps up to the house where the violets grow every year in lush profusion. They are finer here than those in any part of the grounds, for this spot was watered with the tears of the dying girl, on that tragic night so long ago.

Church Hill was for many years the lovely, well-kept home of Mr. and Mrs. E. Wright Noble. Among the improvements and alterations that were made is a huge chimney built of bricks brought from Rosewell.

The classic columns, the commodious proportions of the house, the excellent taste with which modern and comfortable furnishings are combined with fine antiques, all combine to enhance the atmosphere of this truly traditional Virginia country house.

This estate has recently been purchased by Mr. and Mrs. E. Stewart James, of Cappahosic House. They have decided to call their new home Church Hill Plantation.

PIG HILL

PIG HILL, now owned by the Kings, has a lovely location on the Ware River.

Originally a part of Glen Roy, it was formerly called Whiting's Mount, and was the seat of the Whiting family. After their day it passed through various hands. At one time it was owned by the Young Brothers, John G. Young, and W. Oscar Young, and by William C. King, Jr., of Pittsburgh.

It is a large, two-story house, of brick, painted white, and has a wing on either end with huge chimneys. The two-story columned portico has a second-floor balcony with Chinese chippendale railing. A small deck surmounting the roof has a similar railing. The large rooms are tastefully furnished, and the grounds, with big, old trees, shrubs, many flowers and lovely grass, are well-kept.

It was occupied by the Whiting family when the Scaife Whiting incident in Ware Church, about which the following poem was written, occurred. (Scaife's mother was Mrs. Mary Scaife Whiting.)

The Gloucester Herald
Gloucester C.H. Va.
Saturday, April 20, 1872
WM. B. Taliaferro and
Samuel D. Puller, Editors

(Ware Church)

A Tale of The Past.

To the Editor of the Herald: — Some two or three issues back you published in your valuable paper an original ballad, written in such pure and apposite English and combining so many of the excellences of the older and better ballad-writers; that, for myself and many others, I would beg the favor of its republication.

Respectfully,

'T'.

It was per chance, in times gone by,
   Some ninety years or more,
As strange a thing did hap I wot
   As e'er you heard before.

There lived a gay and dashing man,
   Scaife Whiting was his name;
In good old Gloucester, then as now,
   A place of noted fame.

To be afraid he knew not how,
   This was his boast and pride,
But surest things are not yet sure,
   And ill doth oft betide.

Now near him dwelt a jolly youth,
   Who was chock full of fun;
A brawny lad of sturdy mould,
   By name, Dick Singleton.

OLD VIRGINIA HOUSES

It so fell out one stormy night,
  In sunny, leafy June,
What time the storm king's gathering hosts,
  Did rout the pale-faced moon,

That these two gents benighted were,
  As home they hastened late.
Nor either knew the other near,
  Each cursed untoward fate.

Scaife rode a horse full mettlesome,
  Black as the wings of night,
And Dick bestrode one near as good,
  Its hue a creamy white.

Close by the road they both did wend
  A church was situate
"Old Ware," that by disuse had grown
  Ruined and desolate.

This was the only place where they,
  A refuge then might find,
To shelter from the drenching rain,
  And ward the furious wind.

Dick first arrived and doubtingly,
  Rode up the desert aisle,
Reined in his steed close to the wall
  And trembling paused a while.

While still his bosom agitates
  Twixt chilling fear and pride,
Scaife Whiting dashing through the door,
  In speedily doth ride.

Now thought Dick unto himself,
  It proven soon shall be
Whether yon daring Infidel
  Doth boast true bravery.

* * * *

And Scaife found as all alone,
  (At least he fancied so)
Within the church at that dread hour,
  His courage fleeting go.

Quoth he, " 'Tis true I am not afraid,
  And yet I feel not right,
Amongst the dead alone to be,
  At this deep hour of night."

As thus he speaks, the lightning gleams,
  And opposite he sees,
A sight that puts his hair on end,
  That makes his blood to freeze.

A ghostly steed of monster size,
  Doth bear a ghostly form,
Which grim, and stark, and full doth seem
  Lord of the awful storm.

* * * *

"What art thou? Speak," Scaife hoarsely
    shouts;
  A hollow groan replies.
"Fough!" now furiously he spurs
  In frantic haste he flies.

And follows swiftly on his track,
  With equal speed the ghost,
Cries Scaife, "Good steed, now do your best,
  Or I am surely lost!"

Full quickly fled the miles away,
  To him they seemed to stand,
Till to his breast's sincere relief,
  He sees his home at hand.

His courser's speed, no whit he slacks,
  But leaps unto the ground,
Nor till his door-knob firm he clasps,
  Doth dare to look around.

While there for an instant pausing,
  Contending with his fears,
He sees the pale steed pass his gate,
  A jeering laugh he hears.

"Now foul fiends sieze me!" loud he cries,
  "That I this night have run,
And shown a craven crest before the
  Eyes of Singleton!"

"Bear witness, Devils, on my oath,
　　This hand his death shall seal.
Does he to any mortal dare
　　This secret to reveal."

＊　　＊　　＊　　＊

The morrow's sun shone cheerily,
　　A handsome banquet spread,
And laughing Dick to Whiting's comes
　　Invited to break bread.

Scaife meets his guest most graciously,
　　And ushers in his door;
"A glorious day we will have," quoth he,
　　And deep libations pour."

＊　　＊　　＊　　＊

Dinner finished, the board is cleared,
　　The servants now retire,
First on the table placing wine
　　To light convivial fire.

"Ere you to jovial duties turn,
　　I, your attention crave,
A moment, will not long delay
　　Bacchanalian rites," quoth Scaife.

So speaking, to the door he goes
　　And locks and bars it fast
Then from his breast a pistol draws,
　　With ire his face o'er cast.

Reseats himself, "and thus bold Dick
　　The truth you fain must tell,
If that to any you have spoke
　　Of what last night befell."

"I have not breathed a syllable,"
　　Instanter answered Dick,
"But what the thunder ails you, man?
　　What means this savage trick?"

"You hold!" said Scaife "a secret far
　　To me, than life more dear;
In that last night you saw me yield
　　To coward dastard fear.

"And if your life you would preserve,
　　Nor anxious are to die;
This secret promise still to keep
　　And guard most sacredly."

＊　　＊　　＊　　＊

"You must confirm it with an oath,
　　And swear as I dictate,
That never while I live, a word
　　Of this you will relate."

Dick swore and faithfully he kept
　　The oath that night he spoke,
Long years had passed and Scaife was dead,
　　E're he his silence broke.

The above was written by Judge Fielding Lewis Taylor, of Belle Farm, Gloucester, Va.

N. T. S.

At the time of the above incident, Scaife Whiting lived at Pig Hill near the head of Ware River, and Dick Singleton lived at Bloomsbury on North River.

GLEN ROY

ON a peninsula in the Ware River, is the oldest church site in Gloucester. It is here that Glen Roy was built. On one side is what is known as Church-field, on the other is Glebefield. There are still tombs in Churchfield.

Pig Hill, formerly called Whiting's Mount, now belongs to the Kings.

Here the Reverend Armistead Smith, a descendant of the old Smith family, of Gloucester, and of the Honorable John Armistead, of Hesse, member of the Colonial Council, brought home his bride, the former Martha Tabb, of Seaford in Mathews County. He served as Rector of two colonial churches, Abingdon and Ware.

The house in which they lived was burned, and their son, Mr. William Patterson Smith, built the mansion known now as Glen Roy. He married the beautiful Miss Marian Seddon, of Fredericksburg, and together for many years they kept up the traditions of Glen Roy.

This was also the home of the Smiths, Tylers and Seawells, who intermarried.

A later owner was Mr. W. R. Jaeger, who left the estate to John G. Young and his brother, W. Oscar Young.

Although Scaife Whiting's home was Pig Hill (or Whiting's Mount as it was then called), we find a notation which says Colonel Scaife Whiting, of Glen Roy, was Justice in 1794; died in 1821. Pig Hill was originally a part of Glen Roy, and of course it is probable that Colonel Whiting, through inheritance or purchase, acquired Glen Roy and spent his later life there.

It is now the home of Dr. Edwin T. Wellford, and his family. They trace back their line to Mrs. Armistead Smith, wife of the original owner.

This handsome Georgian type home has first floor ceilings sixteen feet high, and second floor ceilings fourteen feet high. It has dormer windows, and stands three stories high. The wide porches, broad lawns, enormous trees and lovely view make Glen Roy a choice place to live.

The present house was built late in the eighteenth century.

LOWLAND COTTAGE

DURING the War of 1812 we find reference, in the writings of General William B. Taliaferro, to Captain Richard Jones, of Lowland Cottage, as being among those who commanded the troops defending our shores. This Captain Jones married Martha, daughter of Warner Throckmorton and Julia Langborne. (Mrs. Page's manuscript; also *Richmond Standard.*)

The Cottage, with its beautiful old trees and wide lawns, is one of the oldest homes in Gloucester. It is an L-shaped house, of early Colonial style. Built about 1690, this was an early seat of the families of Warner, Throckmorton, Jones, Taliaferro, and is now the home of Major and Mrs. Jeffery Montague.

The chimneys and the planting around The Cottage give evidence of its age. With two end chimneys and one middle chimney and with gable windows and gambrel-roof, the structure seems of simple plan, but the rooms

Glen Roy, the home of Dr. E. T. Wellford.

A dependency at Glen Roy.

72

are large and homey. The Cottage is a pleasant place to live in, and the fruit trees and flowing shrubs around it enhance the impression of friendly live-ableness.

HOCKLEY

ADJACENT to The Cottage is Hockley, a spacious, colonial house, which was long the home of the Taliaferros. In olden times the place was called Cowslip Green, also Erin. Hockley has attractive grounds, with old plantings.

It now belongs to Marian Canfield and Annie Hayes O'Neil.

LEVEL GREEN

LEVEL GREEN was the old home of the Robins family, but has been out of the family now for many years. It was built early in the 18th century. Around the house are huge, beautiful old trees, and velvety lawn dotted with box and other shrubs. Built of brick, with gable windows and huge chimneys, the effect is quaint and lovely.

It is here that Henry Clay once landed during a political campaign in this part of the country.

Level Green is now owned by William T. Kilborn.

BAIAE

BAIAE, a small place on the Ware, was formerly owned by John Taliaferro, who probably was the builder. It was later owned by a Mr. Eels. During the Civil War, Baiae became a hospital. After living at Elmington a few years, Colonel Munford, who married a Miss Ellis, and who was author of *The Two Parsons*, bought Baiae, and made it the family home for some years. (Miss Etta Munford, the daughter of Colonel Munford, now lives in Richmond.) Baiae was next owned by Mr. Fox, to whom it was sold by Colonel Munford.

After Mr. Fox, Mr. Augustus Drury, of Richmond, lived at Baiae for some years. It has undergone many alterations, and has been modernized.

ON FACING PAGE

(Above) Lowland Cottage, home of Major and Mrs. Jeffrey Montague.

(Below) Level Green, home of the Kilborns.

A dependency at Lowland Cottage.

The house and the great oaks at Level Green. Notice the river in the background.

76

PART FOUR
ON THE NORTH RIVER

DITCHLEY

IN writing of the social life of Gloucester in the 1890's, Mrs. Sally Nelson Robins, speaking of beaux, says: "Young men are delightful adjuncts, but by no means the perfunctory articles they have gotten to be in 1893." She goes on to tell of a friend who came to spend the day and stayed forty-five years. Social life in Gloucester, no matter of what period, has always, it may truly be said, centered around North River—possibly because the estates there could be reached so conveniently by water. And that is why, no doubt, this section has been called the Venice of America.

The first old house on the left, as one sails into the North from the Mobjack Bay, is Ditchley. It was originally the home of the Singletons, and was called Bloomsbury. In 1862 this place was bought by Professor Edwin Taliaferro, of Belleville. He restored and remodeled the house, and beautified the grounds, calling it Miramer, because of the beautiful and clear reflection it made in the blue water. However, the house was burned down before he moved in.

When the property was acquired in 1863 by Dr. John Prosser Tabb, he built a home on the site of the earlier dwelling, naming the place Ditchley, for Ditchley in England. This was in honor of his wife, who was related to the Lee family, of English Ditchley.

In 1898, Ditchley was purchased by Mr. and Mrs. William Ashby Jones, of Richmond. The house has been remodeled and is now owned by Mr. and Mrs. William Ashby Jones III.

BELLEVILLE

BELLEVILLE, on one of the most beautiful sites on the south side of the North River, was built on the land acquired by John Boswell and John Booth, in a grant from the crown in the seventeenth century. This grant adjoined other land on the North River, already owned by Booth. These two gentlemen were wholesale tobacco buyers, who did an export business between Gloucester and London. Their office, a brick building with a huge fireplace, is still standing. It is close by the Belleville mansion, and for years was used as a kitchen.

The original mansion was an H-shaped brick building, which faced the river. It was built about 1658. When it burned some years later, only a five-room brick wing remained. A substantial frame building was added to this. The parlor, with a large fireplace to the north, had on each side a deep recess, beautifully arched, in which was a window of tiny panes; there was a wide window-seat, on which many a child curled up and read the Standard Works. This room and the adjoining dining room were paneled from ceiling to floor. Both rooms had the deep windows and high mantels.

In 1705 Thomas Booth, a descendant of John, acquired the entire property by indenture. It was passed by inheritance to Frances Amanda Todd Booth and her husband, Warner Throckmorton Taliaferro, and from them to their son, William Booth Taliaferro.

During the lifetime of Mr. Warner Taliaferro, Belleville reached a high peak of production and development. There were large barns, a harness shop, saw-pit, shoe-shop, weaving-house, blacksmith shop and carpenter shop, besides servants' quarters, stables and carriage houses.

Practically everything used on the plantation was made there; even the boats used on the river were constructed of lumber cut from local trees; the nails used were made in the blacksmith shop.

Mr. Taliaferro's second marriage was to Miss Leah Seddon, of Fredericksburg. It was she who laid out a new garden around what was left of the box walk and the enormous crepe myrtles of the old garden. She introduced every variety of flower and shrub adaptable to the climate. With its natural, parklike setting, and lovely view of the river, Belleville became one of the show places of the area.

Some years after the death of General William Booth Taliaferro, his son George Booth Taliaferro sold the place to Mr. A. A. Blow. Thus Belleville passed from the family of Booths and their descendants, the Taliaferros, after it had been in their possession for two hundred and fifty years.

Mr. Blow built a pillared portico, and made other changes in the house.

Dr. and Mrs. H. E. Thomas purchased Belleville early in 1930 and for

The old part of the house at Belleville, originally the home of the Booths.

An avenue at Belleville.

ON FACING PAGE

(Above) Chimneys, dormers and roses at Belleville, the boyhood home of General William Booth Taliaferro. (Below) A massive chimney at Belleville.

80

The Morck's living room at Belleville, from which an excellent view of the river can be had.

a number of years lived there, but they sold it a few years ago to Mr. and Mrs. Wesley C. Morck, who now make it their home. Its magnificent box and beautiful garden draw visitors from all parts of the country.

In the cemetery, Booth tombs, with arms, may still be seen.

WARRINGTON

NEAR Belleville is Warrington, the large comfortable modern home of General William Booth Taliaferro's daughter, Mrs. H. O. Sanders. This place has the advantage of the same magnificent view of the river as Belleville, and now Warrington is as popular a center for social gatherings of the community as Belleville was in days of yore.

82

Dunham Massie, originally General William Booth Taliaferro's home. Now the home of the Worths.

DUNHAM MASSIE

WARNER THROCKMORTON TALIAFERRO, of Church Hill, married Frances Amanda Todd Booth, and went to live at Belleville, the Booth home. When their son (and only child), William Booth Taliaferro, was married, his father built a beautiful home for him on adjoining land near the river. It was a two-story house with steep roof, and pointed gables. There were big center chimneys and a large front porch. It had an English look. It was finished in 1847 while the son was serving in the Mexican War. This place was named

83

Burgh Westra, the home of the Marshalls.

Dunham Massie, in honor of the ancestral Booth home, near Chester, in England—which is still occupied by Booth descendants.

William Booth Taliaferro became a Major General in the Confederate Army, and was an important citizen for many years, serving as Judge of Gloucester County.

At Dunham Massie, on its spacious front porch with an extensive view of North River, were entertained a charming and delightful society of churchmen, statesmen, and gracious ladies of an older regime; but as long as General Taliaferro lived, each guest, so it was said, had to walk under a Confederate flag as he entered the door.

The family sold the place in 1939 to Mr. and Mrs. A. Carlton McKenney, of Richmond, and it is now owned by Mr. and Mrs. Mathew Fontaine Maury Werth.

84

OLD VIRGINIA HOUSES

BURGH WESTRA

NEXT to Elmington, on the North River, the attractive little home known as Burgh Westra was built for Dr. Philip Alexander Taliaferro, by his father, Warner Throckmorton Taliaferro, about 1847. For many years Dr. Taliaferro lived here, where much entertaining was done. After the Doctor's death the place passed first to his wife, then to his sister, and finally to his favorite great niece, Susan Seddon Taliaferro Wellford Marshall (Mrs. Thomas R. Marshall, of Richmond). Built of brick, this substantial building has weathered beautifully the passing of the years. There are many nice shrubs and trees, also flowers, and a lovely river view. Furnished with antiques and reproductions, Burgh Westra is much enjoyed as a summer home by Mrs. Marshall, her children and grandchildren.

ELMINGTON

IN Gloucester, on the North River, approached from the highway by a long straight drive bordered with cedars, is Elmington. Located on a knoll, surrounded by a beautiful lawn, which sweeps out to the river beyond, this century-old mansion of white-washed brick, is one of the most impressive homes in the Tidewater. The white-wash is a kind of plaster treatment that makes the walls look like alabaster. The grounds are dotted with huge magnolias, crepe myrtles, box-woods, cedars and enormous elms.

In November, 1642, a patent to land on which Elmington stands was given to Edmund Dawber, of London. His wife's name was Margaret; she was a daughter of Sir Thomas Gates, a very early Colonial Governor of Virginia. This patent was renewed, or "cleared," seven years later, March 18, 1649, as was customary, to prove that the claim was in good faith, the land "seated," settled, and cultivated. Included in the patent was a tract of 2400 acres on the North River, and other land elsewhere.

Meanwhile, the massacre of 1644 and other circumstances prevented the issuance of further patents in Gloucester for some time.

However, on March 19th, 1652, a patent was issued for this same land, to William Deynes. This patent declared, after quoting dates of the Dawber patent, and renewal, that "—since deserted and granted by order of the Assembly—unto sd William Deines—"

Deynes had to face some disturbing "claymes" to his grant, as is evidenced by a rather formidable document of 1660 in the form of a deed from Dawber's heirs to Richard Young and John Prise, executed in London, and recorded in York County. Apparently Deynes became discouraged and relinquished his claim to at least a part of the North River property.

85

Elmington, the home of Mr. and Mrs. W. S. Rhoads, Jr.

Richard Young was issued a patent for the Elmington tract by Governor Berkeley in 1665. Before his death the same year, Young willed the land to his son, Richard, Jr., saying, "My son Richard to take in satisfaction of his share my plantation which I hold jointly with Dorcas Price, widow, lying at Mobjack Bay, near York River in Virginia."

Richard Young, Jr., was frequently in court about various matters, once in connection with a wager with Mr. Humphrey Gwynn about a servant maid.

There was also, on another occasion, a suit between Mr. Young and Mr. Henry Whiting, over a tobacco house on a certain parcel of land.

Later, Young petitioned the Governor and the Council to have Major John Lewis appointed "to lay out" the borders of his land according to his "ancient knowne bounds." Richard Young, Jr., left the Elmington estate to

The front entrance to Elmington.

his son, but under date of December 22, 1682, a patent for 2673 acres was made to Mr. John Buckner and Major Henry Whiting. This ended a period of twenty-seven years during which the Youngs had resided on the tract.

On a Quit Rent Roll, in Ware Parish, Gloucester, in 1704-5, from Governor Nicholson to England, we find the following acreage; John Buckner, 900 acres; Henry Whiting, 800 acres; Madm. Whiting, 950 acres; Thomas Todd, 884 acres. The conclusion is reached that the land had been divided; that John Buckner was John Buckner, Junior; that Henry Whiting was Henry Whiting, Junior; and that Madm. Whiting was Henry Whiting, Sr.'s, widow. It was during the Whiting ownership that the name Elmington was bestowed on the estate.

Henry Whiting, Jr., married Ann, daughter of Peter Beverley. Their children were: Elizabeth, who married John Clayton, the famous botanist,

87

and lived at Windsor; Catherine, who married John Washington, of Highgate, and became the great-aunt of General George Washington; and Beverley, their son, who inherited Elmington. He married Mary Scaife. He was educated at Oxford, in 1740 was a member of the House of Burgesses, and died in 1755.

Beverley's son, Peter Beverley Whiting, succeeded his father as owner of Elmington. He was educated at William and Mary College, became a vestryman of Ware Parish, and Sheriff of Gloucester. He married Elizabeth, daughter of Lewis Burwell, of Carter's Creek.

Peter Beverley Whiting II married Elizabeth Peyton, who was probably the granddaughter of Sir John Peyton, of Isleham. He evidently did not live long, for during the Revolution, when bad days had come to Elmington, the place is referred to as "Mrs. Whiting's." Mr. Philip Taliaferro reported to General Washington on October 3, 1781, "A party of the Enemy are now at Mrs. Whiting's and have sent out to collect the cattle and sheep adjacent there being no one to stop them."

In July of 1788 "a dreadful storm and highest tide ever known" swept away crops and livestock, thus removing subsistence for the next year. Houses were blown down, and other damage done.

As though this were not enough, in 1790 Mrs. Whiting was called on to settle her late husband's obligations as security for the deputies of Sir John Peyton, when sheriff in 1782-3, of Gloucester County. The Court order said in part: "It shall be lawful for Elizabeth Whiting, Adms. of Peter Beverley Whiting, decd. . . . to deliver and put in the hands of the afore named commissioners . . . all and every slave and Slaves, which now remain in their respective possessions . . . to be sold for satisfying the balance due. . . ."

Peter Beverley III is mentioned in 1800 as being a vestryman of Ware Parish. Old Mrs. Whiting died December 6, 1803. In 1804, after a hundred and twenty years of Whiting ownership, Elmington was sold by Peter Beverley Whiting III, now of Berryville, to Mr. Benjamin Dabney, a prominent lawyer of King and Queen County.

Mr. Dabney died in 1806, in the second year of his residence at Elmington. When some years later his widow arranged for a second marriage, their son, Thomas Smith Gregory Dabney was called to take over possession of Elmington. The house at this time was "of red brick, quaint and oldfashioned," and probably Colonial in style, with some Georgian influences. It was said to have been quite close to the river, and must, even in those days, have been imposing, for when Mr. Thomas Dabney brought home his beautiful bride, the former Sophia Hill, aged sixteen, she was so overcome with awe at the grandeur and magnificence of the place, and the many servants, that she did not dare to take over her housekeeping responsibilities for a matter

88

Elmington river front, showing edge of big magnolia.

of two years. She was Mr. Dabney's second wife. In 1820 he had married Mary, daughter of Chancellor Samuel Tyler. She died three years later. Then, after three years had elapsed, the handsome young widower courted and married the aforesaid lovely Sophia. That was in 1826.

For nine years this young couple lived at Elmington, entertaining hospitably many distinguished guests. In those days, a signal from post or tree meant an invitation to all the families up and down the river, to come for some gay festivity. John Tyler, later President of the United States, was a frequent guest at Elmington. In 1835 the Dabneys moved to Mississippi, and a few years later John Tabb, of White Marsh, bought Elmington for his son John Prosser Tabb, who married Miss Rebecca Lloyd, of Alexandria.

It was in 1848 that the present house was built. The beautiful old place was a wedding gift to Rebecca, who was as lovely a bride as Sophia Hill

*Great hall at Elmington, showing circular stairs, grandfather's clock
and historic scenes on walls.*

had been, and her husband, John Prosser Tabb. There was a fine Hubard
portrait of Rebecca, hanging in the home. The couple apparently lived in
great style. It is said that Rebecca's cupboard was filled with dishes of gold
and silver.

The hospitality and gracious living at Elmington were interrupted by
the coming of the Civil War. Dr. John Prosser Tabb and his wife sold Elmington to Mr. James M. Talbott, of Richmond, and it was paid for with Confederate money.

Mr. Talbott leased the estate soon after, for a term of three years, to
Colonel George Wythe Munford, who wrote *The Two Parsons* while resident
there. The Munfords, however, only stayed at Elmington about two years.

The next owner of Elmington was Mr. Duncan; then just before the end of the century, Mr. Thomas Dixon, the famous novelist, bought and remodeled the house, renaming it Dixondale. It was he who built the pillared portico. While Mr. Dixon was resident here, he wrote some of his best books.

It seems that this spacious mansion on the river was destined to figure further in our literature, for more recently, Mr. Virginius Dabney has made it the scene of *Don Miff,* which was a best seller of the year in which it was published.

Mr. Dixon sold to Mr. Walkup, and he to Mr. Dimmock. The Dimmock possession lasted from 1908 to 1940, when Mrs. Walcott, the former Mrs. Dimmock, sold to Mr. Richard Smith, who in 1941 sold to Mr. and Mrs. Webster S. Rhoads, Jr., the present owners. So reads the list of owners of Elmington, for a period of three hundred and seven years.

Today, Elmington has a pillared portico on each front, and its appearance when approached by water or land, is most imposing. The great hall

Dining room at Elmington.

Sun room at Elmington.

ON FACING PAGE

(Above) Living room at Elmington.

(Below) Drawing room at Elmington.

92

reminds one of the great hall at Monticello. The scenic wall panels here depict episodes in American history. The spiral staircase ascends to the third floor, where there is an observatory with a unique arrangement of windows. A chandelier is suspended from the ceiling of the third floor, dropping down through the stair well, to light the great hall on the first floor.

The rooms are large, and have beautiful windows, mantels and chandeliers. They are furnished in exquisite taste, both in color combination and suitability of furnishing. The sheen of antique furniture, the gleam of old silver, and flowers everywhere, combine to create an atmosphere of charm and beauty as glamorous as what we like to think was characteristic of the fabled days of old.

EXCHANGE

THE Dr. Dabney home on the North River just above Elmington, is called The Exchange. It has been the home of the Dabneys for several generations. The Misses Dabney, whose mother was a Miss Tabb, of Toddsbury, long dispensed hospitality at the Exchange.

Tombs there show that this estate must previously have been the Anderson home.

One tomb reads:

Mary Anderson
born 27 August 1749
died 12 June 1820

Another:

Mathew Anderson, Esq.,
born 6 December 1743
died 24 December 1806

A third tomb has this inscription:

George Dabney Anderson
son of Mathew and Mary
born October 8, 1760
died Sept. 9, 1771
(followed by consoling poetic
quotation typical of the period).

94

Exchange, the home of the Dabneys.

Exchange was lent distinction by the famous artist, Hubard, well known in Gloucester County. The portraits he did which hung at the Exchange were: one of Thomas Todd Tabb; one of his wife, Elizabeth Foreman; one of Martha Tompkins, who married Dr. Henry Wythe Tabb, of Auburn, and left four daughters and one son; and one of Dr. James Dabney. Hubard also did a portrait of Elizabeth Perrin Page Michie, but if this was ever hung at Exchange, it was removed at an early date.

A unique feature of Exchange is the charming living quarters, both comfortable and modern, into which the picturesque old ice-house has been converted.

95

The Exchange was presumably built in the late eighteenth century, and is Georgian style, of frame construction. There is a front porch. Large chimneys are at the ends, and there is one wing.

HAIL WESTERN

JOHN THROCKMORTON married Miss Washington and lived on the Northern Neck, but returned to Gloucester after her death. There were several children by this marriage. After making financial arrangements for the care of these children, he married a Miss Cooke, of Gloucester, and went to England to receive an inheritance which had been willed to him there. When he returned to Gloucester he built a home and called it Hail Western (or Weston) in honor of an old home of the Throckmortons in England.

There was one child of this second marriage, a daughter, Eliza, whom Mrs. Page calls "Cousin Eliza Jones."

Hail Western was burned many years ago, but the outbuildings are still standing. They are frame, and have been converted into modern homes. It is away from the rivers but not far from the Ware.

TODDSBURY

ON the North River, in Gloucester, with its lawns sweeping right down to the water's edge, stands Toddsbury, a silent witness to almost all of Gloucester County's past, for it was in 1658 that the oldest part of the house was built. Thomas Todd, the emigrant, was the builder, and the place remained in the possession of his direct descendants for over two hundred years.

For four generations the owners were Todds; then Phillip Tabb, the son of Lucy Todd and Edward Tabb, married his cousin, Mary Mason Wythe, a daughter of Elizabeth Todd, and inherited Toddsbury from their uncle, Christopher Todd. Both these young people were direct descendants of Thomas Todd, the founder. Their descendants were owners for many years. Various additions and improvements were made to the house up until 1784.

The house is in purest Dutch Colonial style, with gambrel roof and shallow dormer windows. The body is of stucco over brick.

The central hall may be entered from the porch on the river front, or from the triangular terrace, which is now enclosed, on the garden front. Entrance may also be made from this terrace to the hall of the old wing, which stands at right angles to the larger part of the building. (This enclosed terrace is said to have previously been a "mud room," where shoes were scraped, boots removed, etc.)

Deeply recessed windows, beautiful old paneling, staircases and mantels

96

Toddsbury, home of Mr. and Mrs. Gordon Bolitho. Notice garden wall
in background, also river and big trees.

contribute to the beauty of the interior. The woodwork has the coveted patina
that comes from daily polishing, and daily use, throughout the centuries.

Toddsbury is homelike, and gives the impression of having been comfortably lived in for many generations. This is not surprising, since it has
been pretty continuously occupied ever since it was built. There have been
few days during the old mansion's three hundred year life-span that have
not seen smoke curling up out of at least one of the great chimneys, and on
chilly days at twilight, a wood fire in one of the six fireplaces of the house
has always brightened at least one room with its cheerful glow.

There must have been gay parties here; cheerful teas; hunt breakfasts;
romantic courtships. This old house must have been the scene of many wed-
dings, christenings, births, deaths and funerals. The family burying ground
is to the east of the house.

97

Toddsbury river front showing "porch" chamber.

The Motts came after the Tabbs, and they stayed over fifty years.

Now Mr. and Mrs. Gordon Bolitho are the owners. She is a direct descendant of the original builder of the house.

One of the unusual features of Toddsbury is the enclosed chamber above the porch, the "morning room," facing the river.

Some of the dependencies are still standing.

There was originally a beautiful formal garden, enclosed by a brick wall. Mr. and Mrs. Bolitho have restored both.

The large spacious lawns which are bordered by the river on three sides, are studded with ancient oak, elm and pecan trees.

Toddsbury is sometimes referred to as "The Jewel of the Tidewater."

In a letter from Mr. Gordon Bolitho, he says in part:

"Over the almost three hundred years since the original house was built, the place has apparently sunk about two feet. It is estimated that all of Tidewater is sinking one foot per century. However, in our cellar we have found the remains of a Dutch Oven, partially sunken now, with a flu running up what was originally the outside wall, now the wall of the library. In restoring the house we discovered numerous 'dated' bricks. The present sitting-room wing was added in 1722 and obviously the panelling taken out of part of the library for the walls of the sitting-room. The wall between library and hall is an ordinary partition which must have been put in when the sitting-room was added. The panelling of the library and sitting-room are identical but the woodwork in the hall is of a much later period. The present dining-room was added to in 1784 with bricks dated and initialed 'P.T.' (Philip Tabb?) and 'R.D.L.'"

The following Todd Genealogy, compiled from papers of Selina L. Hopkins, of Waverley, Gloucester County, and from family records lent us by Mrs. Nina Taliaferro Sanders, would be of great interest to descendants of the Todd family, the Tabb family, the Booths and Armisteads.

1. Geoffry Todd, sometimes spelled Tood, Toode, Todde, was of Hanghton-le-Sherne, a parish about five miles from Denton County, Durham, England. Buried February 22, 1637/8.

> Married Margaret.
> Their son—

2. Captain Thomas Todd, came from Denton, England to Toddsbury, Ware Parish, North River, Gloucester County, Virginia, and went later to Todd's Neck, North Parish, Patapsco River, Baltimore County, Maryland, where he settled in 1664. His will, and those of his son, Thomas Todd II, and his grandson, Thomas, are on record in the Courthouse of Baltimore County. He died at sea, 1676. Was baptised, September 12, 1619. Married Anne Gorsuch, issue, nine children of which the eldest:

3. Thomas Todd II, or Junior, was born at Toddsbury 1660. Justice of the Peace for Gloucester County from 1698 to 1702. Died January 16, 1724/5. Buried at Toddsbury. His will dated January 1714-15 on file in Baltimore County, Maryland, devises his "Lands in the neck where I now live" to his sons, Thomas and Robert, and if they have no heirs, to his brothers, William or Philip or Christopher on condition that whoever gets them shall live on them. Showan Hunting Grounds in draught of Gunpowder River to his son Robert. "All lands of mine in Virginia to be sold, except that on which I lived, and proceeds to be divided between my wife and children." He married Elizabeth Bernard, daughter of Colonel William Bernard and Lucy Higginson.

Issue of Thomas Todd II. Thomas Bernard, moved to his grandfather's

99

The hall at Toddsbury, showing antique chest with paintings of
Maria Louisa, fourteenth child of James II.

estate in Todd's Neck, Maryland. Robert, who inherited Showan Hunting Grounds, Maryland. William. Anne, who married Thomas Cooke, of Wareham, Gloucester County, Virginia. Philip, Sheriff of Gloucester in 1730. Frances. Frances 2nd. Elizabeth. Christopher.

4. Christopher (ninth child of Thomas Todd II and Elizabeth Bernard). Born at Toddsbury, April 2, 1690, and died at Toddsbury, his home, March 26, 1743. Buried at Toddsbury. Married in 1738, Elizabeth Mason (1701-1764), daughter of Lemuel Mason.

Issue of Christopher Todd. Lucy, born 1721, died 1794. Married in 1749, Edward Tabb, son of John and Martha Hand Tabb; Edward Tabb was born 1719; died 1782. They lived in Cumberland County for a time and came from there to live with her brother, Thomas Todd, after the death of their mother, at Toddsbury. When Thomas Todd died, he left Toddsbury to his sister, Lucy, and thus Toddsbury came into the Tabb family.

5. Elizabeth (daughter of Christopher Todd and Elizabeth Mason), born

100

Detail of alcove and paneling at Toddsbury.

101

The Library at Toddsbury.

ON FACING PAGE

(Above) The living room at Toddsbury (and below) the dining room.

Master bedroom at Toddsbury. Notice paneling and deep windows.

1723; died 1785. Married first, Nathaniel Wythe of Warwick County, and had a daughter, Mary Mason. Elizabeth married, second, Mordecai Booth, of Belle Ville, Gloucester County.

6. Mary Mason Wythe (daughter of Elizabeth Todd and Nathaniel Wythe) married, first, her step-brother, George Booth, of Belle Ville, son of Mordecai Booth and his first wife, Joyce Armistead of Hesse, Mathews County. Mary Mason Wythe married, second, Philip Tabb of Toddsbury, (her first cousin), son of Thomas T. Tabb.

Issue of Mary Mason Wythe and Philip Tabb: John, of White Marsh; Henry Wythe, of Auburn; Philip Edward, of Waverley; Thomas Todd, of Toddsbury.

Guest room at Toddsbury.

105

Newstead, home of the Holcombes, formerly a Tabb home.

NEWSTEAD

ON the North River, near Toddsbury, of which it was originally a part, stands Newstead. This, too, was a Tabb home. Built near the middle of the 19th century by John H. Tabb, it remained in the Tabb family for almost a century. It now belongs to Colonel and Mrs. John Lee Holcombe.

The house, of red brick with many gables and chimneys, and several porches, stands in a grove of large trees. A huge wing runs back at right angles to the main building. The style is Early American. There is a large area of lawn, and extensive gardens are being restored.

The father of the present owner lived for years in China, and Colonel Holcombe, himself, has visited there several times, so it is not surprising that the Holcombes have a magnificent collection of Chinese curios. There are in this collection many valuable pieces of carved ivory, as well as a handsome Chinese bowl, said to be 1500 years old. The Holcombes also have at Newstead a very extensive library and a large collection of 19th century paintings, among which is a Rembrandt Peale, a Sully, a Trumbull, a Hubard, and the famous Charles II, by Edward Wissing.

WAVERLEY

ABOVE Newstead, on the North River, was built, about one hundred fifty years ago, the commodious mansion known as Waverley. It was built by Captain Philip Tabb, of Toddsbury, for his son, Philip Edward, at about the time he built Auburn for another son, Dr. Harry Tabb. Waverley is a Colonial type house in Georgian influence.

Captain Tabb, the builder of Waverley, distinguished himself in the War of 1812 by running the Blockade. He used his own men and his own ships in these adventurous expeditions. Captain Tabb left many descendants who became prominent, among them the late John Lightfoot, Esq., Mrs. Brown, who was a Miss Lightfoot, Judge Crump Tucker, and the late Dr. Beverley Randolph Tucker.

Philip Edward Tabb, Captain Tabb's son, for whom Waverley was built, married Miss Mary Almond of Norfolk. Their daughter became the wife of Judge William W. Crump, of Richmond, and left many descendants in Richmond.

Waverley, a beautiful home of brick construction, was enhanced by a marble porch and steps. This spacious mansion had a wide hall with very handsome curved stairway. There were two large rooms at the back and one to the right of the hall.

Tombs at Waverley indicate that there was a previous house on this site.

One of the tombstones reads:

In Memory of Doctor
Richard Edwards
Who departed
This Life the 8
Day of March in
The Year 1721
Having had two
Wives and at the
Time of his Death
Nine Children
Living
(Skull and crossbones)

Midlothian, home of the Moormans.

Another of the tombs is not entirely decipherable, but we learn that an earlier Richard Edwards died in March 1707.

Waverley was sold first to Dr. Jones, later to Mr. Hopkins, a nephew of Johns Hopkins of Baltimore.

Mrs. Snowden Hopkins, now of River's Edge, Gloucester County, was residing at Waverley at the time it was burned—some years ago. Mrs. R. M. Janney, of Roaring Springs, who was a Miss Hopkins, was born at Waverley. The place now belongs to Lloyd N. Emory.

108

MIDLOTHIAN

BUILT by Mr. Josiah Deans over one hundred sixty years ago, near the head of the North River, Midlothian is a quaint, small, but comfortable home, in Early American style. The building is one room deep, two-stories high, with steep roof and dormer windows.

The parlor and dining room are paneled, and the staircase is built in.

In 1915 this was the home of the Davidsons. Besides them and Mr. Deans, it has been owned by Mr. Charles Talbott, also Mr. Eugene Sanders, of New York. Then Malcolm Matherson, Esq. lived at Midlothian for some years, but after World War I, he sold to Commander and Mrs. Elliott Moorman of Philadelphia. The Moormans still make their home here.

The house faces the river, and there are lovely trees, back and front.

NORTH END

ADJOINING Midlothian, and at the very head of the North River, used to stand North End. The house is long since gone, but it was formerly a Van Bibber estate. "Mrs. Van Bibber, of North End" was the devout congregation of one, who made the responses to Dr. William Taliaferro's readings in Ware Church during the time when there was no minister to conduct the service. Sometimes Mrs. Van Bibber would have to guard against the cold with extra wraps, and a charcoal brazier for her feet.

AUBURN

ON the North River in Mathews County, adjoining Green Plains, Auburn was built in the early 1800's by Philip Tabb for his son, Dr. Henry Wythe Tabb (see Waverley). For many years it remained in his family.

Dr. Henry Wythe Tabb was married three times; first to Hester Van Bibber; from this union there was no issue. His second wide was Martha Tompkins, who left four daughters and one son. His third wife was Ellen Foster, who had three daughters and one son. Henry Wythe Tabb, of Auburn, was born January 12, 1791, died in 1863.

Auburn was originally property of the Mayo family. Mrs. Yeatman, of Auburn, says that her grandfather, Edward Tabb, born February 3, 1719, was the son of John Tabb and Martha Mayo, of Auburn. Records show that John Tabb married Martha Hand. The conclusion is that Martha Hand was a widow who had been Miss Martha Mayo.

Auburn in Georgian style is a magnificent mansion with brick walls

109

three feet thick. The mantels, stairs and panels are of exquisite hand-carved mahogany.

The lawn, with its noble elm trees and excellent river view, is all that could be desired.

This beautiful estate has been lent a special interest by Mr. Joseph Hergeshimer, the famous novelist, who made it the scene of his novel, *Balisand*. White Marsh was supposed to be Welfield in the same story.

During the Civil War the cabinets in the dining room at Auburn were closed up, their keyholes plugged, and their doors made to look like the rest

The great oak at Auburn.

Auburn, the home of Mr. and Mrs. Alexander P. Blood.

111

The dining room at Auburn.

112

The hall and stairs at Auburn.

113

Air view of Green Plains, estate of Mr. and Mrs. Francis Higginson Cabot.

114

of the paneling, to provide a safe hiding place for the family silver.

At one time, Auburn belonged to Mr. and Mrs. Alfred Bell; later to Mr. Charles Heath. It is now the home of Mr. and Mrs. Alexander P. Blood. It is furnished in exquisite taste with beautiful antiques and reproductions, and the library houses a splendid collection of books.

GREEN PLAINS

ON the North River, in Mathews County, stands the large red-brick Georgian house, which Mr. James H. Roy built between 1798 and 1802.

Mr. Roy was the grandson of Dr. Mungo Roy, of Scotland, and the son of Mr. Mungo Roy, of Locust Grove, Caroline County. He married Elizabeth Booth, daughter of George Booth, of Belleville. He was a representative, from Mathews County, in the House of Delegates (1818-1819).

William Henry Roy, the son of James H. and Elizabeth, was also a representative in the House of Delegates (1832-1834). He inherited Green Plains, and was twice married: first to Anne, daughter of Thomas Seddon, of Fredericksburg; then to Euphan, daughter of John MaCrae, of Park Gate, Prince William County. He had two daughters by his first wife. They were Mrs. John C. Rutherfoord, of Rock Castle, and Mrs. Thomas H. Carter, of Pampatike.

By his second wife, he had three daughters; Mrs. Washington and Mrs. Goldsboro, of Maryland, and Mrs. H. McKendree Boyd, of Green Plains.

In 1937 Mr. and Mrs. Higginson Cabot bought Green Plains, and they now reside there. They remodeled and redecorated the house, raising the roof, and setting in dormers; raising the wings, and building large chimneys.

The great central hall, with its magnificent staircase; the deeply recessed windows, with window seats; the chandeliers, the old mantels and paneling; the great fireplaces; the priceless antiques; the handsome oil paintings; the splendid library; all these are only a few of the features which contribute to the beauty and charm of Green Plains. Identical wings built by William H. Roy in 1838 balance each other at the ends of the central building. The two fronts, the towering chimneys, spreading lawn, large old trees and the extensive gardens, go to make a grandeur not often found in Tidewater Virginia.

The river view here is unsurpassed, for Green Plains is on a peninsula, and the blue water sweeps in a semi-circle around the river front.

The garden is enclosed in a scalloped brick wall, four feet high, said to be the only scalloped wall in America. The garden, itself, includes more than an acre, and has a profusion of flowers and shrubs. The tree box is unusually fine, and there are also vast quantities of large and dwarf varieties of box. The crepe myrtles are huge.

Mr. Cabot is quite a farmer and country gentleman, and Mrs. Cabot is a writer.

115

The great oak and a maze of box at Green Plains.

ON FACING PAGE

Two views of Green Plains. (Above) The river front and (below) the land front showing the great oak in early spring.

The scalloped wall at Green Plains.

ON FACING PAGE

Two views of the garden at Green Plains.

The hall (showing staircase and grandfather's clock) at Green Plains.

120

The dining room.

The music room.

The drawing room.

ISLEHAM

THE home of Sir John Peyton, the only English baronet who came to live permanently in Virginia, was called Isleham and was situated on the North River near the Mobjack Bay in what is now Mathews County.

Sir John was an officer in the Gloucester Militia. Although an English baronet, during the Revolutionary War he was ardently devoted to the American cause. His descendants intermarried with the best families of Gloucester. The home was an important center of social life in the early days of the county. It was here that Sharpless, the artist, died, and was buried in the family graveyard.

The house has not been restored, but there are still traces of a wide impressive driveway.

Following ownership by its original owner, Sir John, Isleham passed to the Throckmortons and then the Yeatmans.

In 1860 it was the property of Warner T. Throckmorton. Later it was owned by Mr. Mosby, then Dr. Miller.

It is now the property of Miss Alice Corr, of Norfolk, Virginia.

Old records of Isleham show that:

Peter Beverley (died 1728), who was very prominent in the county, married Elizabeth, daughter of Major Robert Peyton, of Isleham; possibly an uncle of Sir John Peyton.

John Dixon, of Mt. Pleasant, Gloucester, married Elizabeth Peyton, of Isleham, February 1773. Their son was John, of Airville. His son, John, a doctor, died unmarried.

December 11, 1773, Major Mordecai Throckmorton married Mary, daughter of Sir John Peyton, of Isleham.

John Patterson, of England, founded Poplar Grove and married Elizabeth Tabb. Their daughter, Elizabeth, married Thomas Robinson Yeatman, of Isleham.

THE SHELTER

IRONICALLY enough, there is now no house on the property called The Shelter, where this famous old house stood for so many years. But because of the mansion's past importance in the social life of Gloucester we wish to include the article, quoted below, lent by Nina Taliaferro Sanders, and written by Philip Hairston Seawell under date of August 29, 1938:

The Shelter, Gloucester County, Va.

THE SHELTER came into the Seawell family of Virginia in the year 1844. At that time it was purchased by Mr. John Tyler Seawell, from Mr. Walter Jones, the father of the late Dr. Walker Jones, and Mr. William P. Jones. The Shelter throughout the long period of its existence was the scene of many happenings that related to the history of Gloucester County, of Virginia, and of the United States.

Part of this historic old homestead stood long before the Revolutionary War, though it is not known who owned it at that time. This early part was an old-styled Dutch gabled-roof building. It formed the nucleus for the later and larger home. The rooms in this part were very large even for the time in which it was built. There was an inside fireplace in the room used later as the dining room when the house came into the possession of the Seawell family. It was in this room that many of the feasts, so customary in the area, took place, here that the tasty dishes for which the Seawell wives were always noted, were served in abundance. In this wing also was another large room, next to the dining room, and an inside-the-house kitchen.

On the second floor were three very large bedchambers.

There was no porch to this building, as was the custom in the section in Pre-Revolutionary days. This house, later a wing of the completed homestead, was two stories in height. The rooms were on different levels. Two steps up or down led to the hall. It is this wing that is the best-known and remembered of the Seawell home because of its distinctive architecture in a country using English Styles. The drive approached the home on this side, from a long lane.

A very old lady, Mrs. Moore, whose husband owned the place before Mr. Jones got it, said that it was used as a hospital during the Revolutionary War. This is most probable, because the house was built long before, and was located about two miles from Gloucester Court House. This placed it in a section in which much action took place during the war.

The main part of the house was added by the same Mr. Jones who turned the historic place over to Mr. John Tyler Seawell. This consisted of a large hallway used as a room, joining a much larger hallway by a flight of several steps. It was this larger hall that became the main entrance hallway and from which the stairs ascended to the bed-chambers.

There was a porch to greet the guest at the front entrance. At the rear of this same hall another small porch let one out into the garden area. From this hall an enormous parlor opened off. This parlor had an inside fireplace. It was here that gay celebrations began and ended,

123

where campaigns were mapped during the Civil War. It was the reception room for the weary traveller, and the ball-room for those gay young peoples of all ages who made up that far-noted Gloucester society.

The Shelter was at the end of a lane a fourth of a mile long. The lane was bordered by heavily shaded woods and crossed a rambling brook. The home got its name from the wife of Mr. Jones. This lane was known far and wide for its roughness, though people always travelled it to get to the Shelter. Mrs. Jones was being taken as a bride to the place, which consisted then of the Dutch wing only. The night was stormy and the bride weary. When she saw the place she is reputed to have said, "Well, it is at least a Shelter." That name has attached and its roofs have sheltered many famous people. Its hospitality was noted so far, that no distance seemed too great to go for its suppers and parties, of which there were many. Many lawyers gathered in its rooms to discuss cases, for it was always the home of a lawyer, when in the Seawell family. It was from here that John Hairston Seawell went off to the University of Va. to study law, and from there to go with his fellow students to the Civil War. Miss Millie Elliott Seawell, the authoress, lived here and drew on the setting of the place for several of her novels. Tho the place was owned by the Seawell family from 1844, only three children of the family were born there, namely, Henrietta, Millie Elliott and John Tyler Seawell, son of John Hairston Seawell, he being the only one of the three now living. This rambling historic house was destroyed by fire in 1925. With it passed a long reign of gayety and sorrow, for it was a house that was old enough to know life.

Philip Hairston Seawell
August 29, 1938

The property now belongs to W. T. Frary Bros.

PART FIVE

ON THE EAST THE PIANKATANK RIVERS IN MATHEWS COUNTY

POPLAR GROVE

THE huge porticoed mansion with wings and many windows, known as Poplar Grove, stands near the East River, in Mathews County, on land which was part of an original grant from George III to Samuel Williams and his son Thomas. They built the oldest part of the present house about 1750.

Mr. John Patterson bought this property some years later, and enlarged and beautified the house. He planted many Lombardy poplars, which were the party symbol of the Whigs—hence the name.

Mr. Patterson was of England, but fought on the American side in the Revolution. He was breveted by Washington at the Battle of Monmouth, and by him recommended for the Navy.

He married Elizabeth Tabb (born July 31, 1760). They left two daughters, Mrs. Thomas Robinson Yeatman, who lived at Isleham, and Mrs. Christopher Tompkins, who lived at Poplar Grove. Her daughter Sally was born here. Mrs. Christopher Tompkins inherited the place, and in turn it became her daughter's home. Sally was a devoted nurse during the Civil War. She was commissioned a captain by General Robert E. Lee; as a captain she could

Poplar Grove, the home of Mrs. George Upton.

126

The tide mill at Poplar Grove.

127

command service and supplies as needed in her work among the wounded. It is said that she was the only woman commissioned by the Confederacy.

In *Tompkins Family,* by Mrs. J. E. Warren, we find some interesting records:

"Maria B. Patterson born Sept. 1794—second wife of Christopher Tompkins."

She had several children: Elizabeth, named for Mr. Tompkins' first wife, Maria, and (Capt.) Sally Louisa, born Nov. 9, 1833. (Sally died 1916.)

Also in *Tompkins Family,* by Mrs. Warren, we find "Married at Poplar Grove 22ond of July 1828 by the Rev. Mr. Cairne, Martha Tabb (daughter of Christopher and Elizabeth Tompkins) to Dr. Henry W. Tabb, son of Philip and Mary Tabb."

One of the few tide mills left in America is at Poplar Grove. During the Revolution, meal was ground here for Washington's troops. It is said that thirty-two bushels of meal could be ground on a tide. During the Civil War, the mill was burned by the Northern soldiers, but it was rebuilt and used until after the beginning of this century.

The gardens, the serpentine walls, similar to those at the University of Virginia, and the grove, are outstanding features at Poplar Grove, and combine to lend distinction to the place.

Poplar Grove has belonged to the Brown family, to Judge J. Taylor Garnett, and to the Butler family.

Mrs. George Upton, who bought the estate from the Butlers in 1927, still makes it her home.

The house is built on different levels. We find lovely paneling in the west wing, which is the oldest part. The center was the next part to be added. Mrs. Upton has the place nicely furnished in reproductions and antiques. The land now consists of two thousand acres.

HOPEMONT

HIGH on a hill, on the Piankatank River, nine miles from the Chesapeake, stands Hopemont. It is a brick Georgian house and was built about 1750 by the Fritchett family. At that time it was called Providence. Later (in 1799), Providence was owned by the Howletts, who renamed it Howlett Hall.

In 1936 Mr. and Mrs. McComb bought and restored the house, adding one wing. They again called it Providence. The house is noted for its fine paneling.

The garden was originally laid out by an eminent English botanist. It is now being restored by the present owners, Mr. and Mrs. Hope Norton.

With its end chimneys, the third story dormer windows; and classical

Hopemont, the home of Mr. and Mrs. Hope Norton.

129

Gate at Hopemont, showing brick wall with eagles on gateposts.

130

Main entrance of Hopemont.

The garden entrance to Hopemont.

132

Fan steps at Hopemont.

On this and the facing page are views of the garden at Hopemont.

134

A remnant at Hesse.

136

doorway, with fan steps, Hopemont has preserved the purity of its architecture. The columns of the portico ascend from the bricked terrace floor to the second story roof. In restoring the fences, walls and outbuildings, the Nortons are exercising the most punctilious care in developing and preserving the correct surroundings for this architectural gem.

HESSE

WILLIAM ARMISTEAD, the emigrant, was the builder of Hesse. His son, the Honorable John Armistead, was a member of His Majesty's Council in the latter part of the 17th century.

King Carter, of Corotoman, married Judith Armistead, of Hesse.

John's son, Henry, married Martha, daughter of the Honorable Lewis Burwell. She had been a great belle, with many suitors. Governor Sir Francis Nicholson had paid court to her, but she refused his hand. Sir Francis had said that if she ever married anyone else three murders would be committed immediately: that of the bride-groom; that of the officiating minister; and that of the justice who issued the license!

Martha and Henry had three children, first Lucy, who married "Secretary" Thomas Nelson (1716-1782), son of Thomas Nelson the emigrant; second, Martha, wife of Dudley Digges, who was a member of the first Executive Council of the State of Virginia; and finally William Armistead, who succeeded his father as owner of Hesse, and who married Mary, daughter of James Bowles, of Maryland. He died in 1755.

In 1765 William's son, William II, married Maria, daughter of Charles Carter, of Cleve by his second wife, Anne, daughter of William Byrd II.

There is on record some interesting correspondence between Maria and her relatives, the Byrds, of Westover.

She named her son Charles Byrd Armistead. When he died in 1797, he left no descendants, so the big old house of Hesse with 3877 acres of land passed from the Armistead family.

For a number of years the place was deserted, the house neglected and desolate, but the present owners, Mr. and Mrs. John Maxwell, are considering restoration of this fine old mansion. There has been an architect's drawing of tentative plans for the restoration. According to these plans the grandeur of Hesse will be restored, too. All that is left now appears bleak and discouraging, but in its heyday Hesse was an imposing place.

Standing high on the banks of the Piankatank, with terraced gardens reaching down to the water's edge, Hesse extended hospitality to the finest families of Virginia. Hither came the Wormeleys, the Burwells, the Carters, the Byrds, the Cookes, the Whitings, the Booths, and the Pages. Hesse was a Georgian house with end chimneys, and was built of brick. There was a frame wing and small front porch.

It is said that the brick walls at the foundation were nine feet thick, and the rest of the old house of corresponding solidity. Now the most of the old house has been destroyed, and the terraced gardens washed away by the waters of the river.

But Hesse has made its imprint on the state and the nation. Many Americans from all parts of the country can boast with justifiable pride of their ancestors, the Armisteads, of Hesse, and many prideful eyes will come to see the mansion—after the restoration.

KINGSTON HALL

IN Mathews County, on the road from Gloucester Court House, is the magnificent home of Mr. and Mrs. George C. Kirkmyer.

The original house was built in 1730, by Thomas Smith, on a grant named Centerville. The large center building was added by George Tabb, in 1840. The wings were built a hundred years later, by the present owners, who named the place Kingston Hall.

Historically, Kingston Hall is noted for being the birthplace of two Phi Beta Kappa founders, Thomas and Armistead Smith, who were sons of the builder. This place, formerly called Woodstock, was long the home of the Lane family, a member of which was Dr. Thomas B. Lane, the famous Confederate surgeon.

Standing back in a beautiful grove, with its many gables, its vast array of windows, and classic front, Kingston Hall is a magnificent sight. The driveway, the old trees, the wide stretches of lawn are most impressive. The profusion of flowers and shrubs add to the charm of the grounds.

The paneling of the interior has been much admired, and the great staircase with its unique railing is very unusual. The railing has five balusters to each step.

WINDSOR

WINDSOR, on the line between Gloucester and Mathews Counties, has almost disappeared, but it was once famous as home of John Clayton, the colonial botanist, who was the friend and correspondent of many learned scientists in different parts of the world. Mr. Clayton was for fifty years Clerk of the county.

He studied many plants native to Virginia, or imported into the state.

138

Gateway to Kingston Hall.

139

Kingston Hall, home of Mr. and Mrs. George Kirkmyer.

140

Kingston Hall, showing trees and flowers at front.

Kingston Hall, view from the back, showing gables and chimneys.

142

The famed staircase at Kingston Hall.

143

The traces of his elaborate and extensive botanical gardens can still be discerned.

Mr. Clayton wrote, in collaboration with the Dutch botanist, Gronovius, *Flora Virginica,* published at Leyden in 1743.

Among John Clayton's friends were numbered Peter Kalm, of Finland, Linnaeus, of Sweden, Alexander Gardner, of England, Thomas Jefferson, William Byrd and Benjamin Franklin.

The Garden Club has put up a marker at Windsor, honoring Clayton, and is considering making a shrine there. It is only very recently that we have awakened to the fact that Clayton ranks with Liberty Hyde Bailey, of Cornell, and other famous botanists.

SEAFORD

FROM Mrs. F. Snowden Hopkins' account in the *Baltimore Sun* of August 27, 1933, of the Piankatank and vicinity, we find that Seaford was on the creek bank inland from the Piankatank. She says that at that time there was left only —a tree-box avenue, a few magnificent elms, and an overgrown garden.

She speaks of ruins—no house left. Seaford was originally the Tabb home —not far from Mathews Court House.

From old records we find that Thomas Tabb married Elizabeth Teackle, of the Eastern Shore, and lived at Seaford. He became the ancestor of many "Seaford Tabbs."

KENWOOD

KENWOOD, the home of Mr. Norman Cook, while not very old, has some historic interest and a pleasant location. The house itself has traditional and architectural value.

THE HAVEN

THE HAVEN figured in the shipping of the early days and also was a refuge for our ships in times of naval engagements along the coast.

HAVEN'S EDGE

HAVEN'S EDGE, the handsome home of Colonel Fales, which is nearby, played, to a certain extent, a similar role.

Kenwood, home of Mr. Norman Cook.

Kenwood, view from the back.

ON FACING PAGE

Two views of Colonel Pales's home, Haven's Edge.

Roaring Springs, the home of Mr. and Mrs. R. M. Janney.

PART SIX
AWAY FROM THE RIVERS

ROARING SPRINGS

IN Gloucester County off Route 17 onto Road 616 one finds the old Colonial house known as Roaring Springs.

It was built by James Baytop Taliaferro, at, or near the end of the 18th century and in early years it was the seat of the Taliaferro family.

Built on simple Dutch-Colonial lines, with gambrel roof, the interior is beautiful, with its fine paneling and woodwork.

It is, as Anne Page Johns, the Richmond poet, so aptly puts it,—"A sequestered small country manor-house of old-time charm, projected into its useful present."

There are about twelve acres of park and lawn in the grounds, and the elm trees are impressively beautiful.

Paintings from the Johns Hopkins collection, priceless family heirlooms, and outstanding antique furniture decorate this charming farm home.

Roaring Springs is owned by Mrs. R. M. Janney.

BELLE FARM

ALTHOUGH this treatise is of the old houses as they are in the 1950's, we have thought it important to bring in some houses, occasionally, that at this time are only history, legend or tradition, and not "four walls" any more; in short, houses that have been dismantled or destroyed.

Such a house is, or at any rate was, Belle Farm. General William Booth

Taliaferro mentions it as a pre-Revolutionary and colonial home of Gloucester.

Mrs. Maria Edwards writes that Belle Farm, the residence of Colonel Lewis, was the scene of the large dinner party when her grandfather, John Seawell, was proposed as a candidate for the Legislature. The grandfather was a Federalist, but his son, John, who went to William and Mary, returned a Democrat. The votes were taken and her father (John Seawell II) refused to vote for his father, whereupon the latter immediately declined the proposal to nominate him, declaring he would not consent to run if his own son opposed him.

Notes from the records of the Tabb family and their connections, say that Ellen Deans, daughter of Josiah Lilly Deans, married Fielding L. Taylor, of Belle Farm, and had two children, Fielding Lewis (died) and Ellen Y. Deans.

Roaring Springs, house and garden.

The living room at Roaring Springs.

A marriage announcement from the *Virginia Magazine of History and Genealogy* says that Robert Thruston and Sarah Brown were married at Belle Farm in Gloucester County, Virginia, by the Rev. Mr. Smith, December 22, 1804.

Mrs. M. M. Taliaferro (a granddaughter of Robert Munford), in a letter, written in 1895, says that after the death of her grandfather in Charles City County, her grandmother removed to Belle Farm, Gloucester County, at which place her sons, Samuel and Robert died, and lie buried. Belle Farm was owned at the time she moved there by her brother-in-law, Mr. Fielding Lewis, "and my grandmother continued to reside there with her daughter and only remaining child, Margaret Ann Munford, until that daughter (who

151

was my mother) married Mr. John Sinclair, my father, when she went to live with them at Shabby Hall, which my father afterwards sold to Mr. Robert C. Selden, whose widow still resides there, as you know." (Shabby Hall is now Sherwood.)

Mrs. Sally Robins says in 1893, in telling of the destruction of the last old brick mansion in Gloucester town, that "From this house, built by an early colonist named Thruston, whose widow married a Lewis and then a Tabb, two curiously-carved mantel-pieces were carried to the Belle Farm; and this old Lewis home still holds them, together with one of the rarest collections of china, silver and glass, portraits and jewels (heirlooms of the Warners, the Lewises, the Corbins and the Taylors) which this county contains."

Waterman says (in *Mansions of Virginia*) "making the pediment traverse the length of the plan was shown to be undesirable at Belle Farm in Gloucester, where the effect was ungainly in the extreme."

Belle Farm, now the property of Mr. and Mrs. John L. Lewis, Jr., has been dismantled, reassembled and rebuilt on Indian Springs Road, in Williamsburg, and it seems to nestle into its new surroundings, as though it had been there all along. It is a clapboard house, with center hall, and large rooms on each side. Both these rooms have open fireplaces, and paneling about shoulder high. The parlor, or in today's vernacular, the living room, has arches opening into recesses, on each side of the fireplace, and in the back of these recesses are windows, with tiny diamond-shaped panes of glass.

At the end of the center hall, there is a cross hall in which, as at Tuckahoe, is the staircase leading to the second floor. Straight across from the door of the center hall is the door to the dining room. This room also has an open fireplace, and the fine woodwork has carving to represent scenes from Aesop's Fables.

At Belle Farm there is boxwood, other shrubbery, a beginning of a flower garden, and a nice vegetable garden.

Mr. Lewis is a descendant (about the tenth generation) of Augustine Warner, of Warner Hall; and of John Lewis, who married Mr. Warner's granddaughter, and he is also a cousin of George Washington, Robert E. Lee, England's Queen Mother, and of her Majesty, Queen Elizabeth II.

GLOUCESTER PLACE

GLOUCESTER PLACE, a large old house which used to stand on the "Gloucestertowne" Road was important in the early days of Gloucester. It was built by John Seawell, a large importing merchant, and was the Seawell home for some years.

Gloucester Place was also the former residence of President John Tyler.

MARLFIELD

MARLFIELD, in the upper end of the county, was built early in the 18th century, by the Buckners. It was a T-shaped brick house. The first printing press in Virginia was brought to Gloucester County by John Buckner, who was Clerk of the county. Lord Culpeper, the governor, reproved him in 1682 for having printed, without license, the laws of 1680. Further printing was prohibited, and some say his press was destroyed.

Marlfield had a center hall, with a room on each side, downstairs and up, this being only the four big rooms, and the two halls, at the time it came into the Catesby Jones family. Mr. Catesby G. Jones, of Gloucester, tells us that it was bought by his great-great-great-grandfather in 1779 or 1780. The purchaser immediately built a wing in the center back, thus making the building T-shaped. The new part also had large rooms, which were used as dining room and kitchen. In 1904 Mr. Jones's family sold Marlfield to Mr. Z. T. Gray. This made about a century and a quarter that the Joneses lived at Marlfield, and during that time it was one of the social centers of the county. The large chimneys, open fireplaces, lovely staircase, mantels, and paneling were typical of the period.

There was a large amount of timber on the place when Mr. Gray bought it; in fact, that was why he bought the place. He sold large quantities of timber, but today, there still remain at Marlfield, some fine trees.

The grounds are over-grown, the house is in ruins, and the old graveyard, with its fine old vaults and tombstones, is also over-grown. Here lie the ancestors of the Jones family, and also of the Buckners.

CLIFFORD

ON Route 17, between Gloucester and Gloucester Point, one and a half miles from the Court House, stands Clifford, the old home of the Kemp family, of Gloucester County. Miss Mary Kemp, of Richmond, tells us that a unique thing about Clifford was that, in olden days, each bedroom had its own staircase leading up to it from the room below. She said, however, that when the home was remodeled in recent years, all the staircases except two were removed.

The house is of frame construction, and of the Colonial structure, Miss Kemp says, only the old parlor and dining room remain. In her childhood,

Fiddlers Green, the home of the Hutchesons.

seventy years ago, there were the most beautiful flowers in her mother's garden, and magnificent shrubs, which were ancient even at that time. Miss Kemp also recalls the trees, huge, century-old, of different varieties, but among them many walnut trees.

The proprietors of the Antique Shoppe in Gloucester now own Clifford. How they must enjoy it!

FIDDLERS GREEN

FIDDLERS GREEN, the birthplace of Ruth Nelson Robins Gordon (Mrs. Thomas C. Gordon), of Richmond, is not far from Gloucester Court House. It was here her father returned after the War Between the States, when all seemed lost. It was here her mother, Sally Nelson Robins, the illustrious writer, lived.

The house, built late in the seventeenth century, is two-storied, with shingle roof and dormer windows, has large end chimneys and a porch all

154

across the front. After the death of Mrs. Gordon's father, the family removed to Richmond, and Fiddlers Green passed into other hands.

The charming old place is now the home of the Hutchesons.

WALTER REED BIRTHPLACE

ON the road from Gloucester to Cappahosic, one passes near the forks of the roads a tiny three-room white house. Here the greatly beloved Walter Reed was born September 13, 1851. This place is called Belroi. Walter Reed's

Birth place of Walter Reed, Belroi.

Long Bridge Ordinary.

father, a minister, had lost his home by fire, a few weeks previously, and the family found temporary refuge here. Dr. Walter Reed was one of Gloucester's most noted sons. It was he who made long and tedious, as well as dangerous, experiments until at last he discovered the cause of yellow fever. He died in Washington at the age of fifty-one. It is for him that the great Walter Reed Hospital, at Washington, was named. The people of Gloucester have honored his memory, and it is hoped that Belroi will become a national shrine.

LONG BRIDGE ORDINARY

AT Gloucester Court House, Long Bridge Ordinary, a hostelry famous in Colonial days, is still much in the mind of the public. It was built as early, certainly, as 1727. From here a coach service to Fredericksburg was regularly maintained at least from 1736 on. A poster dated that year hangs in Rising

Sun Tavern in Fredericksburg announcing the departure of the stage coach in the morning for Hornets Nest, and Long Bridge Ordinary.

Although this building has only one chimney, it has five fireplaces. Built on a hillside, the garden entrance is into the basement which has a hall, dining room, and kitchen. The first floor, entered at front from hilltop level, has a hall, a large living room, and a powder room, the second-floor a hall and a bedroom where the proprietor slept. The staircase is classically plain, and is sometimes called a platform stairs.

The lower story of the house is of brick, and the upper two stories of wood. The door panels were doubled, with the grain of the wood of the outer panels running straight, and the inner panels slanting. This was to turn the point of the Indian's arrows.

Many distinguished guests have eaten at Long Bridge Ordinary.

Around the beginning of the present century this place changed hands several times.

This may have been due to the fact that with the beginning of the automobile era, Long Bridge Ordinary lost its value as a hostelry.

In 1914, the Gloucester Woman's Club acquired the property by purchase. With the house they bought one and a quarter acres of land. The garden is being beautifully restored under the supervision of Mrs. Edward Newton Cheek.

GLOUCESTER COURT HOUSE

THE present Gloucester Court House was built in 1766, the previous building on this site having been destroyed by fire.

It is of lovely colonial architecture, with brick arches, and white-columned porch. The porch was added after the Revolution. The records of Gloucester have been destroyed three times—the last time when Richmond was burned during the evacuation of the city in the Civil War.

The town of Gloucester, at that time called Botetourt, was laid out in 1769. In olden days great leniency was practised in the keeping of prisoners. Each day near the middle of the day, they were allowed to take a walk from the Gloucester jail to get their exercise. A tall tree about a mile away was the furthest point to which they were permitted to go. No one ever heard of trouble with escapees, but of course the most of them were in for debt!

The interior of the Court House is not only fitted out in the best taste but is also most unusual, and of great historic and sentimental interest. In the courtroom are forty-eight portraits and seven tablets commemorating the great of the county. Among the forty-eight are two portraits of General William Booth Taliaferro, of Belleville, and one of Dr. Walter Reed.

157

Gloucester Court House with monument and green.

One tablet has been put up (by the Gloucester Monument Association) to the Women of Gloucester County, Virginia, during the Civil War, 1861-65—; another to the distinguished men of the Page family; and one to the illustrious Cookes, four of whom had Mordecai as their given names.

There is a tablet to the memory of Dr. Walter Reed, one to Nathaniel Bacon, one to John M. Gregory, Governor of Virginia and Judge of Circuit Court, and one in "Honor of the men of Gloucester, who on land and sea, in field, camp and air, gave themselves and their services to our County."

For a complete list of the portraits, and of the texts of the inscriptions on the tablets, see *Twelve Virginia Counties,* by John H. Gwathmey.

Mr. Gwathmey gives, too, a list of officers of the five companies of infantry and the three of cavalry that went into the War Between the States from Gloucester. He also lists officers from Gloucester who were attached to other commands.

An entire roll of Confederate soldiers from Gloucester is to be found in the Clerk's office.

The circular Court Green, with its group of quaint, beautiful buildings, divides the road. It is a lovely place. The brick wall which surrounds it was built by the Gloucester Garden Club, which was founded in June, 1928, by Mrs. George Mackubin, Mrs. H. O. Sanders and Mrs. William Fleet Taliaferro. The design for the wall was executed by a Williamsburg architect, and W. P. A. labor was used in its construction. Then, also under Williamsburg advice, the walks from one building to another were laid out in patterns in keeping with the period of the buildings, and the Court Green was further beautified. Besides the Court house, there are the Clerk's Office, a brick structure built in 1890; the Old Debtor's Prison, adjoining the Court house (from which the prisoners used to take their noon walk), which dates from early in the eighteenth century; and the tiny Old Clerk's Office, which is also of brick, and was built in 1821. Nowhere in Virginia is there a group of court buildings more attractive, or grounds more lovely than at Gloucester.

WARE CHURCH

NEAR the head of the Ware River and not far from the old "War Path" or "Indian Road," stands Ware Church, the old brick rectangular building where citizens of Gloucester County have worshipped for nearly three hundred years. An earlier building, called The Glebe, stood on the peninsula known as Glen Roy. The present building is on land given by the Throckmorton family of Church Hill, and it was completed soon after 1690. The grove of original growth trees which surround the church consists of cedars, pines, oaks, elms and other varieties usually found in virgin growth of this section.

Gloucester Court House, closeup.

These trees, with the old brick wall which surrounds the church, the old part of the church yard and the quaint old tombstones, with their interesting inscriptions, all evoke the atmosphere of another world, one long since vanished into the past.

The church building has been little changed, just enough for comfort for the congregation. The old box pews which were used by the British for horse stalls during the Revolution, have been replaced by more modern ones. A polished floor now covers the stones upon which once congregations walked

160

and knelt. Lights have been installed, but the fixtures are of Colonial design.

Many generations have buried their dead at Ware Church. The cemetery has had to be enlarged from time to time. It is interesting to note that in each generation the church roll in the clerk's book reads like a list of names from the tombstones outside. The descendants keep the faith, even to this day.

Many persons were buried under the chancel of Ware in early times. Their tombstones are still there. Among those so interred were the Rev. J. R. Fox, Rector of Ware, his wife and child, and the child's nurse; Mrs. Francis Willis; the Rev. John Richards, who died in 1735, and his wife Amy Richards, (1725) and her maid, Mary Ades, who died two days after her mistress.

The very ancient Ware communion service is part of a set presented originally by Augustine Warner to Petsworth Church. When church services were no longer held at Ware, this communion service was preserved and cared for by Mrs. Mary Cooke Booth Jones, the widow of the Rev. Emmanuel Jones; the two chalices and patens were given to the Rev. Mr. Cairns, Rector of Ware, on the night of the marriage of Mr. Jones' granddaughter, Lucy Ann Jones, to George Wythe Booth, of Belleville; the tankard had been lost by the Rev. Emmanuel Jones; a later tankard has been given to Ware by the Rev. Emmanuel Jones' descendants to replace the one he lost.

The building at Ware is a perfect rectangle, forty by eighty feet. The bricks were made in the brickyard west of the church property, and were laid by local bricklayers, with English artisans to glaze the brick ends. The present roof is slate, put on in 1854. The rafters, of hand-riven oak, are twelve by eighteen inches, and were found to be in perfect condition when the roof was replaced.

According to English and American architectural authorities, Ware Church is perfect in its simplicity. The main door is to the west, with the chancel in the east end of the building. There are cross aisles from the north and south, and a cross aisle in the rear of the nave, with two longitudinal aisles extending from this to the chancel.

Each of the twelve large windows is surmounted by an arch. The five windows on each side have thirty-eight panes each, while the two double ones over the chancel have sixty panes each.

Heavy wooden uprights and cross-sections make perfect crosses in each window.

The foundation walls begin six feet below the surface, and are five feet thick to ground level. From ground level to a height of three feet the walls are four feet thick; above that they are three feet thick. The doors are constructed of two layers of wood; each layer is an inch thick, the grain of the wood in one of the layers runs crosswise to the grain in the other. This was a precaution against Indian arrows.

Ware Church.

162

Ware Church, interior.

163

At times in the past there was no minister, but almost always, with the exception of ten years prior to 1826, so the Reverend William Byrd Lee (who wrote the history of Ware Church for *The Southern Churchman* early in this century) avers, a minister came in soon after a vacancy occurred. He says ". . . it appears there was a minister generally at hand to administer baptism, and other rites of the Church."

During one period, when the church had no rector, Dr. William Taliaferro went faithfully every Sunday morning to read the prayers and lessons and Psalms of the service, while the lone member of the congregation, "old" Mrs. Van Bibber, of North End, made the responses. Bishop Meade comments on the devout spiritual character of these two saintly people.

The Reverend Mr. Lee speaks of the high regard in which the ministers of Ware were held by their congregation (as shown by tablets, tomb inscriptions, etc.), and he lists the following as examples of long tenure in the service, in Gloucester and Mathews:

"Mr. Clack served nearly 45 years
Mr. Gwynn, 16; Rev. Guy Smith, 18;
Rev. Emmanuel Jones (in Petsworth) 39;
Rev. Mr. Hughes, 25; Mr. Mann, 40;
and the present pastor 25 years."

"The present pastor" that Mr. Lee referred to, was himself; and his "25 years" eventually became forty years of service, after which he retired and became Rector Emeritus.

The roll of the vestry of Ware, like that of Abingdon, is a list of the names of truly great Americans.

The interest and earnest work of the congregation under the auspices of the Chancel Guild, have effected the restoration and beautification of the interior of the church, and through munificent gifts, several memorials have been erected.

ABINGDON CHURCH

ON the road from Gloucester Court House to Gloucester Point, about six miles from The Point, stands Abingdon Church. It is cruciform in style, built of rose brick, and is said to have been planned by Sir Christopher Wren. The building is eighty-one feet long, and seventy-six and a half feet wide. The eastern and western ends of the "cross" measure thirty-six feet in width on the outside, while the northern and southern outside ends of the cross measure

164

Abingdon Church, showing wall.

thirty-five feet. The walls are in Flemish bond with glazed heads. They are two feet thick.

The silver service still in use was presented by Major Lewis Burwell, of Carter's Creek in 1703. A smaller building preceded the present one, but it seems a little difficult to determine the exact date of the building of either. It is perhaps safe to say the earlier church was built about the middle of the 1600's, and the present church about one hundred years later. William Byrd, of Westover, said of the old church ". . . exquisite little church, the finest I have seen in the country."

It is a fact, however, that much of the original woodwork of the previous building was retained in the present edifice. A distinguished pediment tops the west doorway, which is superb in its symmetry and grace. There is an old flagstone pathway leading to the door.

The Warners, of Warner Hall, gave the land on which the church was built. The family, including Mildred, who married Lawrence Washington and became George Washington's grandmother, attended church here.

Some of the old box pews were used by the British as box stalls for horses during the Revolution. After the Civil War they were removed and replaced by the high-backed pews now in use.

Some of the tombstones in the Abingdon Cemetery have coats of arms carved on them. The cemetery has been enlarged from time to time, and names on the stones are known throughout the county.

Within the churchyard, close to the front door, are handsome "table" style tombstones of the Burwells; one of the family moved to Abingdon from the old Burwell home, Carter's Creek. One of the tombstones is in memory of Mrs. Burwell, who persisted in calling herself "Lady Berkeley," even on the tombstone, though her husband, Governor Berkeley, had died some years before she married Mr. Nathaniel Burwell.

The chancel is in the east end of the cross. Here was placed, probably in the early 1840's, the beautiful pentagonal reredos which still is much admired. It was nicely described by Mrs. Fielding Lewis Taylor in these words:

"It represents the facade of a Greek temple in the bas-relief, about twenty feet in height and extending entirely across the back of the chancel. It is handsomely carved, and painted snowy white. Straight across the lintel of the facade runs the first line of the Te Deum, 'We praise Thee, O God.' The roof of the reredos dividing at the apex, supports a pine apple both in high relief. Between the four fluted pilasters of the reredos are set four long black tablets, framed and lettered in gold. These contain the Creed, the Lord's Prayer, and the

166

Abingdon Church, within wall.

Abingdon Church, interior.

168

Ten Commandments. Alas, the breath of time has dimmed the beautiful words. The light from the great arched windows (in the head of the cruciform building, on either side of the chancel) shines full upon these four foundation pillars of the Faith once delivered to the saints. The effect of the whole is simple, but beautiful, full of deep spiritual earnestness."

Above the apex of the reredos is a gilt cross painted on glass.

The main aisle from the west door to the chancel is crossed by the aisles from the north and south entrances. In olden days the Thruston and Lewis families occupied the gallery in the south arm of the cross, and the Burwells and Pages occupied the one in the north arm. Servants sat in seats placed back of their masters.

Of course a modern furnace heats Abingdon in cold weather now, but in an older day, heated bricks, braziers and warm clothing had to be depended on for warmth.

Near the beginning of this century Mr. Joseph Bryan enclosed the church yard, consisting of about two and a half acres, in an attractive and substantial brick wall. This adds to the impressive beauty of the old church surrounded by the grove of lovely old trees and the tombstones.

In a book called *Virginia Colonial Churches,* second edition, published by The Southern Churchman Company in 1908 in Richmond, Virginia, is the most complete history of "Abingdon Church, Gloucester County, Virginia," that we have been able to find. It is written by the Reverend William Byrd Lee, Rector. Mr. Lee used all sources available, and authenticity of the facts he gives are self-evident. He says that, according to the report of the Reverend Thomas Hughes to the Bishop of London, in 1724, "there were three hundred families in the parish; that services were held every Lord's Day, Good Friday and Christmas, in the forenoon; that there were sixty or seventy communicants; that the Holy Communion was administered three times a year, and that about two hundred Christians generally attended the church."

Mr. Lee goes on to give, as far as possible, a complete list of ministers, wardens and vestrymen of Abingdon. He gives total counts of baptisms, and ends with a list of five hundred seventy surnames of resident families of Abingdon Parish, Gloucester County, Virginia from 1677 to 1761.

BIBLIOGRAPHY

Virginia, a Guide to the Old Dominion. Compiled by Workers of the Writers' Program of the Works Projects Administration in the State of Virginia. New York, 1940. Oxford University Press.

Andrews, Matthew Page. *Virginia, the Old Dominion.* Richmond, 1949. The Dietz Press.

Brock, Henry Irving. *Colonial Churches in Virginia.* Richmond, 1930. The Dale Press.

Byrd, William, of Westover. *Another Secret Diary.* Edited by Maude Woodfin, decoded by Marion Tingling. Richmond, 1942. The Dietz Press.

Byrd, William, of Westover. *Secret Diary.* Edited by Louis Wright and Marion Tingling. Richmond, 1941. The Dietz Press.

Chamberlayne, C. G. *The Vestry Book of Petsworth Parish, Gloucester County, Virginia.* 1677-1793. Transcribed, Annotated and Indexed by C. G. Chamberlayne. Richmond, 1933. The Library Board.

Chandler, Joseph Everett. *The Colonial Architecture of Maryland, Pennsylvania and Virginia.* Boston, 1892. Bates, Kimball & Guild.

Christian, Frances Archer & Massie, Susanne Williams, Editors. *Homes and Gardens in Old Virginia.* Revised Edition. Richmond, 1950. Garrett and Massie, Inc.

Coffin, Lewis A., Jr. & Holden, Arthur C. *Brick Architecture of the Colonial Period in Maryland & Virginia.* New York, 1919. Architectural Book Publishing Company, Inc.

Colonial Churches of Virginia. Richmond, 1908. The Southern Churchman Company.

Davis, Deering, with Dorsey, Stephen P. and Hall, Ralph Cole. Special Article by Nancy McClelland. *Alexandria Houses.* 1946. Architectural Book Publishing Company, Inc.

Davis, Deering. *Annapolis Houses, 1700-1775.* 1947. Architectural Book Publishing Company, Inc.

Davis, Deering with Dorsey, Stephen P. and Hall, Ralph Cole. *Georgetown Houses of the Federal Period, Washington, D.C. 1780-1830.* 1944. Architectural Book Publishing Company, Inc.

Department of Agriculture and Immigration of the State of Virginia, George W. Koiner, Commissioner. *A Handbook of Virginia.* Richmond, 1909. Everett Waddey Company, Printers.

Eberlein, Harold Donaldson. *The Architecture of Colonial America.* Boston, 1915. Little, Brown & Company.

Elliott, Charles Wyllys. *The Book of American Interiors.* Boston, 1876. James R. Osgood & Company.

Forman, Henry Chandlee. *The Architecture of the Old South, The Medieval Style, 1585-1850.* Cambridge, Mass., 1948. Harvard University Press.

Forman, Henry Chandlee. *Jamestown and St. Mary's, Buried Cities of Romance.* Baltimore, 1938. The Johns Hopkins Press.

Frary, I. T. *Early American Doorways.* Richmond, 1937. Garrett and Massie.

Frary, I. T. *Thomas Jefferson, Architect and Builder,* Third Edition. Richmond, 1950. Garrett and Massie.

Freeman, Douglas Southall. *George Washington.* New York & London, 1948. Charles Scribners Sons.

Freeman, Douglas Southall. *R. E. Lee.* New York & London, 1934. Charles Scribners Sons.

French, Leigh, Jr. *Colonial Interiors.* New York, 1923. William Helburn, Inc.

Gloucester County, Virginia. *Educational Survey Report.* Richmond, 1928. State Board of Education.

Gwathmey, John H. *Historical Register of Virginians in the Revolution, Soldiers, Sailors, Marines, 1775-1783.* Richmond, 1938. The Dietz Press.

Gwathmey, John H. *Legends of Virginia Courthouses.* Richmond, 1933. The Dietz Press.

Gwathmey, John H. *Legends of Virginia Lawyers.* Richmond, 1934. The Dietz Press.

Gwathmey, John H. *Twelve Virginia Counties.* Richmond, 1937. The Dietz Press.

Hamlin, Talbot. *Greek Revival Architecture in America.* London, New York, Toronto, 1944. Oxford University Press.

Hergesheimer, Joseph. *Balisand.* New York, 1924. Alfred A. Knopf.

Historic American Buildings Survey. Washington, 1941. National Park Service.

Howells, John Mead. *Lost Examples of Colonial Architecture.* New York, 1931. William Helburn, Inc.

Huntley, Elizabeth Valentine. *Peninsula Pilgrimage.* Richmond, 1941. The Press of Whittet & Shepperson.

Jackson, Joseph. *American Colonial Architecture.* Philadelphia, 1924. David McKay Company.

172

Johnston, Frances Benjamin and Waterman, Thomas Tileston. *The Early Architecture of North Carolina*. Chapel Hill, 1941-1947. University of North Carolina Press.

Johnston, George Ben, M.D. *Some Medical Men of Mark from Virginia*. Richmond, 1905. Reprinted from the *Old Dominion Journal of Medicine and Surgery*.

Lancaster, Robert A., Jr. *Historic Virginia Homes and Churches*. Philadelphia and London, 1915. J. B. Lippincott Company.

Lee, Mrs. Marguerite du Pont. *Virginia Ghosts and Others*. Richmond, 1932. The William Byrd Press, Inc.

Legg, Carrie Mason. Unpublished Manuscript. Elmington.

Library of Congress. *Colonial Churches in the Original Colony of Virginia*. Washington, D.C. U. S. Government Printing Office.

Mason, Polly Cary. *Records of Colonial Gloucester County, Virginia*, Volume I. Compiled by Polly Cary Mason. Newport News, Virginia, 1946. Mrs. George C. Mason. Post Office Box 720.

Mason, Polly Cary. *Records of Colonial Gloucester County, Virginia*, Volume II. Compiled by Polly Cary Mason. Newport News, Virginia, 1948. Mrs. George C. Mason, Post Office Box 720.

Massie, Susanne Williams and Christian, Frances Archer, Editors. *Homes and Gardens of Virginia*. With an Introduction by Douglas S. Freeman. Richmond, 1931. Garrett & Massie, Inc.

Meade, William, bp. 1789-1862. *Old Churches, Ministers and Families of Virginia*. Philadelphia, 1872. J. B. Lippincott & Company. Reprinted, Lippincott, 1931. Two volumes with Wise Index. First published 1857. Second edition 1861.

Moore, Virginia. *Virginia Is a State of Mind*. New York, 1942. E. P. Dutton and Company, Inc.

Mumford, Lewis. *The South in Architecture*. New York, 1941. Harcourt, Brace & Company.

Nutting, Wallace. *Virginia Beautiful*. Framingham, Massachusetts, 1930. Old America Company.

Paxton, Annabel. *Washington Doorways*. Richmond, 1940. The Dietz Press.

Rawson, Marion Nicholl. *Sing, Old House*. New York, 1934. E. P. Dutton & Company, Inc.

Robins, Sally Nelson. *Gloucester, One of the First Chapters of the Commonwealth of Virginia; History of Gloucester County, Virginia, and Its Families*. Illustrated with Photographs by Miss Blanche Dimmock, of Sherwood. Richmond, 1893. West, Johnston & Company.

Rothery, Agnes. *New Roads in Old Virginia*. Revised Edition. Boston and New York, 1937. Houghton Mifflin Company.

Rothery, Agnes. *Virginia The New Dominion*. New York, London, 1940. D. Appleton-Century Company.

Sale, Edith Tunis. *Boxwood and Terraced Gardens of Virginia*. Richmond, 1925. The William Byrd Press, Inc.

Sale, Edith Tunis, Editor. *Historic Gardens of Virginia.* Compiled by the James River Garden Club Committee: Edith Tunis Sale, Laura C. Martin Wheelwright, Juanita Massie Patterson, Lila. L. Williams, Caroline Coleman Duke. Foreword by Mary Johnston. Richmond, 1925. The William Byrd Press, Inc.

Sale, Mrs. Edith Dabney (Tunis). *Interiors of Virginia Houses of Colonial Times.* Richmond, 1927. The William Byrd Press, Inc.

Sale, Edith Tunis. *Manors of Virginia in Colonial Times.* Philadelphia and London, 1909. J. B. Lippincott Company.

Scott, Mary Wingfield. *Houses of Old Richmond.* Richmond, 1941. Valentine Museum.

Scott, Mary Wingfield. *Old Richmond Neighborhoods.* Richmond, 1950. Published by the author.

Squires, W. H. T. *An Anthology of Virginia and Virginians.* A Volume of Manuscripts Presented to the State Library of Virginia.

Squires, W. H. T. *The Days of Yester-Year in Colony and Commonwealth.* Portsmouth, Virginia, 1928. Printcraft Press, Inc.

Squires, W. H. T. *Through Centuries Three.* A Short History of the People of Virginia. Portsmouth, Virginia, 1929. Printcraft Press, Inc.

Stanard, Mary Newton. *Colonial Virginia, Its People and Customs.* Philadelphia and London, 1917. J. B. Lippincott Company.

Stanard, Mary Newton. *The Story of Virginia's First Century.* Philadelphia and London, 1928. J. B. Lippincott Company.

Stanard, William G. and Stanard, Mary Newton. *The Colonial Virginia Register.* Albany, 1902. Joel Munsell's Sons, Publishers.

Stubbs, Dr. and Mrs. William Carter. *Descendants of Mordecai Cook of Mordecai's Mount, Gloucester County, Virginia 1650, and Thomas Booth of Ware Neck, Gloucester County, Virginia, 1685.* New Orleans, 1923. Published by Dr. and Mrs. William Carter Stubbs.

Stubbs, Dr. and Mrs. William Carter. *A History of Two Virginia Families, Transplanted from County Kent, England.* New Orleans, 1918. Published by Dr. and Mrs. Stubbs.

Tate, Leland B. *The Virginia Guide, The Land of the Life Worth Living.* A Manual of Information About Virginia. Lebanon, Virginia, 1929. Leland B. Tate.

Tuthill, William B. *Interiors and Interior Details.* New York, 1882. William T. Comstock, Architectural Publisher.

Verrill, A. Hyatt. *Romantic and Historic Virginia.* New York, 1935. Dodd Mead & Company.

Virginia Highway Historical Markers. Strasburg, Virginia, 1930. Shenandoah Publishing House, Inc.

Wallis, Frank E. *How to Know Architecture.* New York, 1910; 1914. Harper & Brothers, Publishers.

Waterman, Thomas Tileston and Barrows, John A. *Domestic Colonial Architecture of Tidewater Virginia.* New York–London, 1932. Charles Scribners Sons.

Waterman, Thomas Tileston. *The Dwellings of Colonial America.* Chapel Hill, 1950. The University of North Carolina Press.

Waterman, Thomas Tileston. *The Mansions of Virginia, 1706-1776.* Chapel Hill, 1945. The University of North Carolina Press.

Waterman, Thomas Tileston. *Thomas Jefferson, His Early Works in Architecture.* August 1943 number of *Gazette des Beaux-Arts.*

Williams, Henry Lionel and Williams, Ottalie K. *Old American Houses and How to Restore Them.* Garden City, New York, 1946. Doubleday & Company, Inc.

Wilstach, Paul. *Tidewater Virginia.* Indianapolis, 1929. The Bobbs-Merrill Company.

PERIODICALS

Calendar of Virginia State Papers.
Henings Statues of Virginia.
Lower Norfolk County Virginia Antiquary.
Tyler's Historical and Genealogical Quarterly.
Virginia Historical Register.
Virginia Magazine of History and Biography.
William and Mary Quarterly Historical Magazine—First Series.
William and Mary Quarterly Historical Magazine—Second Series.

CURRENT PUBLICATIONS

Commonwealth Magazine.
Virginia and the Virginia County.

NEWSPAPERS

Baltimore Sun.
Gloucester—Mathews Gazette—Journal.
New York Times.
Richmond News Leader.
Richmond Times Dispatch.

OLD VIRGINIA
HOUSES ALONG
THE JAMES

OLD VIRGINIA HOUSES ALONG THE JAMES

BY

EMMIE FERGUSON FARRAR

ILLUSTRATED WITH PHOTOGRAPHS BY

HARRY BAGBY & OTHERS

THIS SERIES AS A WHOLE IS FOR

FRANKLIN FLOYD FARRAR

THIS VOLUME IS FOR

Elizabeth Walker Farrar Martin

and

Annie-Laurie Farrar Berry

CONTENTS

ILLUSTRATIONS

ILLUSTRATIONS

FOREWORD

DURING the years I spent in a Richmond bookshop to a great extent devoted to literature about American backgrounds, we used to occupy our leisure moments discussing among ourselves and with collectors the need for a series of books about old houses in Virginia. That there was such a need, that there was, in fact, a crying need for several volumes describing notable historic homes in the state, volumes which would be well illustrated, we were all agreed. Many books about old Virginia houses have appeared, but most of them were published quite some time ago and have been out of print for some years. Mr. Robert W. Lancaster, Mrs. Edith Tunis Sale, Mrs. Elizabeth Valentine Huntley, and others, have written charming, attractive and informative works on the subject, but all these books are out of print. Then there is the further consideration that a number of these old houses have changed considerably in appearance—some have been restored, others have been added to or otherwise changed—since these books were written.

As time went on, however, our hope that someone would be found to carry out this project failed of realization. Finally it seemed to us that the only way to get the job done, was to undertake it ourselves. So, with a good deal of hesitation, because of the arduous and difficult nature of the task, we set to work on the first volume, OLD VIRGINIA HOUSES: The Mobjack Bay Country, which was published in 1955 and which was generally well received. With Harry Bagby's photograph-illustrations it could hardly have been otherwise.

This encouraged us to go ahead with the second volume in the series, covering that section of the state, perhaps its most historic region, which extends along the James River, from Richmond to the Capes. Many scholars, owners, and many friends have

xiii

assisted us, have given information, have helped in various ways. To these we wish to acknowledge our great sense of indebtedness.

Our bibliography is a long one. We have not merely listed these books; we have studied them carefully. We have done our best to avoid errors, but surely some will have crept in; that is inevitable in a work of this character. We trust our readers will freely offer suggestions for corrections to be embodied in future editions.

For the most part, the houses described and pictured in this volume are still homes, happily lived in, oftentimes by descendants of earlier owners. The concept of "home" as symbolized in a house of brick and mortar, with its warm feeling of a refuge from the outside world, of assurance of the continuity of things, is an abiding and all-appealing one. This is a concept tied to the deepest human emotions and instincts. A house, as such, is not necessarily a home; its occupants make it so by the loving care they lavish on it, and by the experiences they go through in it—the tragedies, the happinesses, nay, even the daily routine of living in it. These old Virginia houses were homes in the truest sense of the word, and still are, for the most part. The graciousness and beauty in which they are clothed, are largely the result of their having been lived in and cared for and embellished by their successive owners.

The labor involved in compiling this book, while it has been arduous, has not been without its compensations. The study of these lovely old Virginia houses, of their history, colorful though sometimes tragic, of the legends and traditions that cling about their ancient walls, has been full of interest and enjoyment. Harry Bagby tells us that he also has had a wonderful experience going around this part of the state making his outstanding photographs of the old houses described by us. It is our hope that our readers will share our enthusiasm and enjoyment, even if only vicariously.

EMMIE FERGUSON FARRAR
CHESTER, VIRGINIA

APPRECIATION

IN the preparation of the manuscript for this book, I wish to express appreciation first of all to my own family, all the members of which have been enthusiastic, sympathetic, patient and helpful;

To Hastings House, Publishers, Inc., who, I felt sure would make as beautiful a volume of this, the second in the series, as it did in OLD VIRGINIA HOUSES: The Mobjack Bay Country;

To Harry and Marie Bagby, who have made such beautiful photographs to illustrate the present volume;

To the Governor of Virginia and Mrs. Thomas B. Stanley;

To the hostesses at the historic Capitol in Richmond, who have extended hospitality in the name of Virginians, to hundreds of thousands of people from other states and other countries; whose names are:

Mrs. Mann Valentine and

Mrs. Julian Trant, official hostesses, and

Mrs. Gordon B. Ambler, who serves as hostess on holidays and weekends;

To Miss India Thomas, at the White House of the Confederacy;

Mrs. Ralph Catterall, at the Valentine Museum;

Miss Ellen Bagby and Miss Elizabeth J. Dance, of the Association for the Preservation of Virginia Antiquities;

Mrs. William B. Jefferson, of the Poe Foundation;

Mrs. David Morton, of Agecroft Hall;

Mr. and Mrs. David Tennant Bryan, of Ampthill House;

Mrs. Frank Upshur, at the Wilton Museum;

Miss Anne Virginia Bennett, who knows the Ellen Glasgow House best;

To Miss Mary Wingfield Scott, who knows Richmond;

To Mrs. Arthur Dugdale, who knows and appreciates antiques;

To Mrs. Thomas C. Gordon, who knows the Tidewater;

To Miss Annie Stewart, of Brook Hill;

To Mr. Thomas Pinckney of Richmond, a descendant of the Brook Hill families;

To General and Mrs. Sheppard Crump, of Meadow Farm;

To Mr. and Mrs. Robert Hiram Sanders, of Bent Pine Farm;

To Mr. and Mrs. A. J. Burlee, of Tree Hill;

To Mr. and Mrs. W. N. Stoneman, of Varina;

To Mr. and Mrs. W. H. Ferguson, of Curles Neck Farm;

To Mr. and Mrs. James F. Lyles, of Henrico County;

To Mr. William Hinds, of Eppington;

To Miss Annie V. Scott, Mr. Hinds' niece, of Eppington;

To Mrs. Maude Atkins Joyner, of Chester, who knows all the old houses and loves them;

To Mr. and Mrs. O. B. Gates, of Chesterfield, whose ancestor, Major William Mayo, laid out the city of Richmond;

To Mr. and Mrs. Hagood Lumpkin, Jr., of Castlewood;

To Mr. and Mrs. S. R. Hague, Jr., of Wrexham;

To descendants of Judge James H. Cox, of Clover Hill;

To Mr. and Mrs. Maynard Powell, of Hedgelawn;

To Mr. and Mrs. Fred Bender, of Half Way House;

To Mr. and Mrs. Thomas S. Wheelwright, of Buckhead Springs;

To Mr. and Mrs. James Pinckney Harrison, of Dogham;

To Mr. and Mrs. Arthur Sackett, of Riverview;

To Mr. C. Hill Carter, Jr., of Shirley; and his family;

To Mr. and Mrs. Benjamin P. Alsop, Jr.;

To Mr. and Mrs. Malcolm Jamieson, of Berkeley;

To Mrs. Bruce Crane Fisher, of Westover;

To Mr. and Mrs. Bergdoll, of River Edge;

To Mr. and Mrs. Cyrus W. Beale, of Greenway;

To Mrs. Percy Walls, of Bush Hill;

To Mrs. John Ruffin, of Evelynton;

To Mrs. Emily Blayton Major, of Charles City;

To Mr. and Mrs. Hunter Sledd, of Mount Stirling;

To Mr. and Mrs. Henry Bohnsen, of Upper Weyanoke;

To Mr. and Mrs. John C. Hagan, Jr., of Lower Weyanoke;

To Mr. and Mrs. J. Alfred Tyler, of Sherwood Forest;

To Mrs. Robert W. Daniel, of Brandon;

To Mr. and Mrs. Harry Clarke Thompson, of Upper Brandon;

To Mr. and Mrs. Mitchell Coury, of Hopewell;

To the Slawson family, of Powhatan;

To the Eggleston family, formerly of Powhatan;

To the McCraes, of Carter's Grove;

To the Ochsners, of Eastover;

To the Franz Von Schillings, of Mount Pleasant;

To Mr. Willis W. Bohannan, of Petersburg;

To Mr. R. M. Hazelwood, of Toano;

To Mrs. Douglas Horne, of Point Pleasant;

To Senator and Mrs. Garland Gray, of Waverly;

To Mr. and Mrs. J. Roland Rooke, of Richmond;

To Mr. and Mrs. Frank T. Bates, Jr., of Richmond;

To Mr. and Mrs. James Walton Carter, of Claremont;

To Mr. Walker Pegram Warren, of Rich Neck;

To Mr. Robert Lachmond, of Montpelier;

To Dr. Alvin Duke Chandler, President of the College of William and Mary;

To the owners, past and present, of Bacon's Castle, Chippokes, Montpelier, Four Mile Tree, Wakefield, Kippax, Jordan's Jorney, Beechwood, Coggin's Point, Flower Dieu Hundred, Cedar Level, Cobb's Hall, Brick House, Point of Rocks, Whitby, Castlewood, Clover Hill, and all other homes mentioned in this book;

To Mr. Roger Dudley, of the College of William and Mary;

To Mr. Richard W. Talley, Senior Warden, Bruton Parish Church, Williamsburg;

To Mr. and Mrs. John L. Lewis, Jr., of Belle Farm;

To Mr. and Mrs. Edward E. Harrison, Jr., of Criss Cross;

To the owners, past and present, of the White House, Cedar Grove, Chestnut Grove, and Eltham;

To Mrs. William Wallace, of Hampstead, and all her family;

To Colonel and Mrs. Benjamin H. Brinton, of Cumberland Farm;

To Mrs. Virginia Braithwaite Houghwout, who restored Providence Forge;

To Mrs. Harry Layfield Bell, of Poplar Hall;

To Mr. and Mrs. John B. Dey, of Broad Bay Manor;

To Mr. and Mrs. Robert E. Laird, of Lawson Hall;

To Mr. Roscoe Thrasher, of the Adam Thoroughgood House;

To Miss Virginia Nelsen, of Yorktown;

To Mr. and Mrs. George Blow, of York Hall;

To Mr. Stanley W. Abbott, Superintendent, Colonial National Historical Park, Yorktown;

To Judge C. H. Sheild, Jr., of the Sheild House;

To Mrs. T. R. Sanford, Jr., Regent, and Mrs. Herndon Jenkins, Chairman, Comte de Grasse Chapter, Daughters of the American Revolution;

To Captain W. P. Chilton, Commanding Officer, United States Naval Mine Depot, Yorktown;

To Lieutenant Commander C. F. Dunbar, U. S. N., Public Information Officer, Yorktown;

To the Reverend Cornelius A. Zabriskie, Rector, Grace Church, Yorktown;

To Emily Blayton Major, of Charles City County;

To William G. Harkins, Librarian at the William and Mary College Library and the Library Staff;

To A. Lawrence Kocher;

To Howard Dearstyne;

To Mr. and Mrs. Bernal Diaz Crymes;

To Mr. and Mrs. LaFayette Blackwell;

To Mrs. Arthur Dugdale;

To Mr. and Mrs. Fred Dorey; and especially

To Teddy Martin, Jr., Franklin Martin, and Martha Lynn Berry;

To the staff of the Richmond Public Library;

To the staff of the Congressional Library in Washington, D. C.;

To the staff of the Virginia Chamber of Commerce;

To the Book Shop staff at Miller and Rhoads;

To the Book Shop staff at Thalhimers;

To the staff at the Cokesbury Book Store;

To the Librarian, and the staff of the Virginia State Library;

To Mr. John M. Jennings, of the Virginia Historical Society;

To the staff of the Library of Richmond Newspapers, Inc.;

and to Henry G. Alsberg, Editor, and Narcisse Chamberlain, of Hastings House Publishers.

INTRODUCTION

THIS, the second book in the series, *Old Virginia Houses*, is, as its title discloses, devoted to the old houses not far from Jamestown, the first permanent English settlement in America.

Beginning with Richmond, the account follows the map from left to right, covering the area along the James River, on both north and south sides, and treating of Jamestown, Williamsburg and Yorktown, together with their neighboring counties, and extending to the coast. This area is certainly the richest in this country in pioneering experiences; here are the beginnings, the "firsts," in American history, in American domestic life and even in American commercial and economic endeavor. There are also "firsts" to be credited to this area in the fields of social welfare and education, and in the development of a rich, new culture and of customs that have since become a part of the American way of life. But the most important "firsts," "firsts" far more significant than any of those mentioned, were the establishment of the first representative government in America, and the inauguration on the soil of our country, of Christian worship.

This book is not a history of an era or of a region, and by no means is it a technical architectural treatise about old houses or period styles; nor does it pretend to offer detailed information concerning Virginia family trees and genealogy. It perhaps contains elements, in varying proportions, of all these ingredients. But first and foremost, it is an account of old homes, how they have in some instances been exposed to the hazards of storms, war and fire, and how they have been affected by the relentless erosion wrought by time. There are some comments on architecture where such comments seemed apposite, some reference to genealogy where this seemed pertinent to the story, and a thread of history, wherever the main stream of history touched the lives of the people who lived in one of these venerable houses. But it is mainly on a foundation of esthetic appreciation and the nostalgia born of studying a wistfully charming *temps jadis,* that these volumes are built. There are also elements of sympathy for the pride that was built and lived into these old homes—pride of family, of course, but also state pride and national pride. This is a study, first and foremost, of people and how they lived—a study of domestic life as it was lived in the best traditions of American culture and civilization.

Architecture, like furniture, is subject to periodic but gradual transitions from one style to another. History, itself, shows few sudden changes, and certainly the arts and crafts of a people show very few, if any, such. Growth and development proceed at a leisurely pace. Building clings to the old, often even while adopting new forms. For thought processes and reversals of opinions, especially in matters of taste, seldom occur in a flash. Unlike death and destruction, culture advances by slow stages.

We feel that these old houses of Virginia, many of them still in good condition, illustrate the evolution of civilization in the state, and that this constitutes a compelling reason for making a record of them. The people who lived in them and their way of life, are interesting not only to their descendants, but also to all of us, since we are, in a manner of speaking, their cultural descendants, after all.

In the treatment of personalities, contemporary or of bygone eras, a sincere effort has been made to present the facts—not merely, however, the bare bones of facts, but also the traditions behind the facts, and the beauty, romantic, happy or tragic, of the setting in which these human beings lived and had their being.

At Jamestown was built the first church of the thirteen colonies, as well as the first capitol. Here the homes of the first Englishmen to arrive in America were built. And here, in 1619, met the first representative assembly in America, and this marked the inauguration of the oldest law-making body, operating continuously through representatives, on this continent.

At Falling Creek, in Henrico (now Chesterfield) County, was established the first iron works. In the same county at Coxen-Dale, was erected the first hospital in America. The first hospital for the deaf and dumb was also established in this county. In 1616, George Yeardley, Lieutenant-Governor, set up the first windmill in America, and only a year after their arrival, the Jamestown settlers established America's first glassworks.

In Henrico County, likewise, was founded the first University in America—the funds for the support of which later went into the coffers of William and Mary College. In Elizabeth City County the early settlers established the first free school in America.

In Henrico County they exploited the first coal mines in America, and the great American tobacco industry had its beginnings in this area. The early colonists kept from starving by learning from the sometimes friendly Indians how to raise corn—the first grown by Englishmen on American soil. And they grew it right here, in this section. It has turned out to be one of America's leading, if not its leading crop.

In this part of Virginia, Bermuda Hundred had the distinction of being America's first incorporated town, and Williamsburg is the oldest city in the thirteen original states. In Williamsburg was built the first capitol building that was so called. This city also claims the honor of having supported the first theater, the first law school, and the first hospital for the insane.

The first duel, of countless duels to follow, was fought in this area, and the first Christmas tree was set up, and, one supposes, properly decorated and illuminated, in the St. George Tucker House in Williamsburg.

On this little strip of land bordering the James, between the Falls and the mouth of the historic river, were born and raised two Presidents of the United States. And in this same section were born and raised three girls who became the wives of Presidents of the United States. Here lived and died the ancestors of seven United States Presidents, and here lived, and served, the illustrious George Washington, Thomas Jefferson, Patrick Henry, George Wythe, John Marshall and Robert Edward Lee.

In this area, where capitulations were made in the Moore House at Yorktown, followed by the signing of the documents of surrender on that 19th day of October in 1781, the thirteen Original Colonies became the free and independent United States of America.

Three wars have spread devastation along the James—but three times have the people slowly but valiantly recovered themselves, their homes, their plantations, and their cities.

The wealth and prosperity of this section of the state—from Richmond to the Capes—is more pronounced after three and a half centuries than ever before. The ancient churches still are objects of veneration and centers of religious worship; the fine old homes still dispense traditional hospitality; the countryside is as beautiful as ever. And yet the region hums with industry; the ports at the mouth of the James are crowded with ships; and the fields yield rich and abundant crops. And everywhere there are schools to train the young, and colleges providing higher education. The practical business of life proceeds uninterruptedly amidst the relics of the revered past, and the continuing development of culture and the arts. No wonder Virginians are proud of this section of their great commonwealth in whose soil were planted the first seeds of a rich and productive civilization. Here, in these historic buildings, they possess a great heritage of which they can justly boast. This heritage inspires them to continue their great traditions of fearless devotion to duty, a devotion, however, which is tempered by kindness, sincerity and human compassion. And they look with optimism toward the future.

OLD VIRGINIA
HOUSES ALONG
THE JAMES

The Virginia State Capitol built from plans by Thomas Jefferson, inspired by the Maison Carrée, a Roman temple at Nîmes, France.
Photo by A. L. Dementi.

PART ONE

RICHMOND

RICHMOND, at the falls of the James River, is the capital of Virginia, "mother of states." It was the capital of the Confederacy during the greater part of the War between the States. Now, in the 1950's, it is a beautiful modern city, of some 300,000 people that spreads and reaches out in all directions, especially toward the west and northwest.

Tobacco and paper are Richmond's chief items of manufacture, although there are many others. The manufacturing areas, the sections for commerce and trade, shipping, and retail shopping, cover many square miles. But this is also a cosmopolitan city, a city of banks, of churches, of schools and hospitals, of fine retail stores and good transportation. In its residential sections and suburban areas are substantial and attractive houses on wide, beautiful, tree-shaded roads and avenues. There are grassy front yards, flower gardens and numerous parks, pleasantly landscaped with shrubs, evergreens and blossoming plants. All these are things of which Richmond can justifiably be proud. They bespeak the presence of a happy and prosperous population.

Richmond, too, takes a very real interest in the arts. It is a city of many cultural clubs; it supports the Virginia Museum of Fine Arts, and carefully preserves its shrines, monuments and the historic cemeteries. The city takes pride in its great past; the citizens have a justifiable pride in their ancestors who played such an important part in the founding of the Republic, in our subsequent history, and fought so valiantly for their ideals. Visitors who tarry for a while soon sense this spirit of the city's inhabitants which imbues the old town with a subtle, nostalgic charm, and are captured and enthralled by it. Those who pass through on a hurried sight-seeing tour, are apt to miss this special all-pervasive quality altogether.

Richmond has a long and colorful history. Its inhabitants have encountered many

1

vicissitudes; they have experienced tragedy, they have endured suffering and they have attained triumphs and victories. Where there have been triumphs and victories, these have been due largely to the courage of human hearts.

The site of Richmond was first visited by men of the white race on May 27, 1607. Captain Newport, with a few men, came up from Jamestown to the falls of the river. He set up a rude wooden cross on a small island near the present 9th Street Bridge. On this cross he carved the words "Jacobus Rex 1607."

In 1609 Captain John Smith sent Captain Francis West and a handful of men on an expedition up the river. West bought land from the Indians and erected a fort, not far from the site of Richmond, which he named Fort West. But trouble with the Indians soon led to abandonment of this outpost.

The settlers at Jamestown were forever talking of, thinking of, and searching for gold—and also for pearls. In 1610 Lord Delaware led an expedition up the river to explore, but mainly to search for gold, silver and pearls. They also went only as far as the Falls, then returned, disappointed, to Jamestown.

In 1637 Thomas Stegg established a trading post "at the head of navigation" and was granted a sizeable tract of land near the Falls. His son, Thomas Stegg II, had property on both sides of the river and eventually left all that he owned to his nephew, William Byrd I, who at that time (1670) was about eighteen years old.

A fort was again established at the Falls after the massacre perpetrated by the Indians in 1644; by order of the Virginia Assembly, as a defense against the savages, tax exemptions and other inducements were offered to families who would settle here. A good many did so, and quite a little settlement grew up around the Falls. The people engaged in farming and their little town enjoyed peace and quiet for about ten years. But in 1656 unfriendly Indians, about seven hundred strong, wandered in and began to make depredations both on whites and on the Pamunkey Indians who were at peace with the whites. The invading savages were called Rechahecrians, but actually they were the cruel Senecas of New York State. Col. Edward Hill, of Shirley, and his force of soldiers were joined by Chief Totopotomoi of the Pamunkeys with a hundred braves. An attempt was made to remove the intruders without "war." But an engagement ensued in which there was so much bloodshed that a stream at the scene ran red with blood. The Senecas won. The encounter was within what are now the city limits and the stream is still called "Bloody Run." It is near Chimborazo Park, and has since been covered by a culvert.

This battle called forth more effective defense measures by the Assembly for Henrico County (which included the land around the Falls) and the passage of laws designating lines beyond which, if Indians came, they could be legally shot by the white settlers.

Nathaniel Bacon lived at Curles, not far from the Falls. When Indian atrocities became unbearable in the settlements, and when Governor Berkeley did little or nothing to prevent them, Bacon led the Rebellion of 1676.

In 1733 Col. William Byrd II decided to found Petersburg and Richmond. In 1737 Major William Mayo laid out the latter for Colonel Byrd on what is now Church Hill.

2

He drew a map that looked like a checkerboard of thirty-two squares. The west side extended to what is now 17th Street and the east side to what is now 25th Street. The width was from what is now Cary Street on the south, to what is now Broad Street on the north. Col. Byrd gave two lots at the top of the hill for St. John's Church, "with any pine timber they can find on that side of Shockoe Creek and wood for burning brick into the bargain."

Major Mayo named the city Richmond, for Richmond on the Thames. When the population of the new "city" reached two hundred fifty, the General Assembly at Jamestown ruled that it be constituted a town. Richmond Town became the capital of Virginia in 1779, and received its charter as a city in 1782.

Many great men have been associated with Richmond. Some have made it their home. Robert E. Lee lived here; so did Patrick Henry, Thomas Jefferson and Chief Justice John Marshall. Culture has flourished, and still does within its gates. Edgar Allan Poe lived and wrote here when he was editor of the *Southern Literary Messenger*. Ellen Glasgow, the great American woman novelist, lived, wrote, and died here, and so did the illustrious Douglas Southall Freeman. James Branch Cabell still makes Richmond his home. Jenny Lind has visited Richmond. John Powell now lives here. Many great artists have been guests in this part of the country, and four Silvettes have called Richmond home.

Yes, Richmond is a city of culture. And although she has suffered through several wars and was burned in 1865, she has come through troublous times with fortitude and dignity; her people have never lost their faith, or their hope, or their courage.

THE CAPITOL

THE magnificent building that is the Virginia State Capitol, which stands on Shockoe Hill, in the eight-acre park known as Capitol Square, was designed by Thomas Jefferson. Mr. Jefferson was not only a statesman and a philosopher, he was also an architect, a designer of gardens, an inventor and a collector. While he was in France he made a study of the Maison Carrée, a Roman temple at Nîmes, which is surely one of the most beautiful buildings left by the Romans. It was built in the time of Augustus Caesar, almost two thousand years before Jefferson saw it; and it was his inspiration for the Virginia State Capitol. Assisted and advised by Charles Louis Clerisseau, a French architect, Mr. Jefferson drew plans for the Capitol and sent them, with a modified plaster model of the temple, back to Virginia. The model now rests in a glass case in the Capitol where it always excites the interest of visitors.

The central unit, from the large south portico with its huge, white Ionic columns, back to the Old Hall of the House of Delegates, is the original part of the building planned by Jefferson. (For economy reasons the structure was not at first as large as Mr. Jefferson intended it to be.)

The cornerstone for this, the original part, was laid on August 18, 1785, and though it was in part unfinished, enough of the new building was completed for it to be used for the meeting of the General Assembly in October, 1788. The House of Delegates came in on October 27, and the Senate on October 29. The General Assembly of Virginia is now, by the way, one of the oldest, if not the oldest, continuously functioning English-speaking legislative body in the world.

The Capitol walls, which are four to five feet thick, and the columns, are of brick covered in stucco. The superintendent of construction was Samuel Dobie. The original building was completed in 1792, but the stucco was not put on until 1798. In 1904-06 the wings and the south steps were finally built. Since that time the House of Delegates has met in the East Wing and the Senate in the West Wing. The architecture of these wings accords exactly with that of the larger central unit. From a distance, the pilaster treatment with Ionic capitals gives the building the effect of having columns the whole way round.

In the center of the rotunda, under the dome, stands the life-size statue of Washington, by Jean Antoine Houdon, the great French sculptor. This is one of the finest pieces of statuary in America and it is said to be Virginia's most priceless art possession. The statue was made from life, when George Washington, six-feet two-inches tall, was fifty-three years old. He saw it after it was placed in the Capitol, and approved of it. Monsieur Houdon carved the statue in Carrara marble, in Paris, where it was exhibited in the Louvre for eight years prior to 1796, when it was set up in the Capitol.

Around the statue, placed in niches in the walls of the rotunda, are eight marble busts. Seven are of the other Virginia-born Presidents: Thomas Jefferson, James Madison, James Monroe, William Henry Harrison, John Tyler, Zachary Taylor and Woodrow Wilson. In the eighth niche is a marble bust of the Marquis de Lafayette.

The Old Hall of the House of Delegates is a landmark of history. It was here that Robert Edward Lee accepted his commission as commander of the military and naval forces of Virginia from the Virginia Convention in April, 1861. On the spot where he stood at that time now stands a beautiful bronze statue of this beloved hero, by Rudolph Evans. Lee graduated from West Point and was a lieutenant-colonel in the United States Army when he resigned. He was offered the field command of the United States Army, but he declined it because he felt he could never fight against Virginia, his native state.

The House of Delegates met here from 1788 until 1906. It was here also that the Confederate Congress met and that Chief Justice John Marshall presided over the trial of Aaron Burr on a charge of treason, in 1807. Edmund Randolph and John Wickham were among Burr's attorneys.

Around these walls are busts of other great men born in Virginia: George Mason; Sam Houston; Cyrus McCormick; General Fitzhugh Lee; Henry Clay; Generals Joseph E. Johnson and J. E. B. Stuart; Commodore Matthew Fontaine Maury; Patrick Henry; and, of course, Chief Justice John Marshall. There is also in this room, in a niche beside the door, a bust of Kentucky-born Jefferson Davis, President of the Confederacy.

The Old Hall is a beautiful room. The draperies are of a color and pattern first selected by Jefferson himself. The little chairs and desks are of a design selected by

4

him also and the little balconies and stairs show the French influence on Mr. Jefferson's taste.

In 1870 the east gallery gave way in the room where the Supreme Court of Appeals was in session. This room was located above the Old Hall of the House of Delegates. When the gallery and everyone in it fell onto the floor of the already crowded court room, the floor of that room also gave way, and everybody and everything in the upper room were hurled into the Old Hall below. This was the famous Capitol Disaster in which sixty-two people were killed and two hundred and fifty-one were injured.

In the Old Senate Chamber the body of the gallant "Stonewall" Jackson lay in state on May 12, 1863. Here also lay in state the body of J. E. B. Stuart and that of Jefferson Davis. Today a great many interesting and valuable paintings hang in this chamber and elsewhere in the Capitol.

One of the most notable events to have occurred in the New Hall of the House of Delegates was in March, 1946, when Winston Churchill and General Dwight D. Eisenhower visited Richmond together and both addressed the General Assembly.

In Capitol Square, in the grounds of the Capitol, stand the Old Bell Tower, the Finance Building, the State Office Building; and the equestrian statue of Washington, around which are grouped statues of Thomas Jefferson, Patrick Henry, George Mason, John Marshall, Andrew Lewis and Thomas Nelson. Then there are statues of Dr. Hunter McGuire, "Stonewall" Jackson and Governor William Smith along the north side of the grounds. The park lawns are always velvety green; and there are many stately old trees, shrubs, and numbers of huge and ancient box. There are two pools with fountains where children gather to watch the fish.

To the east stands the Governor's Mansion.

THE GOVERNOR'S MANSION

THE ample brick dwelling at the northeast corner of Capitol Square, with its walls painted white and four chimneys projecting from the roof, is the residence of the Governor of Virginia. Chief executives and their families have lived within its walls since its completion in 1812.

The Governor's Mansion is in the early Federal style of architecture and is designed with satisfying simplicity. There are two windows on the first floor on each side of the Doric portico of the façade, and five windows across the façade on the second floor.

The grounds of the mansion used to have an iron fence across the front, but more recently this was removed and a handsome brick wall has been built in its place. It is not quite a serpentine wall, but each half of it is built in a long, gentle curve outward, rather than straight across. Evergreens, grass, trees and the fountain decorate the front garden, while to the side is a box and flower garden. There is also a guest house on the garden side, well shaded with trees and approached by brick walks.

Etta Hodges Mann, the wife of Governor William Hodges Mann (1910-1914) has written a delightful and valuable book called *Four Years in the Governor's Mansion of Virginia*. Because almost everyone is enchanted with the vista upon entering the front door, we should like to quote Mrs. Mann's description of the first floor as it was on the day Governor Mann took the oath of office in the House of Delegates, February 2, 1910. After the prayer by Dr. T. P. Epes and the inaugural address, the Manns, with family and friends, went to their new home, the Governor's Mansion. Here is what Mrs. Mann wrote in her diary: ". . . With all the improvements made by our predecessors it is a most lovely and attractive home and I see little to do save to enjoy it to the fullest extent. One is struck on entering the front door by the spacious hall, with wide rooms on either side, parlor and library, and a long reception hall extending across the entire house; in the rear is the dining room, a beautiful room, elliptical in shape, from which stretches a wonderful vista, showing the Washington Monument in the distance. This room really makes the house perfect."

Mrs. Mann goes on to say: ". . . All of the Governors' wives seem to have done their part towards improving the old home which in 1912 will be a hundred years old. I mean to do my share by renovating and improving the bathrooms, putting in modern plumbing and marble flooring and side walls."

Many prominent guests have been entertained in the Governor's Mansion in Richmond, among them Lafayette, Marshal Foch, nearly all the Presidents, and many artists, musicians and statesmen.

THE WHITE HOUSE OF THE CONFEDERACY

IN 1816 Dr. John Brockenbrough, a very prominent citizen in Richmond, bought a lot at the corner of 12th and Clay Streets, for which he paid the sum of $10,000. He had built one home, not far away, a large, lovely place, and his friends decided that the reason he was building another was because he wanted a home planned by the famous architect, Robert Mills, who made the original designs for the Washington Monument and the U. S. Treasury in Washington, D. C., and planned many other important buildings. That, perhaps, was true, for Dr. Brockenbrough had been chairman of the committee for planning the Monumental Church which was built as a memorial to the seventy people who had lost their lives in the great theatre fire at the Virginia Academy the 26th of December, 1811. Robert Mills planned this church, and also planned John Wickham's house diagonally across the street from the first Brockenbrough house. All three men were good friends, so it was natural that Dr. Brockenbrough would enjoy a new home planned by the eminent architect. He was president of the Bank of Virginia on Bank Street, and he was a man of affluence.

The house was built in 1818, at least it must have been almost complete at the end of that year—according to insurance policies taken out during the year.

The front portico is small and formal, but the garden portico extends all the way across the back, and has enormous columns. The building is of brick construction covered with gray stucco. The rooms are enormous and beautiful, the hall and staircase works of art. The building is 67 x 52 feet, and at the time of its construction, rose two stories above the high basement. (The third story was added later.)

From the moment Dr. Brockenbrough and his wife, the former Gabriella Harvie (who was the Widow Randolph) moved in, their magnificent home was a scene of gaiety. Young ladies came to visit, and young beaus to call. Parties were the order of the day (or night). The next lot was bought and a most beautiful garden laid out. It was called a "hanging," or terraced garden, and overlooked the ravine of Shockoe Valley, which at that time was a picturesque rural scene—no trains or factories to mar the beauty of wood, stream and valley.

Mrs. Brockenbrough adopted Mary Randolph, a granddaughter by her former marriage, and Mary was married here in the drawing room that is now called the Georgia Room.

Maria Ward was a close friend of the family, as was John Randolph of Roanoke, and when their love affair broke off it was to Mrs. Brockenbrough that Maria trusted the sealed packet of his love letters, to be destroyed, unopened, at her death. Mrs. Brockenbrough kept the faith, and neither the world nor she ever learned the contents of the letters.

In 1844 Dr. Brockenbrough sold the Brockenbrough House to James M. Morson, and retired to Warm Springs, Virginia. One year later Mr. Morson sold the house to

(*above*) *Governor's Mansion, Richmond, residence of Virginia's governors since 1812.*

ON FACING PAGE

(*above*) *The Guest Cottage, Governor's Mansion.*

(*below*) *Herb garden by the Guest Cottage, Governor's Mansion.*

(above) Ball room, Governor's Mansion.

ON FACING PAGE

(above) Dining room, Governor's Mansion.

(below) Kitchen in the Guest Cottage, Governor's Mansion.

his sister-in-law; she and his wife, Mrs. Morson, had been known as the "two beautiful Bruce Girls." Then Mr. Morson moved to Dover, his home in Goochland County. Miss Bruce was almost immediately married to Morson's cousin and law partner, the Honorable James Seddon, member of Congress from Virginia, and later Secretary of War for the Confederate States.

Evidence seems to point to the fact that the third floor was added during the Seddon occupancy. There was no general increase of taxes at the time, but the Brockenbrough House was assessed for an additional $3,000.00, which would seem to have been for the new upper story.

During the Morson and Seddon residences, the traditional hospitality and the many gay functions made this beautiful home a much-frequented social center in Richmond.

When the Seddon's moved to Sabot Hill, their home in Goochland, near Dover, the home of their relatives, they sold the Brockenbrough House to Lewis D. Crenshaw, who resided there until June 1, 1861, when he sold the house to the city for $35,000.

The city spent $8,000 furnishing the mansion, and offered it as a home to President Davis and his family. The gift was declined, but the Davis family occupied the house, with the Confederacy paying rent to the city.

From then on the building, at 12th and Clay Streets, has been known as the White House of the Confederacy and what happened there is well-known history.

It was here Varina Anne Davis ("Winnie") the original "Daughter of the Confederacy," was born. Here President Davis was baptized by Dr. Minnigerode of St. Paul's. Here President Davis' sister was married to Captain William Waller, and "little Joe," not yet five, was killed when he fell from the back porch, April 30, 1864.

Evidently Mrs. Davis made a determined effort to keep up the morale of the people generally, for she, with the President, gave frequent parties, and entertained the many officers who came so often to the home. They seemed to come to the White House both for conferences with the "Chief," and for a few hours surcease from the grim rigors of the rugged life of war.

In the Rebel War Clerk's Diary we find these words: "Last night . . . the President's house was pretty well filled with gentlemen and ladies. I cannot imagine how they continue to dress so magnificently, unless it be their old finery which looks well amid the general aspect of shabby mendicity. But the statures of the men, and the beauty and grace of the ladies, surpass any I have seen elsewhere, in America or Europe. There is high character in almost every face, and fixed resolve in every eye."

When the President left the White House of the Confederacy, and fled Richmond on April 2, 1865, the Federals immediately took possession. General Weitzel moved right into the former executive mansion, and it is said, ate the meal that had been provided for the President.

On April 5, 1865, President Lincoln paid his first and last visit to Richmond. He came in a steamer, and as far as is known, the only building in the city that he

The White House of the Confederacy, garden front, Richmond. This was the residence of Jefferson Davis and his family during the Civil War. The house was designed by Robert Mills, architect of the Washington Monument, Washington, D. C. Courtesy Valentine Museum, Dementi Studio.

entered was the White House of the Confederacy. He conferred with General Weitzel there, and was given a reception attended chiefly by Union officers.

It was not until 1870 that the White House of the Confederacy was turned over to the city by the United States Government. For many years it was a private school. At least a part of the time the superintendent of this school was Stephen T. Pendleton, "a polished gentleman, and one of Virginia's foremost scholars."

The city turned over the building to the Confederate Memorial Literary Society to house its collection of Confederate material. The transfer was made on Jefferson Davis' birthday, June 3, 1894, with suitable ceremonies. It is now known as the Confederate Museum, and is the Mecca for thousands of visitors every year.

THE WICKHAM-VALENTINE HOUSE

AT Eleventh Street on Clay Street stands one of the most colorful museums in the South. The original part, the corner house, was also designed by Robert Mills.

It was built for John Wickham, a very distinguished gentlemen, and a prominent lawyer of Richmond, and his wife, the former Elizabeth McClurg.

John Wickham was a friend of Aaron Burr and was his attorney in Burr's treason trial at the Capitol in 1807. He was a close friend of John Randolph, of Roanoke, of Dr. John Brockenbrough, Edmund Randolph and many other prominent citizens of his day. Tom Moore, the poet, declared him "fit to adorn any court." His wife, Elizabeth, was a noted beauty; and so she appears in St. Memin's portrait of her.

The house was built in 1812. It is of brick with gray stucco or plaster cover. Its exterior shows Greek Revival influences in the small front portico and the large rear portico (facing the garden), as well as in some of the features of the interior. The house has one of the most beautiful stairways and front halls "ever built in the city."

Mr. Wickham died in 1839, and Mrs. Wickham survived him until 1854. After her death the house had a succession of owners. During the Civil War Charles G. Memminger, the Confederate Secretary of the Treasury, lived here. Then there was Mr. Ballard, of Ballard and Exchange Hotels; Mr. Brooks, who "made his money in trade;" and finally Mr. Mann Satterwhite Valentine III, who bought the property in 1882. When he died in 1892 he left the house, with a liberal endowment, to be used by the city as a museum for his many collections, and the collections of his sons, Granville Gray, Mann Satterwhite III, Edward Pleasants, and Benjamin Batcheldor. There are collections of art, books, manuscripts and many Indian relics; objects of archaeological interest; and also ethnological items.

In 1928 the three adjoining houses were purchased, remodeled and connected with the Wickham-Valentine House, thus making a huge unit to house one of the rarest and largest collections of its kind.

At the rear, facing the garden, is the studio of the illustrious sculptor, Edward Virginius Valentine. This was moved here in 1936, and has become a part of the Valentine Museum.

14

THE JOHN MARSHALL HOUSE

CHIEF JUSTICE JOHN MARSHALL always considered Richmond his home town. He was born in Fauquier County, was educated at Williamsburg and campaigned with Washington through some of the colonies. He moved to Richmond to practice law. He was appointed Chief Justice of the United States in 1801. The John Marshall House was built 1788-90. It is a somewhat small brick structure two stories high, with three porches; a small room seems to have been added at a later period. A substantial, durable house, simple in arrangement and outline, it lays no claim to ostentatious grandeur.

The stairway, while attractive and rather charming, cannot by any means be described as being in the grand manner. The front hall, though small, has dignity. The parlor and library are much larger rooms than one would expect from looking at the exterior of the house; the same is true of the dining room. The paneling in parlor and library is impressive, as are the doors, mantels, window casings and cornices. All the main rooms downstairs have dadoes.

There is a feeling of comfort and hominess in this little house that is not so little. One is awed by the thought that here for forty-five years lived one of the most distinguished citizens of our country.

Mr. Marshall married Mary Ambler, whom he called "Polly," and they lived together in happy concord. She died here in 1831. He died in Philadelphia in 1835 and was buried in Shockoe Cemetery in Richmond.

John Marshall lived in simple, unpretentious style. He had a habit of keeping careful accounts of all the money he spent—and what for. Also he frequently jotted down notes of the things he did, places he went, people he met, and so forth. He would go shopping with his market basket, talk with his neighbors, eat fruit on the way home, and perhaps take home, in his hand, a live turkey or a couple of ducks. He was generally beloved.

The John Marshall House, now owned by the Association for the Preservation of Virginia Antiquities, houses many items of interest connected with the life and times of the great Chief Justice of the United States.

THE OLD STONE HOUSE
(The Poe Shrine)

ON lot No. 32 shown by the old map of Richmond which Major Mayo drew for Col. William Byrd II in 1737, a stone house was built. Some say it was built prior to 1688, and was already there when the map was drawn. This conjecture has its origin in the fact that the letters JR have been carved into one stone of the house; the supposition is that this JR stood for Jacobus Rex. As James II was driven from the throne in 1688, in the "Bloodless Revolution," if the house was built during his reign, it would have to date from 1688 or an earlier year.

Wickham-Valentine House, Richmond, built by John Wickham, attorney for Aaron Burr in the latter's trial for treason. Courtesy Valentine Museum, Dementi Studio.

(below) Wickham-Valentine House, garden view. Courtesy Valentine Museum, Dementi Studio.

Spiral stairway in Wickham-Valentine House. Courtesy Valentine Museum, Dementi Studio.

(below) Music room, Wickham-Valentine House. Courtesy Valentine Museum, Dementi Studio.

Dining room, Wickham-Valentine House. Courtesy Valentine Museum, Dementi Studio.

(below) The parlor, Wickham-Valentine House. Courtesy Valentine Museum, Dementi Studio.

Another story says that the Old Stone House was built in 1737 by Jacob Ege,. either a cooper or a tailor—or possibly both. Members of the Ege family owned the house until 1911.

Some distinguished guests were entertained in this house, certainly Washington, Jefferson, Patrick Henry and Lafayette. Mrs. Welch (or Welsh) told Lossing that she remembered Monroe boarding with her mother there. Her father and mother were Samuel and Elizabeth Ege (Samuel being a son of Jacob Ege, Sr.).

When the Old Stone House was put up at auction December 5, 1911, it was bought in by the Association for the Preservation of Virginia Antiquities—thanks to the generosity of Mr. and Mrs. Granville Gray Valentine. For several years it served as an antique shop or remained vacant. Then in 1921 the Poe Shrine, through the efforts of Mr. and Mrs. Archer Jones, was organized. The Old Stone House became The Shrine, and priceless collections of Poeana are now housed there. Although Poe never lived in the stone house, indeed he may never even have entered its door, yet it was there while he lived in Richmond, and he probably saw it many times.

When the *Southern Literary Messenger* building was torn down, a good deal of the material of which it had been built was used at the Poe Shrine. The bricks were used to build a loggia, or summer house, at the back of the garden. Some of the woodwork and paneling was used in the little old house itself.

The house is so tiny that one is almost afraid to stand up straight when one is inside it. But actually the rooms do not seem too crowded. A hall only four feet wide runs from the front door to the door that opens into the garden. The room to the right is a little larger than the other on the opposite side, and has two windows. All the rooms have fireplaces. The room to the left has one window toward the front, and a door which opens into the garden. At the far end of the small hall, to the left, is a crude, narrow, very steep stairway, which leads to a hall above, opening into rooms on either side. These have dormer windows, fireplaces and sloping attic ceilings.

Housed in this little building are the desk Poe occupied at the *Southern Literary Messenger*, when he wrote for that magazine, his chair and many other objects he used. In the rooms all the Poe antiques and relics are tastefully arranged. About these humble objects, so lovingly collected, seems to hover the spirit of the great poet; one feels his presence in them—they evoke memories of his passionate, tragic life and the strange dreams and visions he transmuted into unearthly beauty of words and rhythm. Meditating on these things, one enters the little garden. Here all is serene, and here grow only the flowers mentioned by Poe in his poems.

The Poe Shrine is now the Poe Foundation. Thousands of people visit the Old Stone House every year. For them it is an unusual and evocative emotional experience.

THE CRAIG HOUSE
(Sometimes called "Helen's House")

IN the square formed by 18th, 19th, Grace and Broad Streets stands the Craig House, a two-story clapboard structure with an ell and three porches. The three outside

Home of John Marshall, the great Chief Justice of the United States Supreme Court. Courtesy Valentine Museum, Dementi Studio.

20

chimneys are slender and tall. There is a white picket fence around the house and garden.

Some facts seem to indicate 1770 as the date when this house was built; others point to a somewhat later time. Adam Craig owned, and his family lived in the house from 1790 to 1822. He died in 1808. He was Clerk in the Hustings Court, the Henrico Court and the General Court. His wife was Polly Mallory, from York County. They had six children. Jane Stith Craig was born in 1793, and lived in the Craig House until her marriage to Judge Robert Stanard. Jane Craig was the girl to whom Poe addressed the lines in the beautiful poem "To Helen." She was already married when he met her, and she lived at that time on 9th Street in the Hay-Stanard House.

After Mrs. Craig's death the Craig House was bought by Sterling J. Crump and Thomas Cowles. It was rented to tenants for several years, when, in 1844, Mr. Wilson Williams bought it for his home. Miss Scott says it must have been he who modernized the two front rooms and front hall on the first floor, which is the only part of the

The Old Stone House (Poe Shrine) which contains relics of Edgar Allan Poe's residence in Richmond. Courtesy Valentine Museum, Dementi Studio.

interior that has been changed since Adam Craig's day. Mr. Williams also may have restored and extended the garden.

After the Civil War the place was acquired by James W. Shields. He made it his home until his death, and was the last private owner of the property. He was a colorful figure and a well-known citizen.

In 1935 the Association for the Preservation of Virginia Antiquities acquired the property, cleared off some incongruous buildings, restored the house, kitchen and beautiful garden. The pine floors are in good condition, and the woodwork is suitable for a house of this type and period. There are tiny closets on each side of the chimney in the downstairs ell-room.

The Craig House is now a Negro Art Center.

THE LEE HOUSE

THE Lee House, 707 East Franklin Street, now the home of the Historical Society, was built in 1844, as one of a row of five, by Norman Stewart, who had come over to Virginia from Rothesay in Scotland before 1806. The row was called "Stewart's Row" and Mr. Stewart, a dealer in fine tobacco, rented out all the houses except No. 707, which he reserved for himself, and here kept "bachelor's hall."

His two nephews followed Mr. Stewart to Virginia. John married Miss Williamson and lived at Brook Hill. Miss Mary Scott has an interesting story, told her by one of Mr. Stewart's great-nephews. He said the younger members of the family used to stop by at 707 East Franklin Street on their way home from St. Paul's, to have a glass of sherry and some stale sponge-cake with their uncle before the long drive back to Brook Hill. He also told that his uncle was rather vain, for the old gentleman hid his red hair under a brown wig; the uncle was also quite thrifty—the Scotch would call it "near"—he had his servant unravel his old stockings so that the yarn could be used to darn his new ones! When Norman Stewart died in 1856 the house was left to his nephew John.

During the Civil War the house was rented to General Custis Lee and some of his brother officers. When Richmond, a city built to hold 35,000 or 40,000 people, suddenly was bursting out at the seams with a population of more than 100,000, it was hard for Mrs. Robert E. Lee to find quarters when she came to the city in January, 1864. General Custis Lee and his friends gallantly let his mother and sisters have their lease. So here in the "Lee House" General Robert E. Lee came home to his family and stayed with them from January, 1864, until April, 1865. It was also to this same house that he returned after Appomattox, to lay aside his sword forever. Lee and his family remained in the old mansion until June, 1865, when he went to the country for the summer; after that he settled in Lexington, Virginia, when he became president of Washington College.

Norman Stewart House, as it is sometimes called, was a comfortable city home, with high ceilings, fireplaces and fine woodwork. For a time it served as the home of the Westmoreland Club. Then, in 1893, Mrs. John Stewart and her daughters presented it to the Virginia Historical Society. Many valuable manuscripts, books and items of priceless historical value are housed within its walls.

THE VIRGINIA HOUSE

THE Priory of the Holy Sepulcher at Warwick, England, was built in 1125 by the first Earl of Warwick. It was generally known simply as "The Priory." Following the dissolution of monasteries in England four hundred years later, Thomas Hawkins came into possession of the old priory and rebuilt it as a residence for himself and his family. In its day it was a magnificent country seat. Queen Elizabeth, with members of her court, visited the Priory, and in her honor her coat of arms was carved on one of the stones of the walls.

Craig House, Richmond, birthplace of Jane Craig, the "Helen" of Poe's poem. Courtesy Valentine Museum.

In 1925, when the old building was about to be demolished, the entire structure was purchased from the house wrecker, shipped to Richmond, Virginia, and rebuilt at Windsor Farms. The project required much time, thought and planning, but was finally carried out successfully. Now it is the beautiful showplace known as Virginia House; set in its ample grounds of ten acres it is an outstanding architectural monument out of a great era.

23

Virginia House has three parts, or sections, and each section has its own architectural character, though all three sections are in perfect harmony. The walls are built of sandstone more than eight centuries old; the moss of past ages still clings to many of the stones. Yet these latter are in a remarkable state of preservation, so that, in fact, the guild emblems with which the 12th-century masons marked some of them, are clearly decipherable. The roof tiles are hand-hewn. Some of these are moss-grown also.

The main section of Virginia House is a modified copy of the Tudor portion of the Priory. The entrance tower shows the architectural influence of Wormleighton, in England, and the west wing is a reproduction of the main part of the original structure of Sulgrave Manor, which was the home of George Washington's ancestors in England.

The interior of Virginia House is magnificent. It would require a lengthy treatise to do it justice. The oaken stairway which came from the Priory, is worthy of special note; it is hand carved. The hand-hewn beams are heavy and still sound. The paneling here and in some of the rooms is beautiful; in the hall are pieces of armor that used to hang in the Tower of London.

The gardens at Virginia House are particularly attractive. There are formal gardens terraced gardens, water and wild flower gardens. Almost all flowers native to this area are cultivated here. The box, the trees and shrubs are the finest specimens. The weeping willow has been grown from a sprig cut off of the weeping willow on the Island of St. Helena.

Virginia House was for years the home of the late Mr. and Mrs. Alexander Wilbourne Weddell; he had been our ambassador to Mexico and Spain. At their deaths, the house passed, in 1948, to the Virginia Historical Society. It contains priceless collections of art, books and antiques.

AGECROFT HALL

IN Windsor Farms, in Richmond, stands a house dating to pre-Elizabethan times. It is Agecroft Hall, the home of Mrs. David Morton. Set in beautiful sloping grounds, which stretch away to the banks of the James, with green grass, occasional apple trees or dogwoods here and there, with some magnificent shade trees, and extensive gardens, the old mansion seems perfectly at home.

The house is of the quaint timber and plaster style, of the period in which it was built, with beautifully carved oriel windows, and richly ornamental gables over the leaded casements. There is one chimney, at least, that Kingsley's Tom might easily have swept, in the days gone by, before he became a Water Baby.

The interior of Agecroft Hall has warmth and beauty, with the rich coloring of the handsomely carved oak paneling, and the sun pouring in through the hundreds of leaded panes.

The old house formerly stood in Lancashire, England, and was the Manor House of the Langley family, which was a branch of the royal family of Plantagenets. In

24

Virginia House, an ancient priory brought from England and
reconstructed in Richmond.

The richly paneled stairway at Virginia House.

(below) Drawing room at Virginia House.

Lower garden at Virginia House.

1925 Agecroft Hall was bought by the late Mr. Thomas C. Williams, who had the materials removed from England to Richmond, where a remarkable reconstruction was effected. The house and its surroundings seem to belong to each other.

According to a bequest of the late Mr. Williams, Agecroft Hall will eventually become a museum for the city of Richmond.

AMPTHILL HOUSE

ORIGINALLY Ampthill House stood on the banks of the James, five miles below Richmond, on the south side in what was then Henrico County. It was built in 1732 by Henry Cary II, son of Henry Cary I, who first owned the plantation.

Both these men were experienced builders, having superintended the erection of the Capitol in Williamsburg, and the rebuilding (after a fire) of William and Mary College; they also were connected with the building of Bruton Parish Church and other notable structures. It was to be expected, then, that the best material and finest workmanship would go into the second Henry Cary's own home.

In 1749 all of Henrico County south of the James became Chesterfield County, so Ampthill found itself in a new county. In the same year Henry Cary II died, and his son, Archibald Cary, inherited the plantation. It was he who gave his home the name Ampthill House from Ampthill Castle in England. He married Mary Randolph.

In the Virginia Convention of 1776, Archibald Cary acted as chairman. In discussing this convention Grigsby says of Archibald Cary, "It was from his lips, as Chairman of the Committee of the Whole, that the words of the Resolution of Independence, of the Declaration of Rights, and a plan of Government, first fell upon the public ear." General Washington was Col. Cary's friend, and related to him. He visited him at Ampthill at least twice, spending the night there. Col. Cary took an active part in the Revolution, advancing supplies and equipment to the troops. He was widely connected throughout Virginia, and many prominent people came to Ampthill to visit him. Among these was Thomas Jefferson. When Col. Cary died, Ampthill passed to his daughter Elizabeth. It remained in the Cary family for a good many years. Later it was owned by the Temple family and still later by the Watkins family.

When Du Pont de Nemours acquired a large acreage for its plant on the James in 1927, the land included the site of Ampthill House, which at that time was not in good repair. The Du Pont Company sold the house to Mr. Hunsdon Cary, a collateral descendant of Col. Archibald Cary, and he moved it up the river and to the other side. It was in Henrico County again, but has since become part of the city of Richmond.

Great care was taken in moving and in rebuilding. While some new material had to be used in the restoration, a surprising amount of the original material was usable. The paneling of the center unit and one wing was intact. All the beautiful old "rose" bricks were used, and most of the flooring was good, and could also be used.

Ampthill and Wilton are neighbors again, and their similarity is somewhat remarkable. Of Georgian architectural style, Ampthill has the great central hall with front

28

Agecroft, a pre-Elizabethan manor house transported piece by piece from Lancashire, England, and rebuilt at Windsor Farms, Richmond.

doors at both ends (river front and garden or street front). The staircase is particularly handsome. Then there are two charming rooms on each side of the hall, downstairs and up, and the woodwork is beautiful. The rose, or salmon brick walls; hip on hip roof; thick high chimneys; and the attached wings, (originally separate depend-

The terrace at Agecroft.

(above) Interior at Agecroft. Note the musicians' pew in the corner of the balcony.

The dining room at Agecroft.

encies) all go to make a most distinctive home. And this lovely house also has a beautiful setting; gardens, trees and lawns, with a view of the river.

In 1949 Mr. and Mrs. David Tennant Bryan bought Ampthill House from the Carys, and are making it their home.

WILTON

WILLIAM RANDOLPH III, son of Col. William Randolph II of Turkey Island, in 1753 built Wilton six miles below Richmond, on the north side of the James in Henrico County. This massive brick house, in Georgian style, with hip roof and four twenty-six-foot chimneys, is sixty feet long and forty-six feet wide. Its wide center hall stretches from river front to garden front, and both halls and all eight large rooms are paneled from floor to ceiling. Even the closets are paneled. The perfect balance in the panels is very pleasing. Above the balustrade type chair rail the panels are tall, in proportion to the space, while below they are short.

The high windows have narrow panes of glass, nine to the sash, eighteen to the window. The stairway is very impressive and in good proportion.

In the drawing room, on each side of the fireplace, there are arched alcoves, with narrow windows in the back and window seats. The door frames of the front doors are supported by handsome Ionic pilasters with brick bases.

The place where Wilton was built was first called "World's End." Just across the river from Wilton was Ampthill, the home of the Carys (see above). Because the plans, the paneling and many other details, such as the marble arches of the fireplaces, were so similar in the two houses, several authorities have considered the possibility that Henry Cary II was consulted in the planning of Wilton.

William Randolph III married Ann Carter Harrison, daughter of Benjamin H. Harrison, of Berkeley. At Wilton they entertained many distinguished guests, among whom were the Marquis de Lafayette, George Washington and Thomas Jefferson. Their daughter, Anne Randolph, nicknamed "Nancy Wilton," was a charming belle and noted beauty. She had many admirers, among whom were Thomas Jefferson, future President of the United States, John Page, future Governor of Virginia, and Benjamin Harrison, her cousin, whom she chose from among her suitors.

Peyton Randolph, "Nancy Wilton's" brother, inherited Wilton, at the death of his parents. He married Lucy Harrison, daughter of Benjamin Harrison, the Signer of the Declaration of Independence.

The estate descended to William Randolph IV, then to William Randolph V, and finally to the latter's daughter, Kate, who was Mrs. Edward C. Mayo, of Richmond. She sold Wilton to Col. William Carter Knight, before the Civil War.

After changing hands several times more, in 1933 Wilton was acquired by the Colonial Dames of America in the State of Virginia. They moved the entire building to Wilton Road, off Cary Street Road, in what was then Henrico County, but now is in the far west end of the city of Richmond. Here it was carefully restored, and the Garden Club of Virginia beautifully landscaped the new surroundings in 1936.

32

Wilton, near Richmond, originally known as "World's End." Here lived Ann Randolph, "Nancy Wilton," who was courted by Thomas Jefferson.

33

(above) Drawing room at Wilton.

ON FACING PAGE

(above) Dining room at Wilton.

(below) Bedroom at Wilton.

34

Interior at Wilton.

36

Wilton is open to the public on certain days, and has had many visitors in the last two decades. The perfection of its restoration and its colorful history charm and interest a large public.

THE ELLEN GLASGOW HOUSE

AT Main and Foushee Streets, on the southwest corner, surrounded by antique shops, little stores and other signs of the commercial world creeping west, stands the house of Ellen Anderson Gholson Glasgow. Richmond is naturally proud of Miss Glasgow and esteems her highly as the city's most illustrious daughter.

Her house of brick, covered by gray stucco or plaster, is large and roomy. There is a small formal front porch, but the rear balcony type porch extends the full width of the building. A wide hall runs through the center of the house and has a handsome stairway rising to the upper floor. There are two rooms on each side of the hall. Miss Ellen had a large library, much handsome silver and many fine antiques.

The room on the right front, upstairs, was the famous author's private study and bedroom. Beside bathrooms, there were four other rooms on the second floor. During the time when other members of the family lived at home, these were their bedrooms. Later Miss Bennett had a large, lovely room, and the other three were guest rooms.

The last half of her life Miss Glasgow spent with her friend and companion, Miss Anne Virginia Bennett, except for the time Miss Bennett did duty as a nurse overseas in World War I. During those months Miss Ellen was alone, except for the servants.

Miss Anne Virginia and Miss Ellen traveled a good deal, sometimes together, and sometimes separately when each went in the company of other friends. Maine was a favorite place in summer, and Europe most any time of the year.

The front yard was small, but green and lovely. There were shrubs and trees, one of which was a fine magnolia, and in the backyard which was enclosed by a high fence, was a shady, peaceful garden with lilacs, boxwood, and old-fashioned flowers.

Although she did some writing during the summer up in Castine, Maine, it was in this house, upstairs in her big room with the open fireplace, that she produced most of her finest work.

Mr. James Branch Cabell, friend of Ellen Glasgow, an eminent writer himself and creator of a new style of satirical allegory, believes Miss Ellen was one of the most important woman novelists of America. She wrote twenty novels, a literary autobiography, *A Certain Measure*, and a personal autobiography, *The Woman Within*. But I shall always remember her poem, *The Freeman*, the title poem of her only book of verse, as her greatest claim to immortality. Of Miss Ellen's novels, young people like *The Battle Ground*, but more mature readers seem to prefer *Romantic Comedians*, *They Stoop to Folly*, *Vein of Iron*, *The Sheltered Life* and *In This Our Life*.

Many of Miss Ellen's readers have wondered whether or not she ever had a serious love affair. The answer to this query is to be found in *The Woman Within*. From what she wrote in this personal account of her life, it would appear that she had two great loves: one in youth, as romantic and sad as such early loves can be; the other, a deeper and more mature experience, in her later years. She never married.

The Glasgow House was built in 1842 by David M. Branch. His daughter sold it to Ellen Glasgow's father, Francis Glasgow, in 1887. It was the Glasgow home until

Ellen Glasgow House, Richmond, home of the famous woman novelist. Courtesy of the Valentine Museum. Photo by A. L. Dementi.

Library at the Ellen Glasgow House, in which Miss Glasgow wrote her books.

Miss Ellen's death in 1945. Now the Glasgow House is the Richmond Area University Center with which Randolph-Macon College of Ashland, the University of Richmond, the Medical College of Virginia, the Richmond Professional Institute, the Extension Division of the University of Virginia, the Extension Division of Virginia Polytechnic Institute, and perhaps some others, have become affiliated.

ST. JOHN'S CHURCH

AT 2400 East Broad Street, on Church Hill, stands beautiful old St. John's Church. The lots which constitute its site were marked on that first map made in 1737 by Major Mayo for Col. William Byrd II. At that time the site was called Indiantown Hill. Four years later, in 1741, the church was built by Richard Randolph, great-great-great-grandson of Pocahontas.

It is said that this church was called by ten different names before 1829. "New Church" and "Town Church" were two of the names it was known by. However, in 1829 and from then on, it was designated "St. John's Church, Henrico Parish."

In the Virginia Convention of 1775, held in St. John's, Patrick Henry made his immortal speech ending with: "The next gale that sweeps from the North will bring the clash of resounding arms. Is life so dear, or peace so sweet, as to be bought with chains and slavery? Forbid it Almighty God! I know not what course others may take, but as for me, give me Liberty or give me Death!"

There were many prominent men as delegates to this Convention; among them were Peyton Randolph, Edmund Randolph, Richard Bland, Andrew Lewis, Peter Muhlenberg, Thomas Jefferson, George Mason, George Washington, George Wythe, Benjamin Harrison, Thomas Nelson, Jr., and Richard Henry Lee. Patrick Henry spoke from pew No. 47. The bell believed to have been used in 1775 is at the Virginia Historical Society.

During the Revolution while the traitor, Benedict Arnold, was marauding in the vicinity of Richmond, he housed his troops in St. John's Church.

The Virginia Convention of 1788, held in St. John's Church, was for the purpose of ratifying the Constitution of the United States.

Of the many rectors who have officiated at St. John's, the first was the Reverend William Stith. George Wythe Munford wrote a book about the Reverend John Buchanan, one of the rectors, a man of ingenious personality, keen wit and great integrity of character; it was entitled *The Two Parsons*. The other "Parson" was the Reverend John Durbarrow Blair, a Presbyterian minister of fine parts. Munford draws their portraits in amusing and entertaining style.

The church now standing is the second on the site, and is a white, clapboarded building, with a square tower in three slightly graduated sections; the tower is capped by a small octagonal section with eight windows. The roof of this little top section is in the form of a very shallow dome surmounted by a cross. The font in the church is said to be the one which was used at the baptism of Pocahontas.

The churchyard at St. John's is of great interest. There are many old tombs, with

St. John's Church, Richmond, where Patrick Henry delivered his oft-quoted speech defying British oppression.

41

quaint inscriptions, and a number of old trees, shrubs, boxwood and dogwood. In the hush of the evening, when the birds' voices are muted and twilight begins to fall, one has a sense of the presence of the spirits of the valiant souls whose bodies rest in this picturesque and historic spot.

ST. PAUL'S CHURCH

ST. PAUL'S Episcopal Church stands on Grace Street at Ninth, just across from Capitol Square. The cornerstone was laid October 10, 1843, by Bishop John Johns, and the church was consecrated two years later. Thomas S. Stewart, of Philadelphia, was the architect.

The edifice is large, and the style of architecture is definitely Greek Revival, inside and out. The iron fence which encloses the front and sides, shows fine workmanship.

The balcony in the interior, which extends around three sides of the nave, is supported by marble columns, with Ionic capitals. The aisles also are of marble. Some of the most beautiful stained-glass windows to be found in America are in St. Paul's, and over the altar is a fine mosaic representing the Last Supper after the famous painting by Leonardo da Vinci.

St. Paul's is a brick structure covered with pale gray stucco. The church once had a spire. This has been replaced by a clock tower with belfry.

The first Virginia meeting of the General Convention of the Episcopal Church in America was being held in St. Paul's Church in 1859, when John Brown's raid on Harpers Ferry occurred. In October, 1860, the Prince of Wales, later Edward VII, attended service at St. Paul's and heard Dr. Minnigerode preach. After President and Mrs. Davis and the capital of the Confederacy moved to Richmond in 1861, St. Paul's was known as the "Court Church of the Confederacy." Here General Lee worshipped. It is said that there were occasions when, besides President Davis and his family, as many as twenty generals, as well as other army officers, would be in attendance at a church service here.

On April 2, 1865, during the service, a messenger quietly entered the church, passed down the aisle to the President's pew, leaned over and whispered a few words in his ear. Mr. Davis rose immediately and followed the man out. This was one of the most dramatic moments in southern history. The message was from General Robert E. Lee. The line at Petersburg had been breached by the Federals, and Richmond must therefore be evacuated.

One week later when word reached Richmond that Lee had surrendered at Appomattox, the Federal soldiers, in exultation, fired two hundred guns in Capitol Square, just across the street from St. Paul's Church—but the South was plunged in black despair.

St. Paul's Church, Richmond, in which Jefferson Davis and other notables worshipped. It came to be known as the "Court Church of the Confederacy."

*Brook Hill, Henrico County, former seat of the Wilkinson,
Stewart and Bryan families.*

44

PART TWO

HENRICO AND CHESTERFIELD COUNTIES

BECAUSE Chesterfield was a part of Henrico County until 1749, when it became a separate county, and because the early histories of both were so intertwined, it seems suitable to tell their story in one and the same account. A good deal of Richmond's early record is also tied up with the happenings in these two counties.

Henrico is twenty-seven miles long and eight wide. It is bounded on the north by the Chickahominy and on the south by the James.

Sir Thomas Dale established the town of Henrico (also called Henricus and Henricopolis) on what is now known as Farrar's Island, in September 1611. It was not as easy as it sounds to do this, for while establishing this settlement, "dyvers tymes" were they attacked by the Indians. A majority of Dale's settlers were "trained in mechanical arts." Within ten days of starting the settlement he "had very strongly impaled" seven acres chosen for the new town.

Dale was a most remarkable man. He handled the Indian situation better than some of the leaders at Jamestown. With "pales, posts and rails," and the trunks of trees he palisaded or enclosed large areas for protection.

Hamor, the historian, was at the time secretary of the colony. He asserts that within four months' time Dale had accomplished more at Henrico than had been done altogether in the colony from its beginning. Hamor said of the town: "There are now in this town three streets of well framed houses, a handsome Church and the foundation of a more stately one laid of Brick, in length an hundred feet, and fiftie foot wide, besides store houses, watch houses and such like; there are also . . . upon the verge of the river five faire Block houses, where in dwell the honester sort of people, as farmers in England and there keepe continual sentinell for the Townes securitie."

There is a big loop in the river at the point where the town was settled (where

45

Dutch Gap now is) and a big ditch was dug, which is partly hidden by tall trees growing along its banks.

On the south side of the river, in what is now Chesterfield County, Dale had his men build an enclosure two miles in extent. Within this area were the tracts called Hope in Faith and Coxen-Dale. Of the forts protecting this area, one was called "Mount Malady a guest house for sicke people." Thus Chesterfield County has the distinction of having had the first hospital in the United States.

Early in 1612 Dale captured the town of the Appomattux tribe, and their food supplies, in retaliation for atrocities committed against the English. He decided to build a town there which he would call Bermuda. He annexed much land, extending out and beyond explored areas. These vast expanses he declared should be called "Hundreds." In one direction there would be "Upper and Nether Hundred," in another "Degges Hundred," "West Shirley Hundred" and so on. Nether Hundred included the planned town of Bermuda—so that is how "Bermuda Hundred" originated. Hamor says ". . . many faire houses . . . near to the number of fiftie."

Dale did not compel the men to work altogether for the common cause, but to stimulate their personal interest, assigned to each three acres to cultivate for himself.

Bermuda was the first town to be incorporated in America (1614).

The governor of Virginia "founded the limits" of the University of Henrico in 1619. The Treasurer of the Virginia Company described the land granted as ten thousand acres for the University to be planted at Henrico, of which one thousand acres were to provide means to be used for the conversion of infidels.

The proceedings of the college were to be reported to the central authorities, it "being a waighty business;" so a court, on June 14, 1619, gave the care of the college into the hands of a committee of "choice" gentlemen. They were: Sir Dudley Digges, Sir John Danvers, Sir Nathaniel Rich, Sir John Wolstenholme, Mr. John Ferrar, Dr. Theodore Gulstone and Dr. Francis Anthony. This was the first college board ever to serve a college in America.

The first iron works in America were at Falling Creek. The massacre of 1622 wiped out the towns of Henrico and Bermuda Hundred, as well as the Iron Works at Falling Creek. There were not more than twenty-one white persons left above the mouth of the Appomattox River after that disaster. The land which later became Henrico and Chesterfield Counties remained for many years the frontier between the settlements and the wilderness full of savages.

With tenacious determination, with courage and patience, the surviving settlers finally conquered this land. Now and again new adventurers drifted in, reclaimed an old cabin or built a new one. A few gentlemen received large grants, brought their families and retainers, and made small settlements. Trading posts, or shoccos, were set up here and there along the river, until by 1676 there was quite a bit of activity up as far as the Falls.

But the old trouble cropped up again. The Indians were once more becoming dangerous, and, as Governor Berkeley did nothing, it remained for Nathaniel Bacon, of Curles, in Henrico, to lead his famous Rebellion, in protest against the Governor's failure to protect the colonists.

After the Rebellion was over, during the period when punitive measures were being taken against the rebels, more people began to move up the river, and by the end of the century more tobacco was being raised and more people were building better homes in this region. William Byrd I was raising his family there, and inviting settlers to make their homes on his land. Thomas Jefferson, the grandfather of President Thomas Jefferson, was living at Osborne, and John Bolling must have been living at Cobb's. The Huguenots were also coming, fleeing from persecution in France.

This land had been called Henrico since 1611 in honor of Henry, Prince of Wales. In 1634, by Act of the Burgesses, it was made Henrico Shire, and by the same body, in 1652, rechristened Henrico County.

For many years coal was mined in Chesterfield County, near Midlothian, and in Henrico County at Gayton.

The members of the Governor's Council from Henrico County (including, of course, present-day Chesterfield County) were:

> William Farrar   1623
> Nathaniel Bacon II ("The Rebel")   1675
> William Byrd I   1681
> William Randolph   1728
> Peter Randolph   1751

In the first House of Burgesses, 1619, representing Henrico were:

> Thomas Dowse
> John Polentine

Members of the Conventions: (Chesterfield had been made a separate county in 1749)

HENRICO	CHESTERFIELD
March 20, 1775	
Richard Adams	Archibald Cary
Samuel Duval	Benjamin Watkins
July 1775	
Richard Adams	Archibald Cary
Richard Randolph	Benjamin Watkins
May 6, 1776	
Nathaniel Wilkinson	Archibald Cary
Richard Adams	Benjamin Watkins

A complete list of members of the House of Burgesses, some of whom were from Henrico, may be found in the Colonial Register.

BROOK HILL

NOW the home of Miss Annie Stewart, Brook Hill was built at Brook Hill near Brook Run, north of Richmond, before the year 1735. It was built for Robert Williamson and his wife, Susanna Williamson, who also was his cousin.

Five generations of Williamsons, Stewarts and Bryans were born in this house, almost all of them in the same room. Mr. Robert Lancaster, in *Historic Virginia Homes and Churches,* gives the succession thus: "They were Robert Williamson II (1735-1796) who married Anne Coxe; their son Robert Carter Williamson (1796-1871) who married Lucy Parke Chamberlayne; their daughter Mary Amanda Williamson who married John Stewart; their daughter Isobel Stewart, (1847-1910) who married Joseph Bryan, of Eagle Point; and their son John Stewart Bryan."

Traditional hospitality has always reigned at Brook Hill, and a great deal of entertaining has been done there. The family has also always maintained its interest in philanthropies, and in all projects for the good of the community and the welfare of its people. John Stewart Bryan was one of the country's foremost citizens; he was for many years president of William and Mary College. He was also publisher of Richmond newspapers.

Brook Hill is a three-story house of brick, built in two sections, each of which has a hipped roof. The chimneys are massive and tall, and there are innumerable windows, also several porches, two of them two stories in height. The interior has magnificent woodwork and interesting paneling.

The mansion stands in a grove, and the gardens are extensive. The boxwood, the blooming shrubs, and many varieties of old-fashioned flowers make an enchanting setting for this lovely old mansion.

MEADOW FARM

THE home of General and Mrs. Sheppard Crump, on Mountain and Courtney Roads, at Glen Allen in Henrico, Meadow Farm was built before the Revolution. It is of frame construction, a story and a half high, and is in the Queen Anne style of architecture. It was built by General Crump's ancestors. The small portico on the front gives access to a center hall, which contains a most interesting stairway; it is a swinging, or "flying" staircase, having no supports, but so constructed that it supports itself. It leads to a hall and three bedrooms above.

To the right of the downstairs hall is the large dining-room, with huge end chimney and open fireplace. A door beside the chimney leads into the kitchen, in a wing which was added in 1850. On the left of the hall is the drawing room, which, like the dining-room, is furnished in exquisite taste with family antiques. Each item has its own history and interesting associations.

An insurance policy with the Mutual Assurance Company of Virginia, taken out by

48

Meadow Farm, Henrico County. In this old house "General Gab'l's" plot for a slave uprising was discovered.

Mosby Sheppard on December 25, Christmas Day, 1812, shows the house to have been of the same size as the main building is today.

General Crump was born here, as were his mother before him (Mary Elizabeth Sheppard) and his grandfather before her, (Dr. John Mosby Sheppard.) It was the home of Mosby Sheppard, the General's great grandfather, and his wife, Mary Glenn Crenshaw Austin, of Hanover. Here they raised a large family. The son, John Mosby, inherited the home. Here he brought his lovely bride, Virginia Anne Young, daughter of Mickelbrough Young, of White Chimneys, in Caroline County. In this connection, it is interesting to note that we found a record showing that Virginia Anne's brother, William R. Young, son of Mickelbrough Young, of "White Chimnies", enrolled as a Junior, at the age of seventeen, at the College of William and Mary, in the year 1838. He was scheduled to take chemistry and natural philosophy, and to live in the home of Mrs. Bowers, where several other students were also listed.

An extraordinary incident occurred here in 1800, when Mosby Sheppard "was sitting in the counting room with the door shut, and no one near except myself; they knocked at the door, and I let them in; they shut the door themselves, and began to tell me what I have before recited." This excerpt from a letter written by Mosby Sheppard to the Governor of Virginia, August 30, 1800, refers to the circumstances which led to the discovery by him of the insurrection planned by the Negroes under leadership of "Gen'l" Gab'l. A slave, by the name of Gabriel, was the instigator of this far-reaching conspiracy which would have resulted in the uprising of the slaves and the slaying of their masters.

The two who entered the "counting room" were Tom, who belonged to Elizabeth Sheppard, Mosby's mother (and General Crump's great-great-grandmother), and Pharioh, who belonged to Phillip Sheppard, Mosby Sheppard's brother. The two slaves revealed something of the terrible plot, but became too agitated to go on. However, Mosby Sheppard was a calm, shrewd, kind man. He told the Governor in his letter that he asked the slaves two questions: "When was it to take place?" "Tonight," they replied. Then, "Who was the principal man?" "Prosser's Gabriel." Mosby Sheppard informed the Governor as soon as possible, and the authorities prevented the outbreak. The two slaves, Tom and Pharioh, were bought by the State of Virginia for $500.00 each, and given their freedom as a reward for their loyalty and courage.

General Crump has an old account book that belonged to Phillip Sheppard, his great-great-uncle. In this book a listing dated 1790 mentions buying shoes and clothing for Pharioh, which were paid for in pounds, shillings and pence.

Mosby Sheppard served with the State Militia in the War of 1812. He was the son

ON FACING PAGE

(above) Hall at Meadow Farm.

(below) Drawing room at Meadow Farm.

of Benjamin Sheppard, who was General Crump's great-great-grandfather.

During the Civil War Meadow Farm was raided by the Federals under General Custer, on the very day that General J. E. B. Stuart was mortally wounded at Yellow Tavern, May 11, 1864. Stuart had just turned the enemy under Sheridan back from the direct road to Richmond. Meadow Farm is only a few miles from Yellow Tavern, and the Northern soldiers were skirmishing and foraging for food in the country. There was quite a little engagement on the hill in front of the house. The Confederates tried to hold the Federals off, but to no avail, for the Northerners entered the house, and took away every morsel of food they could find on the place. The meat had been placed in a locked closet upstairs, the door of which was hidden by a wardrobe, but a Negro slave woman told the soldiers where it was hidden and they took it, too.

General Crump's father was Edmund Parke Crump, a Confederate soldier from Hanover, and his paternal grandparents were Edmund Parke Cary Crump, and the latter's wife, Mary Hall Povall Goodall, of New Kent and Hanover Counties. Through this grandmother General Crump is of the fifth generation of the Parke Goodall family, many of whom have been in the military services. Mary Hall Povall Goodall was the daughter of Charles Parke Goodall, who was the son of Parke Goodall, of Revolutionary fame. John Gwathmey, in *Twelve Virginia Counties,* says: ". . . and it was Ensign Parke Goodall, of Hanover, who with sixteen men, browbeat [Governor] Dunmore into paying for the ammunition," the rebelling colonists used.

General Crump has been a prominent figure in military affairs. He saw service on the Mexican border in 1916-1917, and overseas in the 29th Division in World War I. For many years he was active as an officer in the Virginia National Guard, and served as Commanding Officer of the Richmond Blues. He was also assistant to the Adjutant General of Virginia. He is now Brigadier General and Adjutant General of Virginia. He is the high commanding officer of the National Guard of Virginia.

General and Mrs. Crump, who was the former Miss Elizabeth Young Adam, take a keen interest in civic affairs. For years they have been active leaders in promoting the welfare and betterment of the community. Mrs. Crump is well known in club work—in Garden Club, Gray Lady, and Woman's Club circles. It was she who originated the "Flowers for the Flowerless" slogan in Richmond, which looks to the pooling by club members of their cut flowers for distribution daily in the hospitals. She is also an excellent gardener, and has a very effective "green thumb."

At Meadow Farm the garden has many varieties of flowers, shrubs, and bulbs. There are lovely trees and boxwood. The General raises beef cattle.

Originally there were four hundred acres in the Meadow Farm tract, but it now comprises only one hundred eighty acres.

BENT PINE FARM

NORTH of Richmond, and not far from Yellow Tavern, lies the peaceful dairy farm known as Bent Pine Farm. It has been the home of Mr. and Mrs. Hiram Robert Sanders for more than a quarter of a century.

Bent Pine Farm, Henrico County. At the left stands the tree that gave the old house its name.

The land at Bent Pine is part of a thousand-acre tract comprising an original grant from the King of England to the Royall family of Henrico County. The original tract extended from what is now Greenwood Road to the Chickahominy River, and from the present Winfrey Road to the Richmond, Fredericksburg and Potomac Railroad Line. Following the Revolution, and during the period of general antipathy to anything "royal," the Royall family changed its name to Ryall. Court records, however, in some cases, show the continued use of the name "Royall" until 1820.

In 1817, by a decree filed in Henrico County Court, about two hundred acres of the estate came into the possession of J. Smith Ryall. In his will, probated at his death in 1873, he devised this land to his niece, Mary Jane King, who was largely responsible for the founding of Greenwood Methodist Church. She was married to Henry C. Barnes about 1880, and died several years later. She lies buried in the family cemetery

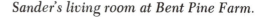

Sander's living room at Bent Pine Farm.

on Bent Pine Farm, beneath a tombstone erected by Greenwood Church in 1884.

The present house is erected over the basement, and uses the two chimneys of the original house, which burned down around 1870. Three different additions were made from 1878 to 1930, to form the present house, which contains a mantel and several doors salvaged from the original structure.

Careful thought was given to the reconstruction of this early American clapboard house. The old-fashioned chimneys, the various floor levels and the quaint old rooms retain the charm of colonial days. Antique furniture enhances the general impression of an earlier era.

The name Bent Pine Farm is derived from a bent white pine set out by the second Mrs. Barnes and Willie Taylor.

Mr. Sanders, the present owner, bought the farm in 1925 from his aunt, Susie Gary Barnes, who had inherited it from her husband, Henry C. Barnes.

Mr. Sanders and Mrs. Sanders, the former Miss Laura Garthright, were prominent in the educational field, before taking up residence at their estate, Bent Pine. They have continued active in the cultural, civic, social and church life of Henrico County, both holding important offices in various clubs. Mrs. Sanders was for some time president of the Presidents' Club of the Parent-Teacher Association.

TREE HILL

TO the east of Richmond, about four miles out on the Old Indian Trail, stands Tree Hill. It is a white clapboard house, two stories high, with four white-washed brick chimneys, two at each end of the central unit of the building. Full length one-story porches extend across front and back, and there are one-story wings at each end of the house that extend to the outer edge of the porches, thus completing the symmetrical plan of a square two-story center section entirely surrounded by a larger square one-story addition. There is a high basement under the entire house. All the windows have outside blinds painted green, and there are high steps to both porches. The woodwork of the interior is suitable for this type of farmhouse; there are two handsome marble mantels. The house is pleasantly located on a rise of land whose expanse of lawn is shaded by beautiful trees. There is a nice rose garden.

Mr. and Mrs. W. J. Burlee, the present owners of Tree Hill (which they inherited,) are dairy farmers. They own herds of purebred Holstein and Guernsey cows. The farm of five hundred and ten acres (ten acres in woodland) produces large quantities of grain and hay. But milk is the chief money crop.

The age of the house is unknown, but indications point to the late 18th century as the period in which it was built. Col. Miles Cary Selden owned the property in the early part of the 19th century.

At one time Tree Hill had one of America's most noted race tracks. It was here that the famous races in honor of the Marquis de Lafayette were held, when he revisited America in 1824. On this occasion "Virginia," a mare belonging to William R. Johnson, of Chesterfield County, won an historic race.

Tree Hill, Henrico County. In 1824 Lafayette watched horse races on this estate's famous racetrack.

56

*An interesting old dependency
at Tree Hill.*

During the Civil War the owner of Tree Hill, Mr. Franklin Stearns, let the Chimborazo Hospital authorities graze hundreds of goats here. The goats' milk and meat were believed to possess especially nutritious food values for the patients. When Richmond fell, in the spring of 1865, the surrender was made not far from Tree Hill; the formalities were carried out by a committee headed by Mayor Joseph Mayo, who used a torn shirttail as a flag of truce.

VARINA FARM

THIS famous old place in Henrico County is noted for two items of history with which it is usually connected. It was here John Rolfe and his bride, Pocahontas, the Indian Princess, lived, and here he raised tobacco that, in flavor and aroma, reminded connoisseurs in England of the "Varina" tobacco from Spain, hence the name Varina. The house that John Rolfe and Pocahontas lived in was small, and built of brick.

The Reverend James Blair, rector of Varina Parish, and founder and first president of William and Mary College, made his home here, as later did William Stith, who wrote a voluminous history of Virginia, and also served as president of the College of William and Mary.

At Varina there stands today a two-story brick house with two chimneys, which is probably the old part of the house. This is a wing which is attached by a long passage

(above) The Varina House, Henrico County. On this plantation John Rolfe
and Pocahontas made their home at one time. Here he raised tobacco of
the same type as the Varina from Spain.

ON FACING PAGE

(above) Engraving, showing the wedding of Pocahontas and John Rolfe,
now hanging in Varina House.

(below) The hall at Varina.

58

THE WEDDING OF POCAHONTAS.

to the present mansion. The mansion is a large square two-story brick building, with four chimneys. The walls have dignified masonry trim, and the cornice with dentils is very effective. The front porch shows a slight influence of the Greek Revival; the small columns have Ionic capitals. The stairway, mantels, doors and other woodwork are in keeping with the pre-Civil War style, in which the main house was built, and the house is furnished with antiques and reproductions.

Varina is now the home of Mr. and Mrs. Wilmer N. Stoneman, in whose family it has been for at least three generations.

RUINS OF MALVERN HILL

THE Malvern Hill house, burned in 1905, has often been grouped with two others in Virginia as unique in architectural style. In plan and structure, in its austerity and rugged simplicity, it has been compared with Criss Cross (Christ's Cross) in New Kent, and Bacon's Castle, in Surry. It seems fairly certain that it was built in the 17th century. Thomas Cocke, the builder, came from England in 1630. He was the son of Richard Cocke, of England.

There were end chimneys and a center hall, said to have been partitioned off the original great room at a later period with one room on either side, upstairs and down. There was also a unique feature not often found in Virginia, a porch chamber—that is, a room over the front porch. The main part of the house was built of brick; it had thick walls, but the room to the left of the hall was built of wood. The house was a story and a half high.

After the Revolution Robert Nelson, of Yorktown, (brother of Governor Thomas Nelson) bought "Malvern Hills." (Spelled with an "S" until after the Civil War.)

Because of its strategic position on the James, the heights of Malvern Hills were chosen for Lafayette's encampment as a precaution against a British attack on Richmond, during the Revolution. Again, in 1813, a large garrison was held here to watch for British ships on the river.

During the Civil War, the Battle of Malvern Hill on July 1, 1862, took place very near the house. Part of the engagement actually took place in the wheat field to the west. Both armies were in sight of the house, which fell to the Federals in June, 1864.

Not far from Malvern Hill was Turkey Island, first owned by Colonel James Crews. He was with Bacon in the Rebellion, and was hanged during Governor Berkeley's reprisals against the rebels. William Randolph I bought the plantation from Crews' heirs, and for many years it was a Randolph home. The Randolphs, descendants of William Randolph, have played a notable part in the social and political life of Virginia. Turkey Island House was burned by gun boats in James River at the time of the Battle of Malvern Hill.

EPPINGTON

FRANCIS EPPES, Jr., built Eppington on the Appomattox River in what was then

Henrico County, now Chesterfield, soon after 1730. The plantation consisted of four thousand acres, and the house was erected back on an eminence which sloped down about a mile to the river.

Two and a half stories high, with hip roof set with dormer windows and towering chimneys, the house has a one-story wing at each end and a porch at front and rear. The house is of white clapboard, and the windows have outside blinds. The cornice has dentils. A hall or passageway runs the length of the front of the house connecting the two wings. The center hall which has the living room—or parlor—on the right, and the dining-room on the left, is reached from this passageway. All main rooms have lovely paneling. The original locks and hinges are still in use on cross and Bible doors.

Mr. Eppes and Mr. Thomas Jefferson married half sisters, the daughters of John Wayles, of The Forest, not far from Williamsburg. The family of Mr. and Mrs. Francis Eppes, Jr., consisted of six daughters and one son. The son, John Wayles Eppes, married Maria Jefferson, the daughter of Thomas Jefferson. The Jeffersons and the Eppeses were very close. Mr. Francis Eppes was an expert horticulturist and agriculturist. Of course, this was an added bond between him and the author of the Declaration of Independence, for it is a well-known fact that Mr. Jefferson was interested in all phases of horticulture and agriculture. He remarked of Mr. Eppes that he "was not only the first horticulturist in America, but a man of the soundest practical judgment on all subjects that he had ever known."

John Wayles Eppes, Francis' son, became a leader in Congress, and probably would have attained to a high place in the government, but unfortunately, he died while still a young man. After Francis Eppes, Jr., and his wife died, the Eppington estate passed to a succession of owners.

In 1876 Mr. William Hinds, of Pittsburgh, Pennsylvania, acquired the property, and his descendants still own it.

COBB'S HALL

AMBROSE COBB patented three hundred and fifty acres on Appomattox River in 1639. The patent was granted him in order that he might bring over himself, his wife, his son and three others to Virginia and settle on the patented land. He was in business in York, and from the records, there were two other sons, Ambrose II and Thomas. (Bishop Meade mentions Ambrose Cobb, vestryman at the Church in Williamsburg, some time between 1674-1769.)

Cobb built the first mansion at Cobb's. Its site was on the north side of Appomattox River in what is now Chesterfield County. Later John Bolling (the great-grandson of Pocahontas and John Rolfe) and his wife, Mary Kennon, of Brick House, bought Cobb's, and it became a Bolling home for many generations. John Bolling went into mercantile business and carried on extensive trade with the Indians as well as the English.

John and Mary had a son, John, who was something of a gay blade and liked dancing, fishing, hunting, dogs and horses. He was devoted to his family. He became

Eppington, in Chesterfield County, at one time the home of Jefferson's daughter, Maria, and her husband, John Wayles Eppes.

a justice in the courts, while the family acres were still a part of Henrico, and later presided over the first Court of Chesterfield County. John had a son, Thomas, who married Elizabeth Gay. She rode about the country and to church with her coach and four, with coachman, footman and postillion in bright yellow livery.

Many distinguished Americans, including the second Mrs. Woodrow Wilson, were descendants of this family.

The burial ground at Cobb's is surrounded by a high brick wall, and many Bollings are buried here. There is a granite monument on which is inscribed, "Around this stone lie the remains of Colonel John Bolling of Cobbs. Great Grandson of Rolfe and Pocahontas—Born 1676—Died 1709."

Some members of the Bolling family were deaf, so William Bolling engaged a teacher, John Braidwood, of Washington, and in 1815 organized the first school for the deaf in America. It continued for only four years.

Cobbs suffered damage both during the Revolutionary and the Civil Wars.

It eventually burned down but was rebuilt. After the Bollings sold the place, there was a succession of owners and several changes of name. Now, since Mr. M. T. Broyhill, of Hopewall, purchased the property and subdivided it into small farms, there are many people living at Cobb's.

62

BRICK HOUSE

THE oldest brick house in Chesterfield County, and thought by some to be the oldest in Virginia, is located on the promontory between Swift Creek and Appomattox River, and is simply called Brick House. The peninsula on which it stands is sometimes referred to as "Conjuror's Neck," because an old Indian conjuror used to live there.

Brick House was built in 1685 by Richard Kennon, an English gentleman of wealth, whose family received large land grants in Virginia. Kennon came to Virginia prior to 1670, and became a merchant of Bermuda Hundred; he also represented Henrico County in the House of Burgesses. Richard Kennon, Jr., was also a member of the House of Burgesses. He married the daughter of Col. Robert Bolling, the emigrant, and his second wife, the former Anne Stith. Richard's sister was married to John Bolling, half-brother of Richard's wife—John was the son of Col. Robert Bolling and his first wife Jane Rolfe. They lived at Cobb's.

The Kennons and their descendants intermarried with many of the most distinguished families, the Blands, Randolphs, Tuckers, and others.

The social life of their families absorbed much of their leisure—music, dancing, cards, winters spent in Williamsburg, entertaining many distinguished visitors in their homes.

Brick House was damaged by fire in 1879. It passed from the Kennon family soon after. The Comstock family acquired the property in 1909, restored the old house, and have made it their home for almost half a century.

POINT OF ROCKS

ONE of the most beautiful spots in eastern Virginia is the site of the little home called Point of Rocks. Just at the spot where Swift Creek flows into Appomattox River, rocks eighty-feet in height project from the shore line. Tradition says that this used to be a favorite haunt of Princess Pocahontas. It was certainly a camp site or hunting ground for Indians, for many artifacts such as arrowheads, hatchets, etc., have been found in this vicinity.

Judge E. P. Cox says in his *History of Chesterfield County* (1936): "Point of Rocks was patented in 1642 to one who was destined to be a leader in Colonial affairs, Abraham Wood. Another grant of tract was made in 1736 to an ancestor of the present owner, John Alexander Strachan."

The Strachans inherited the place through their ancestors, the Battes and the Strattons.

The present house was built early in the 1800's, but the original house on the site was still standing after the beginning of the twentieth century. The dependencies have long since disappeared.

The existing house, which has been modernized, is a one-story building with the original wide-board floors and cornice with dentils. The original weatherboarding is well preserved. After the Reverend John Alexander Strachan died, Point of Rocks passed to his grandson, Mr. Thomas Cox, who is the present owner.

During the Civil War a shell fired from a gun-boat on the Appomattox crashed through the wall, and the occupants of the dwelling at the time narrowly escaped being killed. This place was occupied by the Federals under General Butler during the latter part of the war. The house was used as a hospital center. The surgeons occupied it as their headquarters, while a hospital was set up in the grounds, either tents or cabins, or perhaps some of each. During the occupation by the Union soldiers the owners of Point of Rocks, the Strachan family, took refuge at Locust Grove, the home of Mr. Daniel Atkins, Mrs. Strachan's father.

WHITBY

THE ancestral home of the Goode family in Chesterfield County should be of considerable interest, especially to the many Goodes still residing in the county, and those of them who have migrated to other parts of the state and nation.

John Goode, who came to Virginia from England in or about 1650, built Whitby on the James four miles below Richmond, in what is now Chesterfield County. It was an English type of house, with dormer windows, and chimneys at each end.

Horse racing was one of the chief interests and pleasures of the early family of the Goodes in Virginia. The first track in the county was at Whitby. The race horses, too, were a home product. Many racers were bred in Henrico County, especially in that part of it that is now Chesterfield County.

John Goode's plantation consisted of five thousand acres. There is a Goode's Creek. Goode's Bridge across the Appomattox River had been destroyed during the Civil War, and some authorities claim that Lee's army forded the river, on the retreat to Appomattox; some suggest that a pontoon bridge was thrown across, but Maude Atkins Joyner says that Goode's Bridge had been rebuilt in time for Lee's army to cross over on it from Chesterfield into Amelia on the way to Appomattox.

John Goode, who built Whitby, was married twice. He raised several sons and daughters. The Goode genealogy, in the Virginia State Library in Richmond, records more than five thousand descendants of John Goode. There are many distinguished citizens among them. Col. Robert Goode, of Whitby, led the County Militia against Tarleton's marauding troops during the Revolution. Whitby was burned during the Civil War.

CASTLEWOOD

AT Chesterfield Court House, the old estate of Castlewood is conspicuous not only for its beauty, but also for its quaint originality and memorable age. The central unit is two stories above a high basement, and the wings are connected to the center by colonnades that have been enclosed and are used as passages. The wings are of the early American type of architecture. They stand a story and a half high and have large chimneys and dormer windows.

The oldest part of the house, the back part of the central unit, was built around the middle of the 18th century or even earlier. The left wing was built by Charles Poindexter in 1776, and the right wing added somewhat later. The front of the central unit was added much later, to be used "as a ballroom on the occasion of the marriage of a daughter of the owner at that time, a Mr. Anderson." (Maude Atkins Joyner in *Historic Sites and People of Chesterfield County.*) The ballroom is now used as a living room. It has a front porch with high steps. The floor of this room is on a higher level, and steps lead down to the passages and thence to the wings. There are fireplaces in all rooms, and three stairways. The woodwork is very attractive throughout the house, but the mantel in the ballroom is especially fine, being carved in a pattern of oak leaves and pineapples.

The original part of Castlewood was used as the parsonage for the Central Methodist Church, which was nearby. Later the church was removed, and the parsonage became a private residence.

Castlewood saw military action during the American Revolution, when General William Phillips and General Benedict Arnold ("traitor Arnold") of the British Army, after much maneuvering, destroyed the barracks at Chesterfield Court House. They also destroyed a great deal of valuable tobacco stored here. This was near the end of the war.

There were celebrated guests at the courthouse during the Revolution, and if they did not visit Castlewood, at least they saw the attractive old house. Baron Von Steuben was at the courthouse for some time, training militia. And George Rogers Clark brought back a distinguished prisoner captured in Vincennes in 1779. He was Harry Hamilton, Governor General of Canada. He was kept in the prison at Williamsburg for some time, but was removed to Chesterfield Court House, which he said he liked much better.

Castlewood has had many owners. Mrs. Hagood Lumpkin inherited it from the Pilkinton branch of her family. It is now the home of Mr. and Mrs. Hagood Lumpkin, Jr. Mrs. Lumpkin is very interested and gifted in interior decoration. It is possible that Castlewood is more beautiful today than it was even in its heyday.

WREXHAM

A pre-Revolutionary house that has been restored by its present owners, Wrexham, is located at Chesterfield Court House. The owners, Mr. and Mrs. S. R. Hague, Jr., bought the estate in 1941, when it was in a run-down condition. A previous owner had even removed the mahogany staircase.

Of frame construction painted white, a story and a half above the high basement, Wrexham has enormous red brick chimneys, which are covered with ivy. The house is T-shaped and it has dormer windows set in the front and rear parts of the roof of

(above) Wrexham, at Chesterfield Court House, a pre-Revolutionary home.

ON FACING PAGE

(above) Bedroom at Wrexham.

(below) Dining room at Wrexham.

the main building. It also has dormer windows set in both sides of the roof of the "stem" part of the building, which runs back at right angles from the main section. There is a small front porch in Queen Anne style. A long porch extends the full length of the stem section. This was a later addition. Gable windows peep out from each side of the chimneys, and the first floor windows have green blinds and each sash has nine panes.

The interior woodwork is all original, the floor boards, the chair rails, the enclosure of the back stairs, which is the stairway now in use, and the mantels. The latter are exquisitely beautiful, with hand carving in different designs.

Since the Hagues restored, redecorated and refurnished this old mansion, it is undoubtedly even more beautiful than when it was first built.

The Hagues have herds of white-faced Herefords, and Black Angus beef cattle. There are seventy acres in the estate, which has stretches of handsome white board fences surrounding it and cross-dividing its pleasant green pastures, fields of clover, alfalfa and succulent lespedeza, all of which makes a charming rural landscape. The house is set in a spacious lawn dotted with shade trees, and there is a lovely garden— All in all, a beautiful, peaceful old house in an enchanting country setting.

CLOVER HILL

AN interesting home on Winterpock Creek in the southwestern part of Chesterfield County, was that of Judge James H. Cox. The original name of "Winterpock" was changed to Clover Hill when the Judge was admiring the panorama of his six hundred acres of beautiful growing clover.

The original house, an English cottage, was a story and a half in height, with basement and a front and a rear porch. Mrs. Joyner says, "It was picturesque, with dormers, gables and rose-covered porches."

There are three interesting stories told of Clover Hill; two are tales of local superstition, ending in tragedy, and one tells of an historical event.

The Judge was in his sitting room, when a bird flew in from the porch, circling him. The colored servants declared it was a sign of a coming death in the family. Edwin, the son of the house, was brought home ill soon after, and he died within a short time.

Judge Cox's brother lived nearby. One night, in January, 1857, he was caught in one of the worst snow storms in the history of that part of the country. He froze to death, at his brother's gate, buried in a snow drift.

On April 3, 1865, Lee was retreating to Appomattox. The army had been on the march since early morning. Judge Cox heard that the great southern hero and his men were pausing for rest at Summit, one mile away. So he sent a messenger to invite General Lee and his staff and General Longstreet and his staff to dine with him. Judge Cox's granddaughter, Lily Logan Morrell, gives an account of this visit in her memoirs of her mother, Kate Virginia Cox Logan. She tells of the mint juleps passed around in the crowded drawing room, and that the guest of honor accepted only a glass of ice water. She recalls the bountiful dinner, and the coffee which was served (coffee was hard to get and all of the family had been drinking a substitute made of parched wheat). General Lee had, for a long time, been sending his ration of coffee to the hospitals.

After General Lee had shaken hands, mounted his famous charger, Traveler, and ridden away, the Cox family must have been under the spell of that extraordinary occasion for a long time. Years later Kate Cox Logan said: "The night of that day came, and folded us in mystery."

Mrs. Joyner tells us that the dining table, at which General Lee sat that day, is treasured in the family still.

HEDGELAWN
(Bleak Hall)

WHEN Chesterfield County was still a part of Henrico, Bleak Hall was built near what is now Centralia, in 1723.

There is an interesting story told about the material which went into the construction of this house. It is said that some lumber of very special quality was sent over from England with which to build a church. However, the members of the congregation could not agree on a location, so, because the merchant was pressing for his money, the lumber was sold. A Dr. Anderson bought it and built a house with it, a story and a half in height, with dormer windows. Later a more imposing structure was built at the front of the original building, with which it was connected by a colonnade. Eventually the colonnade was incorporated in the main structure.

This Doctor Anderson also built a hospital near a spring here. It was said to have been one of the oldest hospitals in America. During the Civil War Bleak Hall was the Wooldridge home, the ancestral estate of the mother of Judge Edwin P. Cox.

Mrs. Maude Atkins Joyner, in her *Story of Historic Sites and People*, goes on to say that, "Hearing the railroad had been blocked by the Federals, Mr. Wooldridge rode to Richmond and advised the authorities of the fact. For this service, it is said, the Atlantic Coast Line Railroad gave the family passes on their cars for life."

The house still bears bullet marks, in paneling and door frames, made by the Federal army.

The floors are made of heart pine, wide boards, and the woodwork is attractive, the rooms on the third floor being paneled. Wooden pegs were used on the woodwork. H and L hinges are almost intact.

The name of Bleak Hall was changed to Hedgelawn, in honor of Mrs. Thomas Wheelwright, Sr., who planted a beautiful hedge around the large lawn, when a friend of Mr. Wheelwright's, Mr. William Northrup, acquired the place. Later, Hedgelawn was used as a Y. W. C. A., but now it is the home of Mr. and Mrs. Maynard Powell. Mrs. Powell says that she and her husband moved from a modern home in Richmond to Hedgelawn in the coldest month in the year, and their friends told them they would freeze in a country house, but they have never been uncomfortable.

She says there is a current legend to the effect that during the Civil War when the Yankees were coming, the owners of Bleak Hall buried all the valuables; each member of the family buried something in a hiding place known only to him- or herself. The individual who buried the silver tea service subsequently died without revealing where it had been concealed, and so it was never recovered. Mrs. Powell asserts that this lost tea service furnishes her with an incentive for digging in her rather extensive garden. With every stroke of the spade or hoe she hopes to hear the sound of the implement striking against the case in which the precious tea service was kept. Thus far, she laughingly admits, she has unearthed nothing of value. But the garden has benefited considerably by her treasure-hunting labors.

Hedgelawn, Chesterfield County, was known as Bleak Hill when its oldest section, shown in this photograph, was built in 1723.

Front hall at Hedgelawn.

(below) The Old Room at Hedgelawn.

HALF WAY HOUSE

PROBABLY the most outstanding landmark on the Richmond-Petersburg Turnpike is the famous old inn known as the Half Way House. It is half way between the two local cities, and also half way between Albany, New York, and Atlanta, Georgia. On the main highway between the north and the south, this notable old hostelry has entertained many famous and distinguished guests. George Washington, Lafayette, Patrick Henry, Robert E. Lee, Thomas Jefferson, Ulysses S. Grant, Washington Irving, and James Whitcomb Riley are a few of the many who have stopped here.

The Half Way House was built in 1760 by William Hatcher, who patented land in 1743 during the reign of George II. Mr. Hatcher was ancestor of many prominent citizens of this part of the country—one of them Mrs. F. G. Laine.

At first a boarding school was established here. Later the substantial old house became an inn. It was during its career as an inn that it became so well known. During the Civil War it was used for a time as headquarters of the Union army, and around it swirled the battle of Drewry's Bluff.

Built right on the highway, as most inns are, the front entrance opens directly into the interior, and there is no porch or stoop. At the rear, however, there is a handsome two-story porch extending the full length of the house. The old inn stands two stories above a very high basement, and has exceedingly long chimneys, one at each end. At the back are some dependencies, and a beautiful formal garden of flowers and boxwood.

At the time Mr. W. Brydon Tenant acquired the property not many years ago, he restored the house properly, and furnished it throughout with antiques and reproductions. The Chesterfield Court House Garden Club, the Chester Garden Club and others, assisted in restoring the garden.

The present proprietors of Half Way House, Mr. and Mrs. Fred Bender, are operating it as an inn once more, and the public of today is enjoying excellent accommodations and hospitality in the same hostelry in which their ancestors were entertained.

BUCKHEAD SPRINGS

THE land on which the old mansion of Buckhead Springs stands was part of an original grant of three thousand acres. The estate was called Upper Paradise Plantation. The mansion was named Mineola and was situated a mile or a mile and a quarter from the site of Buckhead Springs. Mineola has long since disappeared and been replaced by a large, more modern house.

In 1726 the overseer's cabin, a log home, stood where Buckhead Springs is now situated. An original door from the cabin is incorporated in the later house. The door is low, so tall guests have to be careful. The fourteen-room house now on the site has a Dutch roof, is shingled, and has windows set in. It also has huge chimneys and

(above) Half Way House, in Chesterfield County—so-called because it was halfway between Richmond and Petersburg, Virginia— was a famous inn.

Buckhead Springs, in Chesterfield County.

three fireplaces. There are two English dormer windows, set in a steep-roofed part of the frame building. All interior woodwork, mantels, stairs, floors, and chair rails, are the original ones used when the present house was built, presumably about a hundred and fifty years ago, or soon after the beginning of the nineteenth century.

Mr. and Mrs. Thomas S. Wheelwright purchased Buckhead Springs near the turn of the present century from the Damon family, soon after Mr. Damon's death. Some of the locks and hinges have been replaced by some from the ancestral home of the Wheelwrights in the valley of Virginia.

Mrs. Thomas Wheelwright was a gifted gardener, and a pioneer garden club member in Virginia. On the beautiful eminence upon which the house is built, Mrs. Wheelwright laid out and planted a handsome garden. The boxwood grew prodigiously, and the shrubs took on the proportion of young trees. She had old rosebushes, and all the old-fashioned perennials. She went into the woods and had small holly trees brought out and planted in a row, thus making a lovely holly-hedge, thought by some to be the first holly hedge in Virginia. There are still at Buckhead Springs two magnolia trees and two cypress trees that Mrs. Wheelwright grew from seeds.

Laura Martin Wheelwright's (Mrs. Thomas Wheelwright) name became well known in Virginia for her interest and work with the American Red Cross, and in the Woman's Suffrage Movement. She was also on the Committee of the James River Garden Club, along with Carrie Coleman Duke, Lila L. Williams, Juanita Massie Patterson and Edith Tunis Sale, Chairman, which brought out the large handsome book entitled *Historic Gardens of Virginia*. This volume turned out to be a great success; its first, second, third and fourth printings were quickly exhausted; then it was revised and this edition also soon sold out. Today book collectors consider themselves lucky if they can buy a copy of this book in a shop dealing in rare books, for eighty or a hundred dollars.

During the first World War Mr. Thomas S. Wheelwright served as Chairman of the Eastern Virginia District Executive Committee of the Federal Fuel Administration.

Buckhead Springs is now the home of Mr. and Mrs. Thomas S. Wheelwright, Jr., and their daughter, Miss Laura Wheelwright. Mr. Wheelwright, Jr., headed the Chesterfield County British War Relief Committee in the second World War. Mrs. Thomas S. Wheelwright, Jr., was the former Genevieve Sweeney, whose father was the famous illustrator.

ON FACING PAGE

(above) Living room at Buckhead Springs.

(below) Dining room at Buckhead Springs.

Owing to the increase and pressure of suburban population, Buckhead Springs, like many other large estates, has suffered a decrease in acreage. Ninety acres of the old property were sold by the Wheelwrights a short time ago, but thirty acres still remain, including some of the most beautiful woods in the county.

OTHER HOUSES OF CHESTERFIELD

A dozen books could be written about the homes in Chesterfield County alone, and still there would be more to tell. We recommend to the reader a valuable little book, by Maude Atkins Joyner, called *Story of Historic Sites and People of Chesterfield County.*

Mrs. Joyner, although erudite and meticulously accurate, writes with charming freshness and verve. Her home is in Chester, and we received a great amount of assistance from her and her book, concerning some of the Chesterfield houses of which we have written. In her book she describes and gives histories of many more of them than we could include. She tells interesting reminiscences of childhood days at her aunt's home, Bay View. Other houses of which she wrote are Forkland, Old Tavern, where Lee and his staff watered their horses on their way to Appomattox, Salisbury, where Patrick Henry once lived, Hebron Church, where Lee wrote his last orders, Magnolia Grange, Strawberry Hill, Locust Grove, where Mrs. Joyner's father, Daniel D. Atkins, was born, Salem Academy, Salem Church, Violet Bank, where Lafayette fired on the British in Petersburg during the Revolution, and where Lee had headquarters in 1864, Enon Church, Burgess, the Clay home, Mont Blanco, Rochdale, Howlett House, Campfield, Sheffields, Gravel Pit Farm, Bellona Arsenal, Hallsborough Tavern, Blackheath, Aspen Shade, Willow Hill (the Miller home), Lone Oak, Gravel Hill, Physic Hill, Poplar Grove, Olive Hill, Belle Vue, and Wood's Church. Another interesting old home of the county is Bellwood, which is now the Officers' Club at Richmond Quartermaster Depot.

Mrs. Joyner has a rare talent; she can evoke for her readers the poetic charm of bygone days in an entertaining fashion.

PART THREE

CHARLES CITY AND PRINCE GEORGE COUNTIES

IN the early days of the colony the land now comprising Charles City County and Prince George County had many different names, of local origin, such as: Martin's Brandon, Shirley Hundred, Bermuda City, and so on. Although these names have lingered, formally and officially—by act of the General Assembly—all this area became Charles City Shire in 1634; then in 1652 it became Charles City County. In 1702 Prince George was organized as a county.

Because there is no city at all in Charles City County, and because it is by and large a county of plantations, whatever history it is necessary to tell about it in this book is told piecemeal, in stories of the plantation houses. All American wars affected both Charles City County and Prince George County.

Charles City County is the only county in the United States that has the distinction of having sent a President and a Vice-President to Washington who held office simultaneously. Also it has the unique distinction of having one of its citizens succeed a President, also one of its citizens, who died while in office. These two famous sons of Charles City County were William Henry Harrison, 9th President of the United States, and John Tyler, Vice-President until Harrison died, whereupon he became the 10th President.

The Charles City Court House is on Route 5, the Old Indian Trail. During the Civil War the court building was ransacked and the records were scattered; some were destroyed, some thrown into the fields, and some taken to the North. Some of those taken away have years later been returned.

Prince George County, all that part of old Charles City County south of the James, organized in 1702, has one city, laid out and named Bermuda City in 1613; it finally actually became a city in 1915—though instead of Bermuda City it was called Hopewell, for the good ship that brought over the planter, Col. Francis Eppes, who was granted the land on which the city was built. In fact, he, himself, had named part of the land Hopewell Farm almost three hundred years previously.

Prince George Court House has had four sites. First, while still a part of Charles City, the courthouse for the county was built at Merchant's Hope on Chappell's Creek near Merchant's Hope Church. The second site was at the Frog Hole Place near the present site of Hopewell. This was used until the seat was moved to Blandford. The courthouse is now at Prince George, a little to the west-northwest of the center of the county.

Prince George is almost a triangle, and is approximately twenty-eight miles long on the longest side, and about twenty-two wide at the widest point.

In connection with the history of Prince George County, an interesting event is to be recorded that took place at, or near, Cummins' Store during the Civil War. Just north of the cross-roads at the old site of Sycamore Church, General Wade Hampton attacked some Union cavalrymen, who were guarding a drove of grazing beef cattle. This was on September 16, 1864. By making a wide sweep around the Federal army, he was able to launch a surprise attack from the south, whip off the cavalrymen, and round up the herd. Of these fat beeves there were 2486, and General Hampton did not lose one. He drove all of them through Black Water Swamp, and on into the Confederate lines, providing a boon to the hungry soldiers, to whom fresh beef was somewhat of a rarity. It was quite a blow to the Federals, and they were also led to believe on the evidence of this coup, that the Confederates were preparing for a general offensive. Some time later, when a Union trooper ventured to shout ridicule at a Confederate soldier who had a dirty face, the latter replied (referring to the capture of the Union cattle): "I'm greasy from eating you-all's beef meat, Yank."

Prince George County is crowded with the remains of forts, defenses, battlefields, fortifications, camp sites, cemeteries and monuments of former wars, not to mention its battle-scarred river houses and farmsteads. All the wars have affected this area, and most all of them, especially the Civil War, left scars, many scars.

The first time the white man saw the land of this county was "the eight of May," 1607. That day the first colonists trying to decide where they would settle first "landed in the countrey of Apamatica." They stayed four days, then re-embarked and sailed back down the river, and, on May 13, 1607, landed at Jamestown where they made the first permanent English settlement in America.

The members of the King's Council from Charles City and Prince George Counties were:

> William Tracy—Berkeley Hundred   1620
> George Thorp—Berkeley Hundred   1620
> Mr. Ouldsworth (died same year) 1621
> William Perry—Charles City County   1632
> George Menifie (also James City)   1635
> Francis Eppes   1637

78

The picturesque Court House at Charles City, built in 1730. Charles City County was incorporated in 1634, which makes it the oldest political unit in America.

Thomas Pawlett—Westover   1641
Edward Hill I—Shirley   1651
Abraham Wood   1657
Warham Horsmanden   1657
Theodorick Bland—Westover   1665
Edward Hill II—Shirley   1688
William Byrd II   1708
John Carter—Shirley   1724
William Byrd III   1754

Delegates from Charles City and Prince George Counties to the Conventions were:

Convention Assembled March 20, 1775

CHARLES CITY	PRINCE GEORGE
Benjamin Harrison	Richard Bland
William Acrill	Peter Poythress

Convention Assembled July 17, 1775

CHARLES CITY	PRINCE GEORGE
William Acrill	Richard Bland
Benjamin Harrison, Jr.	Peter Poythress
(until August 9 as alternate for father)	
Benjamin Harrison	
(after August 9)	

Convention Assembled December 1, 1775

CHARLES CITY	PRINCE GEORGE
William Acrill	Richard Bland
Benjamin Harrison	Peter Poythress

Convention Assembled May 6, 1776

CHARLES CITY	PRINCE GEORGE
William Acrill	Richard Bland
Samuel Harwood	Peter Poythress
(alternate for Benjamin Harrison)	

DOGHAM

THE name, Dogham, said to be a corruption or variation of D'Aughams, a stream in Normandy, belongs to a home in a very lovely part of Charles City County. There is a stream here, too, shady, rippling, and cool. The house is just off the Old Indian Trail (Route 5 between Richmond and Williamsburg) without doubt one of the oldest roads in this country.

In 1635 eleven hundred acres of land was granted to Joseph Royal by the King of England. On this land a number of persons were to be settled who were being brought to the colony by Royal. By 1635 a better class of settlers was coming in. At first most of the immigrants were either gentlemen—who did not know how to do the things necessary for survival in a raw country—or they were adventurers, or outlaws, who

(above) Dogham, in Charles City County, is a lovely house, the oldest part of which dates from 1635.

Hanging on the wall in Dogham is this facsimile of a will executed by Henry Isham, Jr., nearly three centuries ago, bequeathing Dogham to his two sisters.

(above) The garden at Dogham.

ON FACING PAGE

(above) Bedroom at Dogham.

(below) Living room at Dogham.

could not have been expected to contribute very much to the well-being of the colony. Dale, in 1611, brought over artisans, mechanics, carpenters and farmers. On the other hand, the settlers who came with Royal were from well-known families.

The land lies between Turkey Island and Shirley, "on Turkey Island Creek and the James River, above Shirley Hundred."

Dogham is a charming old house, very quaint, and with quite an English atmosphere. It is built in two almost identical sections which stand at right angles to each other, as though identical twins had turned halfway about to face each other. Both sections are covered with white clapboard; the house itself is a story and a half high with chimneys at each end, three dormer windows on each side of the roof, and outside window blinds. The two sections are connected by one of the small, one-story wings, which flanked the original part of the house. The other wing has been converted into an end porch which is enclosed or screened. Each section has a center hall, with a room on each side, upstairs and down. The earlier part of the house was built in 1652.

Some boxwood, several nice old trees, a grassy lawn, a flower garden and a picket fence add to the homey air of the attractive old place.

When Joseph Royal died his widow married Henry Isham. Henry Isham, Jr., in his will of November 13, 1678, said—"I give and bequeath my plantation in Charles City in Virginia . . . commonly knowne by ye name of Doggams, with all the land thereto belonging, all the houses fences woods underwoods etc. to be equally divided betweene my two Sisters Mrs. Mary Randolph & Mrs. Anne Isham aforesaid to them & their heirs forever." A framed photostatic copy of this will hangs in the old hall at Dogham.

The property passed by inheritance for two and a half centuries. In 1928 Mr. James Pinckney Harrison purchased it from Miss Alice Royal, a direct descendant of Joseph Royal. Mr. and Mrs. Harrison still make this their home for most of the year.

RIVERVIEW

NOT far from Dogham, and built on a part of the original tract of eleven hundred acres granted by the crown to Joseph Royal, stands the magnificent old mansion called Riverview.

The house, whose one side faces the river, is well-named, for the lawn that stretches out from the portico slopes very gently right down to the water's edge, a broad expanse of which is visible from here both up and down the river.

Riverview was completed before the Civil War. It is in the Greek Revival style, has a hip roof, with a wide, shallow gable and a fanlight set in the roof on the river-front side of the house, and tall, inside chimneys. The basement is brick painted white, and the two stories above it are of frame construction. The house stands three stories high, and has a handsome, two-story portico, with Ionic columns, facing the

Riverview, in Charles City County, is a beautiful example of pre-Civil War, Greek Revival architecture.

river; this portico is balanced by a somewhat less impressive one on the side facing the main road.

The front portico floor is actually a stone terrace at ground level; and the house is entered, at this front, with no steps—either up or down. Then, on the other side, at the road front, one enters by going down a few steps—three, to be exact. In other words, the ground floor might be termed an English basement. This floor has a center hall opening from which are: a beautifully paneled living room; a dining room; and a handsome guest bedroom. There is a large, handsome, old-fashioned kitchen that has been modernized.

The stairway in the hall is very wide, and the steps are quite shallow. This leads to the second or main floor. The hall on this floor is large and lovely, with a handsome

(above) The boxwood garden at Riverview.

ON FACING PAGE

(above) The salon at Riverview.

(below) The paneled library at Riverview.

drawing room about eighteen or twenty feet by forty. This room is beautifully furnished with French antiques and reproductions. Across the hall is the master suite, sitting room, bedroom and bath. On the third floor are four exquisite bedrooms, in each of which a different color scheme is carried out.

There are huge old trees shading the lawn; there is also a notable boxwood, one section of which is said to be the largest box plant in Virginia. It is about thirty feet tall and of enormous girth. But the glory of Riverview is its garden. It lies at some little distance across the shady lawn to the east of the house, and is quite large. An ivy-covered serpentine brick wall surrounds it and inside the space so enclosed is a gorgeous and brilliant mélange of color. It seems that there is a sample of every flowering plant in existence in this garden, and there are masses of blooms in all seasons; but in the spring, when the dwarf boxwood seems so richly green, when the pink and white dogwood are in bloom, and thousands of tulips of every hue flaunt their flaming colors, it is then that the garden at Riverview seems at its best.

George Y. Webster owned the plantation for many years, but in 1936 he sold the property to Mr. and Mrs. Arthur J. Sackett, of New York. They still make it their home.

SHIRLEY

SIR THOMAS WEST (Lord De La Warr) was first Royal Governor of the Colony of Virginia. His wife, Cecilly, was the daughter of Sir Thomas Sherley. In 1613, when Lord Delaware, with his three brothers, Francis, Nathaniel and John, owned land along the James, and Sir Thomas Dale was establishing the city of Bermuda Hundred, and naming "Hundreds" in all directions, one grant was called Westopher (for the West family), and another was called Sherley for Cecilly's family. The land was occupied that year (1613). This was the beginning of Shirley, owned by the first Royal Governor—and named for his wife. Two other West brothers also became Royal Governors of Virginia.

The first mansion at Shirley was built by Col. Edward Hill I. He had led the English and friendly Indians under Totopotomi against the cruel Susquehannas in the battle of Bloody Run. Totopotomi was killed, and Hill was defeated. This was in 1656. In 1660 or earlier, Hill acquired possession of twenty-five hundred acres of land at Shirley Hundred. He served in the King's Council, and was Speaker of the House of Burgesses. This house, known as "The Old House," was torn down in the 19th century and rebuilt at Upper Shirley (see below).

At the death of Edward Hill, Shirley descended to his son, Edward Hill II (1637-1700). He was Speaker of the House of Burgesses, Treasurer of Virginia, and Judge of His Majesty's High Court of Admiralty. He was also Commander-in-Chief of Charles City County. Edward Hill III inherited Shirley next. His wife was Miss Williams, daughter of Sir Thomas Williams, of Wales. Her portrait, showing her to have been a beautiful young girl, hangs at Shirley now. A portrait of Edward Hill III in velvet and lace and a flowing peruke, also is there, as well as one of their daughter Elizabeth, very like her mother: she is portrayed with her arms full of flowers. There

(above) Shirley, one of the most notable great mansions on the James, has been owned by "King" Carter's descendants down to the present day.

(below) Ancient dependencies at Shirley.

is also a portrait of Edward Hill IV, the young brother of Elizabeth. He, too, appears clad in velvet and lace. He died young (aged about sixteen) and his sister, Elizabeth Hill, and her husband, the Honorable John Carter II, of Corotoman, were the next owners of Shirley. After John Carter died in 1742 or thereabouts, Elizabeth married Bowler Cocke, who lived at Shirley until their deaths (1769 and 1771).

Elizabeth Hill Carter Cocke's son, Charles Carter, who lived at Corotoman until his mother's death, inherited Shirley, and immediately began an extensive building program. Mr. Waterman thinks it was at this time that the present mansion was built, but in a letter from a Mr. Richard Adams to his brother, Thomas, dated 30th September, 1771, the former says, "Our friend C. Carter will remove to Shirley as soon as he can get the House repaired, which he expects will be done in about 12 or 13 months." This would seem conclusive proof that the present mansion was "repaired" or remodeled (mainly the roof and porticos) rather extensively at this time, and had actually been built at the time the four buildings of the fore-court were erected, previous to the death of John Carter II in 1742.

Charles Carter was twice married, first to Mary Carter, daughter of Charles Carter, of Cleve, second to Anne Butler Moore, daughter of Bernard Moore and Katherine, daughter of Governor Alexander Spotswood who is remembered as having led the Knights of the Golden Horseshoe across the Blue Ridge.

Charles Carter was the father of twenty-three children who intermarried with many of the most prominent families: the Randolphs, Lees, Burwells, Braxtons, Nelsons, Fitzhughs, Berkeleys and others of the early regime in Virginia. He has many distinguished descendants who proudly claim Shirley as a family roof tree.

Ann, a daughter of Charles Carter, became the wife of "Light Horse" Harry Lee, and the mother of Robert E. Lee. (As a child, General Lee loved Shirley and visited there frequently.) Another daughter, Elizabeth, was the grandmother of Bishop Alfred M. Randolph.

Hill Carter inherited Shirley in 1816.

Captain Robert Randolph Carter, of the United States Navy and later of the Confederate Navy, inherited Shirley and married Miss Louise Humphreys, of Annapolis, Maryland. She was familiarly known as "Miss Lou," a friendly, charming hostess.

Her daughters, Mrs. Bransford and Mrs. Oliver, inherited Shirley in 1906. Mrs. Bransford died many years ago, but Mrs. Oliver, the former Miss Marion Carter, and widow of Admiral James Harrison Oliver, reigned as a charming, hospitable hostess at Shirley for almost a half-century. After her death in 1950, C. Hill Carter, Jr., ninth-generation descendant of Edward Hill I and sixth-generation descendant of the Honorable John Carter II, became the owner of Shirley. Mr. Carter is a successful farmer who uses the most up-to-date equipment on his acreage. He and his family, mother, father, and sister, live at Shirley.

It is hard to describe the spell cast by Shirley upon the visitor. There is the vast plantation, the huge square mansion, with its fore-court of four exquisitely built brick dependencies; and the ever-present river, softly lapping the edge of the huge, gently sloping grassy lawn shaded by great trees that have weathered the centuries. Last but not least to be remembered, is the ancient garden, where the boxwood grow as tall as a house, the ancient walks, the old-fashioned perennials above which flutter many-hued butterflies, and the warm sunshine. Together with the fine old mansion, all this evokes the spirit of a splendid era that flourished three centuries ago.

The house, which is of brick, was built with a lavish disregard for cost seldom displayed in the building of even great mansions. It stands three stories high above the basement, and has dormer windows in the hip roof on all four sides, five on each of the two fronts, and four on each of the other two sides. The two heavy inside chimneys rise above the roof, and between them is the traditional, carved pineapple, denoting hospitality.

Two identical, handsome two-story porticos, with four pillars to each story, embellish the mansion; they make delightful, restful, outdoor sitting rooms. On the river front and on the garden front as well, massive steps seem to grow up out of the ground; they are of a piece with the mansion.

On entering the house from the drive (the garden side) one comes into a large square hall which has the famous Shirley walnut staircase, called the "flying" stair, because it has no support, but is so constructed that it supports itself. This extends to the third floor. There are a fireplace in the hall and doors opening into the parlor, the salon or drawing room, and the dining room. The door into the parlor has a double transom. The little leaded glass panes are of different shapes, in the two sides. The big square locks on the doors have little handles or pulls, instead of knobs, and the hinges are the old H and L kind. The windows have twelve panes to the sash. The paneling and mantels as well as the stairs and door and window facings are of exquisite workmanship, showing most elaborate handcarvings in designs such as the Tudor rose, the pineapple, the egg and dart, the Wall of Troy, and others as pretty. There are three St. Memin pictures and many handsome, practically priceless portraits in the parlor, the hall, the salon, and the dining room. The door heads, frets and pediments with broken arch, and pineapple insets, have been admired by many visitors to this handsome old mansion.

Shirley contains notable antiques and family silver; things that have descended from mother to daughter, from father to son. It was in the salon that Robert E. Lee's father and mother were married. They had met in the dining room at Shirley when Anne, a beautiful slip of a girl, was desperately trying to hold on to the slipping punch bowl and was rescued from her dilemma by the quick intervention of the gallant young officer, "Light Horse" Harry Lee.

The famous life-size, full length portrait of Washington, by Peale, for many years hung in the dining room at Shirley. It now hangs in the Capitol at Williamsburg.

Ninth generation of a family in one home—and that place first owned by the first Royal Governor of Virginia, and named for his lady—

That is Shirley.

UPPER SHIRLEY

ALL the background and tradition that belong to Shirley, belong also in a way to Upper Shirley, for the land is part of the original tract included in the grant of Lord De La Warr, first Royal Governor of Virginia, in 1613, and later possessed by Col. Edward Hill, King's Councilor and Indian fighter.

As was customary among wealthy Virginia gentlemen, Hill Carter, who inherited Shirley in 1816, provided plantation land for each of his five sons. The Forest went to one; Shirley Mills and High Hills to others. Upper Shirley was given to Fitzhugh Carter, who had married Ann Lightfoot.

The original brick house at Shirley Plantation, built c. 1650-1660, and called "The Old House" after the present mansion was built, was torn down and rebuilt on the new site as Upper Shirley. The seventeenth-century bricks, which had been made of native clay, were covered with plaster in the style of the day, similar to the Governor's Mansion and the Wickham House (now the Valentine Museum), both in Richmond. The house faced south down an avenue of trees leading towards Shirley, and consisted of three stories, each of two rooms, separated by a wide hall.

Extensive additions were made to Upper Shirley about 1870, when Mr. N. E. A. Saunders bought it from the Carter family and gave it to his son, Herbert Saunders, upon his marriage to a popular local girl, Rosalie Bell. Its size was doubled at that time, rooms being added on each floor to make the house square. Its chief feature became the wide cross halls, running east and west, as well as north and south.

The place was noted for its hospitality. The Saunders were beloved hosts. Upper Shirley was also noted for Mrs. Saunders's roses, which included a wide variety of the old-fashioned ramblers popular in Virginia at the time.

Many of the roses are gone now, but every year the "hosts of golden daffodils" from more than 100,000 bulbs planted at Upper Shirley, spread a gleaming carpet of blooms from around the old ice-house down to the river bank as early as February. Besides the pleasure the sight of them affords visitors, they also bring joy to many Richmond homes, for they are sold annually to provide funds for charitable purposes.

Among the surviving dependencies at Upper Shirley, besides the old ice-house, are the original smoke-house, with its interesting meat-hooks, and the out-door kitchen. The latter was used as such until the 1930's. The present kitchen is in the English basement, and the old smoke-house is now a tool house.

Mr. and Mrs. Benjamin P. Alsop, Jr., the present owners, have cleared a new view of the James River, and are planning a garden, which will be centered around the enormous and ancient scuppernong vine, which has been there no one knows how long.

Each year Upper Shirley is the scene of a luncheon, honoring the distinguished visiting authors who come to Richmond for the Junior League Annual Book and Author Dinner. Under its present ownership, this lovely old home is continuing its tradition of hospitality.

Upper Shirley, also originally a Carter home, has a wonderful display of
100,000 daffodils early every spring.

BERKELEY

IN 1618 the London Company gave a large grant of land on the James River to Sir William Throckmorton, Sir George Yeardley, and Richard Berkeley and John Smith of Nibley. The next year the "good ship Margaret" of Bristol sailed for Virginia bearing thirty-five settlers for the new "Town and Hundred of Berkeley" (which was named for Richard Berkeley). These people were under the care of Captain John Woodlief.

The Reverend John Paulett (or Pawlett) a relative of Lord Paulett, was minister of Berkeley Hundred in 1621, and probably lived at the main settlement of the Berkeley Plantation—or possibly stayed there a part of the time.

George Thorpe, a person of considerable importance of the time, a member of the King's Privy Council, had been appointed by the London Company to manage the University of Henrico. He was at Berkeley and although he had lovingly and with brotherly concern worked with the savages, teaching them the precepts of the Christian religion, he was one of the nine people at Berkeley who were brutally slain on Good Friday, 1622, the day the first of the two terrible massacres in Virginia took place.

After this tragedy the beautiful land of Berkeley Hundred, comprising about eight thousand acres, lay abandoned for several years. William Tucker and others got possession of Berkeley from the "Adventurers of the Company of Berkeley Hundred" about 1636.

Soon after this the plantation became the property of John Bland, a merchant of London, whose son, Giles Bland, made his home at Berkeley. He was prominent in Colony life, but was hanged by Governor Sir William Berkeley in 1676, after he (Bland) had participated in the Rebellion under Bacon.

Benjamin Harrison III, the next owner of Berkeley, was three years old when Giles Bland died. Evidently the Bland estate was slow in being settled, or perhaps the confusion of Berkeley's controversy with the Commission, and later the Crown, caused delay. On the other hand, Benjamin III was the son of the Honorable Benjamin II, of Wakefield, and brother of the Honorable Nathaniel Harrison I, of Wakefield, so it may be the father purchased the Berkeley property for him (Benjamin III), while he was still young.

Benjamin Harrison III lived at Berkeley, was Attorney General, and Speaker of the House of Burgesses, and Treasurer of the Colony. He died at the age of thirty-seven, and his massive tomb may be seen today at the site of Old Westover Church, on the river near the house at Westover. The inscription on the tomb is in Latin and Greek. His wife, the former Elizabeth Burwell, rests beside him. Her tomb bears her family coat of arms. She was the daughter of the Honorable Lewis Burwell II.

After the death of Benjamin Harrison III his son, the fourth Benjamin Harrison, inherited Berkeley. He was the builder of the present house. He also served for years in the House of Burgesses. His wife was Anne, the daughter of Robert Carter ("King"

Berkeley, on the James River, the ancestral home of the Harrisons and one of the finest houses in America.

(below) The main house at Berkeley, birthplace of William Henry Harrison, 9th President of the United States.

Carter,) and their son, Benjamin Harrison V (1726-1791,) inherited Berkeley at the death of his father in 1744.

Benjamin Harrison V held many high offices and was a signer of the Declaration of Independence. He married Elizabeth Bassett, daughter of Colonel William Bassett, of Eltham, New Kent County. Their eldest son, Benjamin VI, inherited Berkeley, but a younger, the third son, William Henry Harrison, became the ninth President of the United States, and William Henry Harrison's grandson, Benjamin Harrison, of Ohio, became twenty-third President of the United States.

William Henry Harrison made his home in Ohio, but he came back to write his inaugural address in his mother's room at Berkeley. President Benjamin Harrison came to visit Berkeley, the home of his ancestors, during his residence in the White House. All the Presidents from Washington through Buchanan have been entertained at Berkeley.

After Benjamin Harrison VI followed Benjamin Harrison VII as owner of Berkeley. The house was sold by the Harrisons shortly before the Civil War. Berkeley was a camping ground for Benedict Arnold's forces during the Revolution.

During the Civil War, Berkeley was used as headquarters by Union General McClellan and his staff. This was in 1862, and his army was camped for miles along the north side of the James. McClellan kept Confederate prisoners in the cellar at Berkeley and embarked his own forces from Berkeley Wharf, shown on maps as Harrison's Landing.

In 1882 Judge Henry F. Knox, of New York, bought Berkeley. At that time there were fourteen hundred acres in the plantation.

The owner of this plantation also owns "river rights" beyond those of other plantation owners along the James. Fishing was at one time engaged in commercially along the three mile river shore. Mr. Robert Lancaster in *Virginia Homes and Churches* says that as many as 22,931 shad and 200,000 herring have been caught there in one season.

A few years after the turn of the twentieth century Mr. John Jamieson purchased Berkeley, and he left it to his wife and children. Now, completely restored and more beautiful than ever, Berkeley is the home of Mr. and Mrs. Malcolm Jamieson.

A perfect type of Georgian architecture, Berkeley, built of red brick, stands two and a half stories above a high basement. The gently sloping roof has three dormer windows set in each side, facing the road front and the river front. There are also small windows, set high in the gables, above the heavily decorated cornice, which extends all around the building at the level of second story ceilings. Two tall, very thick chimneys rise high above the roof. The windows have twenty-four panes to the window, and there are outside window blinds, painted green.

ON FACING PAGE

(above) The kitchen at Berkeley.

(below) The dining room at Berkeley.

(above) Central hall at Berkeley.

ON FACING PAGE

(above) One of the drawing rooms at Berkeley.

(below) Another drawing room at Berkeley.

The doors at both fronts have pediment hoods. The approach is by stone steps, with iron hand railings. At each end, a little way from the house but in line with it, are two smaller, perfectly proportioned brick buildings, in Georgian style. The one on the east is the office or school building, and the other, on the west, is the kitchen and laundry. Both are two stories high and have chimneys at each end.

The main, or central building, is 41 x 60 feet, and the wings or dependencies 21 x 48 feet. On the west end of the main building, cisterns are at each corner, and lead down below to an underground room which is circular, sixteen feet in diameter. This was arranged for a hiding place from the Indians.

The hall at Berkeley extends from door to door. In the center is a wide arch (elliptical) which enhances the vista, especially when looking out through and beyond the far door. This arch has fluted pilasters. The chair rails are eleven inches wide, and are given a fluted effect by hand-tooled treatment. The door heads and casings are elaborately patterned; some have dentilled frets and applied decorations. The paneling in the dado is given accent with applied moldings. All the woodwork is painted white. In the drawing room and library, also in the dining room, the decorations of the woodwork are even more elaborate. On each side of the chimney in the drawing room is a beautiful arched alcove in the back of which is a door leading into the library. The arches are elaborate with fluted pilasters and beaded keystones. The staircase is interesting. The Musicians' Balcony on the second landing is supposed to be the only one in Virginia.

All about the grounds at Berkeley are lovely shade trees, some very old, but some new ones put in during the restoration.

WESTOVER

FRANCIS WEST, who first selected the site for the Westover estate, was granted a large number of acres here at the same time that his brother, Lord Delaware, acquired Shirley (1613.) Called West Hundred and Westopher in honor of the West name, it remained for Thomas Pawlett (or Paulett), brother of Lord Paulett, to bestow the name Westover.

After the massacre of 1622, when six persons were killed at West Hundred, the place was more or less abandoned, as were many of the other settlements. It was in 1637 that the patent for the vast acreage at West Hundred gave possession of the property to Thomas Paulett, and at that time it was given the name Westover. After Paulett's death, his brother, Lord Paulett, sold the estate to Theodorick Bland (1666.) As purchase price Bland paid three hundred pounds sterling, and ten thousand pounds of tobacco, for twelve hundred acres of land and all the buildings thereon. Theodorick Bland was an ancestor of John Randolph, of Roanoke. He (Bland) is buried at the Old Westover Church at Westover. Bland was a member of the King's Council, and it was he, at this time, who established a county seat for Charles City. He gave ten acres of land, a church, a court house and a prison. Theodorick Bland, though born an English subject, had, before coming to Westover, been a Spanish merchant.

Westover, on the James, rivals Berkeley in splendor. It was once the home of the famous Byrd family.

William Byrd I (1653-1704) came to Virginia about 1674 and, with his wife, Maria Horsemanden (called Mary) settled at "The Falls" by 1685. He called his stone house there Belvedere. In 1688 he purchased the plantation of Westover from Theodorick Bland.

When William Byrd II (1674-1744) inherited Westover and 26,231 acres of land which his father had acquired at Westover, the Falls, and at many places in between, William, a brilliant, highly educated, polished young man, contemplated selling the whole property—to avoid responsibility for certain debts. Instead of selling, however, he built the magnificent mansion of Westover. (1726-1730.) He married Lucy, daughter of Colonel Daniel Parke (1669-1710.) After her death he married Maria Taylor, a widow of Kensington.

By his first wife William Byrd II had Evelyn, the noted beauty, and Wilhelmina. His second wife's children were Anne, Maria, William and Jane. The girls were all beautiful. Evelyn, the eldest and most beautiful, died of a broken heart, aged twenty-seven, because her father had thwarted her marriage to Charles Mordaunt, the son of the Earl of Peterborough, after he had romantically wooed and won her in England when she was but eighteen. The charming young Virginia belle, on that same visit, had been presented at Court. It was on this occasion that the King made the much quoted remark about his colony producing such "beautiful Byrds."

Evelyn's tomb is near the river at Westover, where the old church stood. It is bound in iron bands to prevent disintegration. Her spirit is said to haunt the mansion at night, and the garden when the sun shines softly in Indian summer, and quiet reigns under the trees. A portrait of unhappy Evelyn Byrd hangs at Brandon. She is in court dress, with curls and wears a rose. The portrait was made when she was eighteen.

Wilhelmina was married to Thomas Chamberlayne; Anne was married to Charles Carter, of Cleve; Maria was married to Landon Carter, of Sabine Hall, and Jane was married to John Page, of North End.

William Byrd III first married Elizabeth Hill Carter, daughter of John Carter, of Shirley, and after her death married Mary, daughter of Charles and Anne Shippen Willing, of Philadelphia.

William Byrd II had a wonderful disposition; in fact, he was blessed with many gifts. Like his father, he held many important offices. He was popular, a good conversationalist, and an inveterate reader. His library was supposed to be the best in America. He wrote in his diary and "did my dance," daily. He was moderate with regard to his own food (often eating only bread and milk) but lavish in this respect with guests, family, and servants. His diaries are interesting, since they disclose many amusing and intimate details of his own and his family's life.

William Byrd II laid out the cities of Petersburg and Richmond in 1734, and gave land for St. John's Church in Richmond.

He had a very real appreciation of the arts. This is evidenced by the beautiful buildings he caused to be erected, and the many beautiful furnishings and other art objects he either had made on his own order or bought, for his home, and the many fine portraits that he hung on the walls of Westover. He also had a fine taste in music.

Kitchen wing of Westover.

*(below) A view of the river from
Westover.*

When the "Black Swan" (as he was known) and his family visited England, they, with their beautiful clothes, their polished manners and interest in cultural matters, were the wonder of court circles.

There was a music room at Westover, and a large room for his priceless library. He was gay. He loved cards, and gambled a good deal. He rode and hunted and danced with a zest usually found only in much younger men.

His tomb, which bears an epitaph he, himself, composed, is in the garden at Westover.

William Byrd III (1729-1777) followed in the footsteps of his father and grandfather in service to the public. He was a member of the Council and served as a colonel in the French and Indian War. His "spirit and liberality in the service" were highly commended by the English Commander-in-Chief in America. Colonel Byrd III was, like his father, fond of cards, and became so addicted to gambling that he left his estate in bad shape when he died during the early part of the Revolution.

During that war the regular correspondence between Mrs. Byrd's family and Benedict Arnold, added to the latter's visits to Westover, aroused suspicion that Mrs. Byrd, formerly of Philadelphia, was sympathetic, and perhaps helpful to the British cause. Nothing was proven, however, except that many of her friends were Tories.

During the Revolution Marquis de Chastelleux and many of the young French officers frequently visited Westover, for Mrs. Byrd, the widow of William Byrd III, had been left with several beautiful daughters, and these charming ladies were, no doubt, very attractive to the handsome young officers so far from home and country. The Marquis said in his memoirs that Westover was the most beautiful place in America, which it is still considered to be by many Virginians.

On a large, level bluff, perhaps fifty yards back from the river, with green lawn and fine old tulip poplars and other shade trees, Westover faces both the river and the garden. The land or road entrance is through large double iron grillwork gates, which are swung from ten-foot brick piers surmounted by brass falcons perched on balls; the grillwork arch over the gates is very fine. The initials of the "Black Swan" are interwoven in its fine design. The posts of the fence around the grounds have finials in the form of pineapples, urns and balls.

The Westover house is one of the finest examples of Georgian architecture of colonial times in America. The foundation is of whitestone and the walls of soft red brick. The center of the mansion is three stories high above the basement, with off-center hall running from front to front. This divides the rooms into unequal sizes. The reception room and music room on the east side are considerably larger than the dining room and chamber in corresponding positions to the west. Four huge chimneys rise high above the roof of the main section of the building, and there are four more chimneys, one at each end of each wing. The story-and-a-half wings are connected with the center building by large story-and-a-half passages, to each of which there is access from the outside, back and front, and from the two nearest rooms in the main building. Thus, the passage to the east is entered from the large reception room or the

104

music room, and gives access to the library in this wing. This passage is used as a living room.

At the front, gray stone pyramid steps approach the magnificent marble doorway. The door-head is massive, decorated and pedimented, with broken arch and pineapple in the center.

The window frames are painted white and a white band course extends around the center building at second floor level. This white trim with the soft red of the bricks, the sombre color of the roof, green ivy growing on the walls, and flecking shadows from the old trees all combine to make a picture not often equaled.

The interior of Westover is as elaborate as it is beautiful. Rocaille ceilings, paneled walls, and the fine stairway with steps five feet wide and spirally turned balusters, with mahogany balustrade and wall stringer, are only a few of the charming features of the great hall and the first floor rooms. The step ends of the stairway are decorated with modillion-like scrolls.

The mantels of dining room, music room and reception room (or drawing room) are all beautiful and unusual. In the dining room the chimney breast has no shelf. In the music room a dentilled entablature, accented with fluted pilasters, makes the chimney end the keynote of this room.

The mantel in the reception room is of beautiful black marble profusely decorated with elaborately carved white marble. The pediment has a white marble cornice, and the architrave is treated with the white marble carved in egg and dart design. The set-in oblong mirror is surrounded by white carved marble in the pattern of grapes and leaves. This mantel is flanked by fluted white pilasters. The paneling in the central house and the east wing is all painted white.

During the Revolution the British came to Westover—twice under Benedict Arnold, and once under Cornwallis. Later, in the terrible days of the Civil War, McClellan's forces camped here, and the house was used as headquarters for General Pope. The east wing was burned, and a lookout was built on the roof, but the restoration of the east wing has been effected to perfection, and war scars have been erased.

After the death of Mrs. William Byrd III her children inherited Westover. In 1814 William Carter bought the plantation. Later Col. John Selden was its owner for thirty years. Then Major Augustus Drewry, the hero of the battle of Drewry's Bluff during the Civil War, acquired the property. While he was owner he made many repairs. Mrs. Sears Ramsey, the next owner, rebuilt the east wing, and connected both wings with the center building. She also did many other things to restore Westover to its former beauty.

Under the ownership of Mr. and Mrs. Richard Crane, a revival of entertaining and hospitality brought back memories of the old plantation as it had been in the days of its grandeur in the time of the "Black Swan." The Cranes' daughter, Mrs. Bruce Crane Fisher, is now owner and hostess at the beautiful old place.

The garden at Westover has displays of all kinds of old-fashioned flowers, and much handsome boxwood. There is a yew tree, planted by George Washington on the lawn, and besides the tulip poplars there are elms and sycamores.

(above) Entrance gate at Westover.

ON FACING PAGE

(above) The long dining room at Westover.

(below) Parlor or second drawing room at Westover, showing a fine overmantel.

106

(above) The main drawing room at Westover, showing the unique black marble mantel with white marble decorations.

(left) A view of the hall at Westover; notable is the fine plaster work of the ceiling.

There is among the outbuildings at Westover a tool house, under which is a dry well. In the walls of this well are doors leading to two small paved rooms, which in turn lead by underground passages to the river.

WESTOVER CHURCH

THE ancient Parish of Westover, in Charles City County, was established before the middle of the seventeenth century. The old church was near Westover, right on the river, and here the tomb of Mary Byrd, wife of William Byrd I, may be seen, as well as that of her beautiful granddaughter, Evelyn Byrd, who fell in love at eighteen, but died of a broken heart at twenty-seven. Hers was the last tomb placed in the old churchyard. The date on it is 1737. The earliest tombstone with legible inscription in the new churchyard bears the date 1748.

The Reverend Peter Fontaine, of a Huguenot family, was rector of Westover at the time of the moving of the church. It was moved, brick by brick, and rebuilt not far from present Route 5, called the Old Indian Trail, on land that belonged to Mrs. Byrd—which she called Evelyngton. The neighbors used to say Mrs. Byrd moved the church to save herself from having to entertain the whole congregation at Sunday dinner, every Sunday. She was hospitable—but that was a little beyond the scope of even her generous hospitality.

The rectangular church building, constructed of the bricks of the seventeenth century church, was much damaged during the Revolution and the War of 1812. The British used the building to stable their horses. During the Civil War the Northern troops, under McClellan, built entrenchments on Evelyngton Heights to help defend their camp at Harrison's Landing. Thus the church was within the Northern entrenchments.

Now the church has been restored and is used regularly. The pews, the floors, the windows and the walls and doors are perfectly appointed, being classically simple, which adds charm to this ancient rural sanctuary. A grove, a well-kept old cemetery, some beautiful box, and velvety lawns surround the quiet old church. These with the muted bird songs evoke in the visitor the feeling that time matters not—that the ages lie behind—and that eternity stretches out beyond.

RIVER EDGE

ORIGINALLY consisting of ten thousand acres, the land lying in Charles City County between Gunn's Run and Herring Creek, and bordering on the north side of James River, is the site of the home called River Edge. This land was a grant from the Crown to William Cole, a native of Warwick County, England. Mr. Cole was a trustee of William and Mary College and a member of His Majesty's Council in Virginia. He was also Secretary of State.

William Cole II inherited the estate, and he, like his father, held important offices

(above) Westover Church, built in the 17th century, scarred by three wars
but beautifully restored.

(below) Interior of Westover Church.

in the colony. He went in for trade and commerce, and warehouses were built on his land near the end of the seventeenth century. Although records have been destroyed, and there is no actual proof of the fact, it is generally believed that the house was built at about this time, by this same William Cole II. Perhaps a quarter of a century later the original house was moved from its river site to its present location. In 1769 William Byrd, of Westover, bought from William Cole IV four thousand acres of this property. Then Cole went west to Albemarle County.

More than half a century later Dr. Edward Wilcox owned and occupied the house at River Edge. At this time it was a story-and-a-half house, not large. It remained in the possession of his descendants for many years. After the Civil War there were many transfers of ownership, but in 1925, Mr. and Mrs. Lamar Curry Thomas bought the property, and restored the house and garden.

Later Mr. and Mrs. Sam Mason bought, remodelled and enlarged River Edge, transforming it into a large, beautiful home. After some years they sold the place to Mr. and Mrs. Bergdoll, of Philadelphia, who are making it their family home.

River Edge, late 18th-century home on the James River, has been considerably enlarged by later owners and restored.

The main historic significance of the River Edge plantation is to be found in the fact that through it passed practically the entire Union army of the Potomac, just before crossing the James on the way to Windmill Point, to begin the long siege of the city of Petersburg. This was in June, 1864.

Architecturally, River Edge is in the old English, or early American style. It has enormous chimneys, many dormer windows, both on the old part of the house and the main part of the new section, as well as on the wings, which are connected to the central unit by lower-roofed passageways. The house is sided with clapboarding painted white, and the windows have outside blinds. The interior is in keeping with the period of the house, the woodwork, doors, mantels and stairs are all charming.

The garden is very lovely. On the lawn are handsome trees, enormous boxwoods, a number of dwarf English box, and the grass is lush green.

GREENWAY

THIS old, story-and-a-half clapboard house, with a steep roof and many dormer windows is of considerable architectural and historic interest. It is the second oldest original house in Charles City County, dating from c. 1650-1700, and is a fine example of Colonial architecture. It is located on present Route 5, the Old Indian Trail, recently renamed the John Tyler Memorial Parkway. The interior has the original woodwork and hardware still intact. The present owners of Greenway are Mr. and Mrs. Cyrus Wendell Beale, of Charles City County and Richmond.

It was at Greenway that Governor John Tyler (1747-1813) made his home and raised his family. The place had been known as Marlee, but when Tyler's little daughter exclaimed at the greenness of the grass roundabout, her father changed the name to Greenway. Tyler married Miss Mary Marot Armistead, daughter of Robert Armistead, of York County, in 1776, and their son, John Tyler (1790-1862) who also became Governor of Virginia, and then tenth President of the United States, was born here, March 29, 1790.

John Tyler, the elder, who was the fourth of his name in Virginia, was born and raised in York County, educated at William and Mary College (during which time he "versified and fiddled" as relaxation from his studies); then for five years he was a student of law under Robert Carter Nicholas. By birth an aristocrat, he became a democrat by choice. A liberal in politics, a conservative at home, John Tyler was said to have been a most interesting individual. He was a close friend and admirer of Patrick Henry, of Thomas Jefferson and other great men of his time. He was present when Henry uttered his famous peroration ending with "If this be treason, then make the most of it," and quoted the speech to historian William Wirt who, in turn, recorded it for posterity.

John Tyler had been appointed to the Committee of Safety of Charles City County in 1774, and in 1775 he led a company of volunteers, which he had raised, with Patrick Henry, against Lord Dunmore. In 1776, he was appointed one of the judges of the High Court of Admiralty for Virginia. From one success to another, Tyler continued on his way. He was elected to the House of Delegates in 1777; vice-president of the Virginia Convention of 1788. When transferred from the High Court of Admiralty to the General Court of Virginia, he was one of the first judges to assert the power of the judiciary over the other branches of the government.

In 1808 Tyler was elected Governor of Virginia, and when his term was over, in 1811, he was appointed judge of the Federal Court for the district of Virginia. The State Literary Fund was established as a result of one of Governor Tyler's urgent messages. He died in 1813, and was buried at Greenway.

The greatest historic significance of Greenway, however, is to be found in the fact that it was the birthplace of John Tyler, son of the earlier John Tyler; he was elected Vice-President when William Henry Harrison was elected President. They were both born in Charles City County. Their respective birthplaces are separated from each other by only a few miles, for Harrison was born at Berkeley. When Harrison died while in office, Tyler succeeded him as President.

Greenway, in Charles City County, was the birthplace and boyhood home of John Tyler, 10th President of the United States.

OLD VIRGINIA HOUSES ALONG THE JAMES

The only other Presidents born in the same county were Washington and Monroe, who both first saw the light of day in Westmoreland County, Virginia, and John Adams, and John Quincy Adams, his son, both born at Braintree, Massachusetts.

John Tyler, the Younger, lived at Greenway till his marriage to Letitia Christian. The newlyweds moved to Monssacre, at that time still a part of the Greenway property, to spend their honeymoon. Later Tyler purchased Greenway and lived there while Governor of Virginia. He sold the place in 1829, about the time he bought Sherwood Forest. Since then the old house has had a succession of owners. Mr. Robert Bradley, during his ownership, bred fine race horses here, one of which won the American Derby in 1901. After his death the property fell into disrepair until acquired by the Beales, who have carefully restored the mansion to its former condition. In the English basement there is a most interesting fireplace with a hearth laid in bricks made on the place about three centuries ago.

BUSH HILL

ABOUT a half mile east of Charles City Courthouse, on an eminence, facing south, is the tall clapboarded house called Bush Hill. Locally known as the House of Doctors, it is not the home of a physician at present, nor has it been for many years, but four prominent doctors have made it their home during its history. During the residence of Dr. Junius Roan, and also during McClellan's occupation of the Peninsula in 1864, there was an encampment of Confederate troops at Bush Hill, presumably as a protection for the Court House near by. The Federals, however, approaching from an unexpected direction, took the Confederate soldiers by surprise. There was quite a lively engagement for a few minutes right near the house. Several Confederates were wounded, and almost all the others were taken prisoner. The house was not injured.

Besides Dr. Roan, Dr. James B. McCaw, Dr. Edmund O. Christian and Dr. Cary Wilkinson have lived at Bush Hill. Dr. Wilkinson was a member of the Committee of Safety for James City County in 1774.

It is not definitely known just when Bush Hill was built, but it is thought that it was during the last half of the eighteenth century. A deed dated 1811 refers to this property as "being a part of the tract of land formerly belonging to William Greene Munford." His father had the same name, and had been Justice of Charles City County from 1769 to 1781, Major of Charles City Militia, and a member of the House of Delegates. As appears from his will dated February 8, 1786, his four sons inherited his land.

(above) Drawing Room at Greenway.

(below) Views of the interior of Greenway.

115

Bush Hill is architecturally unique, inasmuch as it resembles no other house of its period. The small front porch does show an influence of the Greek Revival style. But this porch is to the side of the front, and the hall upon which it opens is a corner room. The pine stairway extends to the third floor. The third floor is lighted by dormer windows. There is only one chimney, but there are several fireplaces. In the dining room the paneled mantel with little concealed cupboards was said to have been copied from—or modified on the lines of—the one in Raleigh Tavern, in Williamsburg. The floor of the wing is a step down from the dining room. This is a bright, cheery room, and has a secret chamber above it. The only method for approaching the latter is by a narrow, steep stairs concealed in a closet of the lower room.

Although most of the dependencies are gone, the old office, the smoke house and the slave quarters still stand.

Bush Hill has had a succession of owners, but after the turn of the twentieth century it remained for many years in possession of the Waddill family. Mrs. Louise Waddill McIntyre painstakingly restored the house about fifteen years ago.

It is now the home of Mrs. Percy Walls.

MOUNT STIRLING

IN Charles City County, not so far from the Court House, and near Providence Forge, stands beautiful old Mount Stirling, on land patented in 1662 by Henry Soane, who was a member of the House of Burgesses. Mr. Soane was of prominence in social and official circles of the early colony. His granddaughter, Elizabeth Soane, became the wife of the Reverend David Mossom, rector of St. Peter's Church in New Kent County, who is remembered as the officiating clergyman at the wedding of George Washington and Martha Dandridge Custis. Elizabeth Soane and her husband, the Reverend Mr. Mossom, were buried in the family burying ground of the old estate. Her tombstone is dated 1759, and is still standing, but the cemetery is no longer a part of Mount Stirling.

Francis Jerdone, a merchant, came from Scotland and settled in Yorktown in 1746. He acquired Stirling Plantation, as it was then called, in 1771. The place remained in the Jerdone family until 1940.

The present mansion, a very fine example of Greek Revival architecture, was built by William Jerdone (a grandson of Francis) in 1848. Some of the dependencies of the earlier mansion, dating back to the beginning of the 18th century, are still standing and still in use.

The handsome fifteen-room, two-story brick home has a high basement and a full attic. The bricks were handmade on the plantation, and the heart pine lumber, used throughout, for joists, sills, floors and paneling, was cut from the forest trees of Stirling. The floor boards are wide, and cut full length for each room. The only departure from the use of pine is to be noted in the stair rail and newel post of the main stairway; they are of native black walnut.

Bush Hill, in Charles City County.

Living room at Bush Hill.

Garden front of Mt. Stirling.

The preparation and assembling of material was done by the slaves on the place, and required a period of two years. The lumber was all hand-sawed.

The ceilings of the main floor rooms are thirteen feet high, and the mantels in the front rooms are of Italian marble, while those of the back room are of Georgia marble. The parlor contains a very unusual lard lamp chandelier, and the dining room has an imported crystal chandelier with more than five hundred prisms. In the basement are two huge fireplaces, which are by no means the least of Mount Stirling's many attractive features. The Greek portico is typical of the period in which the mansion was built.

The grounds are extensive and beautiful. Native trees, green lawns, a formal box-wood garden, a luxurious flower garden, a vegetable garden, an orchard and a natural hillside garden, joined by walks and foot-paths, combine to make a setting worthy of the lovely old home.

118

(above) Living room at Mt. Stirling.

Mt. Stirling, in Charles City County, front view. This home is a fine example of Greek Revival architecture.

Drawing room at Mt. Stirling.

(below) Dining room at Mt. Stirling.

The old mansion has a certain historic interest. General McClellan's forces encamped here, and judging by remaining traces of trenches and gun emplacements, there must have been considerable military activity on the place. According to tradition, General Sheridan for a time used the Mount Stirling parlor as his office. Soane's Bridge, over the Chickahominy, not far from Mount Stirling, was crossed by General J. E. B. Stuart, on his memorable sweep around McClellan's Army, on June 14, 1862. The Ninth and Sixth corps of Grant's Army crossed here, also, on June 13-14, 1864. William Byrd refers to this bridge in his *Secret Diary*.

In 1940 Mount Stirling was bought by Mr. and Mrs. Hunter C. Sledd, of Richmond, and it could not have fallen into better hands. No one knows his history better than Mr. Sledd, and together, he and Mrs. Sledd have furnished the magnificent old mansion with a collection of interesting and valuable antiques. Both are experts, too, in gardening and horticulture, and this has contributed to creating Mount Stirling's charming setting.

THE GLEBE

ALTHOUGH the Crown had ordered that suitable quarters be provided for ministers, Governor Berkeley paid this ordinance no heed. But in 1732 Colonel Wm. Byrd II, with John Smith, Samuel Howard and John Carter, as a committee, bought the Glebe from Philip Lightfoot, to be a rectory. It is located on a road running from present Route 60 to Charles City Court House, and is near Providence Forge and not far from Ruthville. The Glebe served as a rectory for nearly one hundred years.

It is a T-shaped house, and has walls three feet thick, of brick laid in Flemish bond, has a center hall with a huge room on either side, and one at the rear of the hall. There are large chimneys, and fireplaces in all rooms. From the hall a wide stairway ascends to the second floor. Above the front door is a handsome, fan-shaped transom, with fan-shaped, leaded panes. The window-panes both downstairs and in the arched dormers are of leaded glass. The wide floor boards, fine mantels and stairway are original. The north wing dates from the present century. It is said that the initials, diamond-cut into the parlor and dining room window-panes, were incised by impatient couples waiting for the minister.

A few old box trees survive, and near the back of the house stands a stump of a tulip poplar, which still leafs out in spring, said to have been the largest tree east of the Rockies, measuring fifty-seven feet in circumference.

Upon the death of Rev. Seawell Chapin, last minister to occupy the house, the Glebe was sold in 1807 to Mr. Patrick Hendron who renamed it Cromwell Grove. Finally, in 1942, it was sold to Col. and Mrs. Richard Parker Crenshaw. The house had been occupied in the middle of the 19th century by the Colonel's grandfather and grandmother, Augustus Pemberton Crenshaw and Ricarda Parker Crenshaw. The Colonel's father had lived there as a boy. During the Civil War, while the elder Crenshaws were living in the Glebe, Federal forces camped in nearby fields. But the redoubtable Ricarda dared the "Yanks" to cross her threshold. None ever did.

121

*The Glebe, Charles City County, where impatient couples, waiting for the
minister, scratched their initials on the window panes.*

Because the Colonel was called into active service in World War II, the Crenshaws
did not move into the Glebe until 1946, when they made extensive repairs and improvements to the old house. In 1949, because the Colonel was again called back
into the service, the Crenshaws sold the Glebe. Today it is the property of Mrs. John
Ruffin.

LOWER WEYANOKE

WEYANOKE, in Charles City County, stands on the spot where Captains John Smith
and Christopher Newport found the Weyanoke Indians in 1607. In 1740 William
Harwood replaced an earlier building on the plantation with the main part of the
present mansion. Two generations later Agnes, daughter of Major Samuel Harwood,

122

who married Fielding Lewis, son of Col. Warner Lewis, of Warner Hall, inherited Weyanoke. Thereafter, the estate passed by inheritance to the Douthats; but in 1876 that part of it on which the mansion stands was sold. Later owners, Mr. and Mrs. Lawrence Lewis, remodeled and enlarged the house. It is now owned by Mr. and Mrs. John C. Hagan, Jr.

UPPER WEYANOKE

JUST before the Civil War Fielding Lewis Douthat married Mary Willis Marshall, granddaughter of Chief Justice Marshall, and they went to live at Upper Weyanoke, part of the original larger tract on which Lower Weyanoke had been built. Fielding Lewis Douthat inherited this part of the original tract as his share of the estate of his mother, Eleanor Lewis, and her husband, his father, Robert Douthat.

The house, an ancient looking English type story-and-a-half brick structure, has large chimneys at the ends, and dormer windows. It stands on low level ground, near the river.

Here Mary Johnson laid the scene for her novel, *To Have and To Hold.*

This small structure was for years owned by Dr. and Mrs. Alexander Yelverton Peyton Garnett. There is a handsome, modern red brick mansion nearby where for years lived the descendants of Mary Willis Marshall and Fielding Lewis Douthat. The whole place is now owned by Mr. Henry Bahnsen.

SHERWOOD FOREST

SHERWOOD FOREST was first called Walnut Grove, and was built on a tract which originally comprised twelve hundred acres "across the river opposite Brandon." The house is of "framed timbers" and stands in a beautiful ten-acre grove of original-growth oaks. At the back is a lovely park planted in choice trees, some of which came from the Botanical Gardens in Washington, D. C.

President John Tyler, while living in the White House, bought this beautiful old place from Collier Minge in 1842.

When President Tyler and his family came home to the country to live, he renamed the place Sherwood Forest, on account of his having been outlawed from the Whig party, and also because of the beauty of the "new green wood."

The main part of the house is two and a half stories high. The various passages and wings are of different heights. There are a great many dormer windows in the picturesque old clapboard mansion, with its numerous first floor windows, its several entrances and many chimneys. It stretches out to a length of three hundred feet, said to have been the longest house in America of its time.

President Tyler was a gifted individual, a gentleman, a writer, a statesman, a musician and a horticulturist. His second wife said of him, after she and her father had visited the White House, soon after Mr. Tyler and she had met, ". . . he welcomed us with an urbanity which made the deepest impression upon my father, and

Sherwood Forest, where President John Tyler retired after serving his term in office.

124

we could not help commenting . . . upon the silver sweetness of his voice, that seemed in just attune with the incomparable grace of his bearing and the elegant ease of his conversation."

To recount all the things Mr. Tyler accomplished while Governor of Virginia, United States Senator and President of the United States (not to mention many other public offices which he held) would take volumes, as would a discussion of his writings. One who saw him while he was President said of Mr. Tyler, "In his official intercourse with all men, high or low, he was all that could be asked: approachable, courteous, always willing to do a kindly action, or to speak a kindly word. . . . He was above the middle height, somewhat slender, clean-shaven, with light hair. His light blue eyes were penetrating, and had a humorous twinkle which aided the notable faculty he possessed for telling a good story, and for making keen conversational hits." ("W. O. Stoddard, William Henry Harrison, John Tyler, and James Knox Polk, 1888," p. 55, from T. P. A. *Dictionary of American Biography,* Vol. XIX.)

He was educated at William and Mary College and, like his father, found relaxation in violin playing and poetry. He married Letitia Christian, daughter of Robert Christian, of New Kent County, on his birthday in 1813. She bore him seven children. After her death, in 1842 (he had become President in 1840), he met the beautiful Miss Julia Gardiner, of New York, and they were married June 26, 1844. She has written most interestingly of life at Sherwood Forest, where the Tyler family retired when Mr. Tyler left the White House. ". . . There are between 60 and 70 slaves on the estate. They were all brought to the house this morning to recognize their new 'missus.' "

Julia changed things in the interior of her new home as much as Mr. Tyler had changed its appearance from the outside. She imported beautiful French mirrors, new rugs, and a chandelier from New York. She furnished the house in lavish style, a whole boat-load of furniture sent down from New York.

When visiting around the neighborhood, or driving from New York, they rode in a fine carriage attended by coachman and footman in livery. For visits to friends on the other side of the James, there was the beautiful *Pocahontas*, a bright blue row boat, and four Negro oarsmen in livery, described by Julia herself as follows: ". . . bright blue and white checked calico shirts, white linen pants, black patent leather belts, straw hats painted blue, with 'Pocahontas' upon them in white, and in one corner of the shirt collar is worked with braid a bow and arrow (to signify from the Forest) and in the other the President's and my initials combined."

Julia Gardiner Tyler had seven children, among whom was the late Judge D. Gardiner Tyler, whose children, two girls and two boys, inherited beautiful Sherwood Forest. It is now the residence of Mr. and Mrs. J. Alfred Tyler.

BRANDON

JOHN MARTIN, one of the first colonists who came to Jamestown in May, 1607, was a member of the original council. He stood strongly for holding on and not

ON FACING PAGE

(above) Living room at Sherwood Forest.

(below) Drawing room at Sherwood Forest.

(below) Ball room at Sherwood Forest.

abandoning the settlement during the starving time of 1610. He was the only one of the original members left alive in Virginia at the time the first House of Burgesses met in 1619. He received a large grant of land, which he called Martin's Brandon. It was bounded by Chippokes Creek on the southeast and by James River on the northeast. The original grant is still treasured at Brandon. A settlement was established here, and Thomas Davis and Robert Stacy represented this settlement in the first assembly.

There were seventy-three persons massacred by the Indians at Martin's Brandon in 1622. John Martin was discouraged and distraught after the massacre, and after a fire at the settlement. In prison, in England, for debt, some time later, he made an appeal for freedom in order to straighten up his affairs. In 1643 Martin's grandson, Captain Robert Bargrave, conveyed the plantation of 4,550 acres to three men who already owned Merchant's Hope Plantation. Their names were William Barker, John Sadler and Richard Quincey. Later Quincey and Sadler, who were brothers-in-law, each owned a half interest in Brandon and Merchant's Hope Plantation. Richard Quincey's son, Thomas, inherited his father's interest, and passed it on to his great-nephew, Robert Richardson.

On August 19, 1720, Nathaniel Harrison, son of Benjamin Harrison II, of Wakefield, had conveyed to him by Robert Richardson "a moiety or halfe part of two tracks of land called Merchant's Hope and Martin's Brandon . . . devised to the said Robert, by the last will and testament of Thomas Quincey, late of the city of London."

Harrison had without doubt acquired the other half interest from Sadler's heirs previously.

Records show that Nathaniel Harrison I owned seven thousand acres of land in the tract called Brandon, and he built the oldest part of the house (the old wing) soon after buying the plantation.

Nathaniel I and his wife, Mary Cary Young (who had been a widow), had seven children. Mr. Harrison was a prominent man in the colony: a Burgess and a Councilor; also naval officer of the Lower James; County Lieutenant of Surry and Prince George; and finally, Auditor General for the Colony.

Nathaniel Harrison II, one of the seven children, inherited Brandon and built the present house. Indications are that he built the second wing some years before the center section, the latter showing the influence of Thomas Jefferson after he came back from France.

Nathaniel Harrison II was a member of the Council. He married first, Mary, daughter of Colonel Cole Digges; second, Lucy, widow of Henry Fitzhugh, and daughter of the Honorable Robert Carter of Corotoman.

His eldest son, Nathaniel Harrison III, the son of his first wife, was heir to Brandon. His portrait is among the many beautiful family portraits at Brandon. His first wife was Anne Randolph, of Wilton, who had no children. His second wife was Evelyn Taylor Byrd, of Westover, niece of the beautiful Evelyn Byrd who languished and died for love. Evelyn Taylor Byrd, the daughter of William Byrd III, was a beauty

Brandon, in Prince George County, was another famous Harrison house.
The east wing dates from the 18th century.

in her own right. She brought with her from Westover many fine antiques, portraits and other things, which are still at Brandon. She had two sons, George Evelyn Harrison, who inherited Brandon, and William Byrd Harrison, who inherited part of the vast acres belonging to the estate, and built Upper Brandon.

George Evelyn Harrison, who inherited Brandon, was a member of the House of Delegates. He married Isabella Ritchie, daughter of the noted editor, Thomas Ritchie. They had two children, George Evelyn Harrison II, and Isabella. When George Evelyn Harrison died in 1839, at the age of forty-two, his wife inherited Brandon, and until 1898 she presided, kind, gracious and charming, not only over Brandon, but over the whole community, as well. Everyone called her "Old Miss." She entertained lavishly. "Miss Belle," her daughter, who never married, remained by her side, assisting in hostess duties and honors.

There is an old story that on one occasion, when all the current expense money

ON FACING PAGE

(above) Hall at Brandon.

(below) Dining room at Brandon.

(below) Drawing room at Brandon.

had been spent on one of the famous May parties at Brandon, "Old Miss" heard that the President of the United States, who was visiting one of the other river houses, was coming to see her. She was in quite a flutter. She called the cook into conference. He reassured her, telling her all would be well.

"But you must remember, this is the President of the United States," she remonstrated.

"But you, Madam," he replied, "must remember how blest we are in our cook." It was as nice a luncheon as President James K. Polk ever enjoyed.

George Evelyn Harrison II married Miss Gulielma Gordon, of Savannah, Georgia. He died early in life, leaving several children. When "Old Miss" died in 1898, Mrs. Gulielma Gordon Harrison was hostess at Brandon. The estate passed to her children at her death.

In 1926 after more than two centuries of Harrison ownership, the Harrison heirs sold the estate to Mr. and Mrs. Robert Daniel, who made many improvements, and entertained many distinguished guests at the lovely old place. Mrs. Daniel is now owner of Brandon, and is as gracious a hostess as any of her predecessors.

The trees around Brandon are impressive. They are large and old and awe-inspiring. The lawn has wide stretches, and the gardens, leading down to the river's edge, are very extensive. Every old-fashioned flower, shrub and bulb imaginable is to be found there.

The house itself, of red brick and white trim, consists of seven parts: a large square two-story center, with two one-story wings, one on each side; then there are the two connecting passages and the two-story wings, each having a center hall with a room on each side, upstairs and down, and a chimney at each end of each wing.

The center hall runs through the house and opens onto porches, showing the Jeffersonian influence, on both fronts. The hall has a magnificent triple arch, a broader one in the center and two others of the same dimensions on each side, the three spanning the width of the hall. These arches are supported by elaborate columns with composite Corinthian-Ionic capitals. The arches and columns, like all the other woodwork, are painted ivory white—that is, all except the stairway, which is mahogany. In one wing is a very curious but interesting Chinese Chippendale stairway. In the other wing one of the fireplaces is immense.

The carving of the mantels, paneling and other decorations at Brandon are all truly elegant. The walls of the drawing room and the dining room are hung with many fine family portraits. Fine silver, antiques and many rare *objets d'art* embellish and beautify the various rooms.

The several wars have left their scars on Brandon, but loving patience in restoration has erased most of the traces of damage done.

132

Upper Brandon, built by William Byrd Harrison in the early 19th century.

UPPER BRANDON

EARLY in the nineteenth century William Byrd Harrison, youngest son of Benjamin Harrison III, of Brandon, and Evelyn Taylor Byrd, daughter of William Byrd III, of Westover, built a home. An older brother would inherit Brandon, so William Byrd Harrison built his handsome home, similar to the old family mansion, on the south side of the James, in Prince George County, about three miles from Brandon, on acreage that was the part of the Brandon estate that he would inherit.

The central part of the house is larger and more imposing than the center section at Brandon, but the wings are somewhat smaller, although they are two stories high. While very impressive and more massive, and in better proportion, Upper Brandon, of course, does not possess the quality of antiquity, nor the fine points of carved details, nor many of the other features that characterize the older place.

At Upper Brandon the trees are remarkably large and fine, and the way the land slopes away to the river is very lovely. There was a very fine garden, but during the Civil War it was almost entirely destroyed. The interior of the house, too, was damaged by Federal occupation. Serpentine walks and fine English dwarf boxwood

133

(above) Brandon Church, in Prince George County, a 19th-century structure. It is in Plantation Parish, which has been in existence since the year 1616.

ON FACING PAGE

(above) Hall at Upper Brandon.

(below) Interior at Upper Brandon.

remain, as well as many bulbs and some shrubs, such as lilac, syringa, and japonica.

William Byrd Harrison was a highly educated man (Harvard and William and Mary) and a disciple of Edmund Ruffin in scientific farming.

Evelyn Taylor Byrd brought to Brandon some elegant and beautiful things from Westover. There were two lovely portraits among her possessions which passed to her son at Upper Brandon.

William Byrd Harrison was very prominent in his state. He was twice married; first to Mary Randolph Harrison, daughter of Randolph Harrison, of Elk Hill, Goochland County; then to Ellen Wayles Randolph, daughter of Colonel Thomas Jefferson Randolph, of Edge Hill, Albemarle County. William Byrd Harrison had three sons who were officers in the Confederate Army. Captain Benjamin Harrison was killed at Malvern Hill.

After the death of William Byrd Harrison, Upper Brandon was sold. Mr. George Harrison Byrd, of New York, bought it, leaving it to his son, Francis Otway Byrd, who made his home here for some years.

In 1948 Mr. and Mrs. Harry Clarke Thompson purchased Upper Brandon, and they now make their home here.

KIPPAX

A two-storied clapboard house with hipped roof and large end chimneys now stands at Kippax in Prince George County, on Route 648, where once stood the home of Jane Rolfe, daughter of Thomas Rolfe and Jane Poythress, and granddaughter of John Rolfe and Pocahontas. And there John Bolling (1676-1729), Jane's only child was born. He had many distinguished descendants, among others, John Randolph, of Roanoke, and Edith Bolling Galt Wilson, second wife of Woodrow Wilson.

JORDAN'S JORNEY

CAPTAIN SAMUEL JORDAN came to Virginia in 1609, which was just before the "starving time." He patented four hundred fifty acres of land just below the confluence of the Appomattox and the James, and called his plantation Jordan's Jorney, or Beggar's Bush. The same year (1619), he represented his own and neighboring plantations in the first House of Burgesses. When the Indian Massacre occurred in 1622, Jordan's Jorney and all its inhabitants were saved. He gathered his neighbors into his home "where he fortified and lived in despite of the enemy."

Burgess Jordan died the next year. On the day of his burial, Rev. Greville Pooley, who had conducted the funeral services, proposed to the widow, who had been left alone to face the perils of the frontier with her children. She told him, since apparently she would have to marry someone to be her protector, she would as soon it were he, but asked for time to think the matter over. She cautioned him not to cause a local scandal by talking about his rather premature proposal. But the overjoyed minister

136

stopped to drink toasts on his way home and apparently "blabbed." This incensed the young widow, and when Pooley later repeated his proposal, she remained silent. Soon after this, Widow Cecilly Jordan became engaged to Col. Wm. Farrar, "an honorable member of His Majesty's Council," and proprietor of nearby Farrar's Island in Henrico County. Pooley thereupon flabbergasted the local courts by instituting the first American breach of promise suit. Finally Cecilly won out. The minister was required to pledge 500 pounds sterling "never to have any claim, right or title to her." However, the Governor and Council thereupon enacted a law which prohibited women from engaging themselves "to two several men at the same time." Soon after this Cecilly married Col. Farrar and moved to his home in Henrico County.

At Jordan's Jorney, in 1676, the volunteers of Charles City County south of the James assembled to join in Bacon's Rebellion.

For a hundred years Jordan's Jorney was the home of members of the Bland family. Richard Bland, an ardent patriot in the struggle against the British, owned it at the time of the Revolution. The old plantation house he would have occupied has long since vanished.

MERCHANT'S HOPE CHURCH

THE old church of Merchant's Hope derived its name from Merchant's Hope Plantation and stands in the northern part of the county, not far from the James. The date of erection is accepted as 1657, the date cut into one of the great rafters.

The church measures sixty by thirty feet, has walls twenty-two inches thick, built of bricks laid in Flemish bond, with glazed headers accenting the full red of the old bricks. The entrance is in the west, with a small window above the door to light the gallery. The windows are arched; there are two in the east end, three, and the chancel door, in the south wall, and four in the north wall. Modillions decorate the edges of the roof. The flagstones in the aisles are originals.

There is a curious old Bible here. Though its title page is missing, it is believed to be a New Testament of 1639, appended to an Old Testament of 1640. This Bible is thought to be the "great Bible" given by John Westhorpe, a London merchant, in 1658. At the time he gave the Bible he also gave one thousand pounds of tobacco and "caske" to contain same, to be used to buy a "Communion Cupp." The "Cupp" is now at Brandon Church.

BEECHWOOD

BETWEEN Route 10 and the James River, on Route 641, and not far from Tar Bay House, is Beechwood. It was built before 1843 by Edmund Ruffin, who made many agricultural and soil experiments, proving that soil reclamation in Virginia would be profitable.

Edmund Ruffin also fired the first gun at Fort Sumter, and in retaliation many Federals on gun-boats on the James frequently used to take pot shots at Beechwood.

COGGINS POINT OR MERCHANT'S HOPE PLANTATION

EDMUND RUFFIN was born at Evergreen and lived at Beechwood, but in between he lived at Coggin's Point, moving there from Evergreen.

This old place on the James was a part of Merchant's Hope Plantation acquired by Captain Nathaniel Powell in 1619. He had the distinction of serving as Acting Governor of Virginia for a few days between the departure of Argall and the coming of Yeardley.

In 1720 Nathaniel Harrison purchased Merchant's Hope. His son inherited the plantation, which then consisted of nineteen hundred seventy-three acres. The estate was entailed, so special legislation was passed in 1765, by the General Assembly, to permit Harrison to sell the entire property, in order to be able to purchase slaves for Brandon. About this time Coggin's Point was acquired by Col. Richard Kidder Meade (1746-1805), who had been on the staff of General Washington during the Revolution. It was to Col. Meade that General Washington assigned the duty of supervising the execution of Major André. About this tragedy Col. Meade said, "I could not forbear shedding tears at the execution of so virtuous and admirable a person." It was by his second wife that Col. Richard Kiddler Meade became the father of the distinguished Bishop William Meade, who wrote *Old Churches, Ministers and Families of Virginia.*

Few traces of the old home remain.

FLOWERDEW HUNDRED

IN 1609 Sir George Yeardley and his wife, the former Temperance Flowerdew, sailed for Virginia with Sir Thomas Gates. Yeardley received a grant of one thousand acres of land on the James River, along Flowerdew Creek, and named the place Flowerdew, in honor of his wife's family. He built the first windmill in America, and to this day the point on which it was built is called Windmill Point.

Sir George Yeardley was twice Governor, and when in 1624 the House of Burgesses was suspended by Royal decree, it was he who went over to confer with the King and plead for the rights of the people. He effected the restoration of representative government.

Abraham Peirsey bought Flowerdew from Yeardley, and his daughter, Mrs. Stephens, inherited the estate. In 1635 her patent was entered for "Floer deue Hundred." This was the first deed for land recorded in America.

Joshua Poythress acquired the property in 1725, and it remained in the possession of his descendants until it was bought by J. Roland Rooke in recent years. The original house is no longer there.

The house standing when the Rookes bought the place was late Colonial, with a weather-boarded center with flanking wings. There were remnants of the old garden, with terraces descending the slope towards the river.

In June, 1864, a Federal host, 130,000 strong, under Grant, crossed over the James from Wilcox Wharf to Windmill Point. They marched over on a pontoon bridge which General Grant's engineers had built.

CEDAR LEVEL

THE home of Robert Bolling (1682-1749), son of the immigrant, Robert Bolling and his second wife, Anne Stith, is called Cedar Level. It is located near Kippax Mansion, and was a part of the original Kippax land. This early eighteenth-century home is a story and a half high with two huge chimneys at each end, and three dormer windows, front and rear. The gabled roof is extended over porches at each end.

At one time Cedar Level was a tavern called Half Way House, since it is halfway between City Point and Hopewell.

OTHER HOUSES OF PRINCE GEORGE

PRINCE GEORGE county contains many relics of past wars; but it also has many new churches and lovely new homes. That means hope and faith, and looking to the future. But the county's sons and daughters also revere and cherish the old. The old homes of Prince George are very dear to the hearts of its people. Besides those described above, mention should be made as well of the following:

St. John's Church
The Site of Cawsons
The John Randolph Hospital
City Point House
Evergreen
Sion Hill
Beaver Castle
Rosewood
Bykars or Rosewood
Goodgame
Tar Bay House
Briarfield
Maycock Plantation
Aberdeen
Rose Cottage

Aspen Grove
Belsches
Site of Mitchells
Northing
John Van Buren House
Belfield
Temple House
Ralphis
Washington
Pinkards
Shellbank
Old Town
Hickory Grove
Harrison House
Roseland

Memorial Church, at Jamestown. In front is the ruined tower of a church built between 1676 and 1686. In an earlier Jamestown church Pocahontas and John Rolfe were married.

PART FOUR

JAMESTOWN AND WILLIAMSBURG

Including James City County,
Surry County and a Few Places East

ALL school children in Virginia, and many throughout the nation, know the story of Jamestown, Williamsburg and Yorktown, the famous Historical Trinity. In Part IV, we are telling of Jamestown, the Cradle of the Nation; and Williamsburg, the seat of cultural growth, education and the development of government up to the Declaration of Independence. We are including in our account the nearby homes of planters and lawmakers. The story of the full glory of Yorktown and its two nearby counties will be presented in Part V.

In 1607 the three little ships, the *Sarah Constant,* the *Goodspeed,* and the *Discovery,* bearing one hundred five colonists under Captain Christopher Newport to the first permanent settlement in America, stopped at Cape Henry on April 26. There the passengers went ashore and prayed, rested, explored and, on the third day, April 29, erected a cross on which was inscribed "Dei Gratia Virginia Condita."

They then re-embarked and proceeded up the broad river, which they called the James for their King. They visited in what is now Surry County, but on "the eight of May," these first white Anglo-Americans went ashore in the "land of the Appamatica"—what is now Prince George County. Their stay here was of four days' duration. They decided, however, to go back down the river to a beautiful peninsula on its north bank, bordered on its northern side by the Back River.

Here the English came ashore on May 13, 1607. On May 14 there was general disembarkation. The first crude altar was erected, church services were held by the Reverend Robert Hunt, and holy communion was administered.

It was just after these services were held that Captain Newport gathered around him the potential leaders of the colony, and opened the sealed orders given him by the Virginia Company in London, which contained the names of those who were

141

to serve on the first Colonial Council. These were: Bartholomew Gosnold, John Smith, Edward Wingfield, Christopher Newport, John Ratcliffe, John Martin and George Kendall. These members chose for the first President of the Colony, Edward Maria Wingfield. He served until September 10th of the same year, when he was replaced by Captain John Ratcliffe. On that same day, May 14, 1607, construction for the settlement began.

Soon palisades were built and a village started. An account of these early proceedings says, "A three-cornered palisade started May 14th and finished June 15th." The account goes on to tell that a year later there was "a street of houses by each wall," and in the "middest," a market place, a storehouse, a guard house, and a chapel.

From the first the colonists labored under many disadvantages. Although the place was beautiful, vegetation was lush and the natives at times friendly and kind, there were many hardships. Disease, pestilence, cold and starvation, together with Indian atrocities, caused many deaths and much suffering in the colony. Mosquitoes were swarming in "fine natural grass," which was worthless marshgrass.

"Supplies" (additional colonists with food and commodities for the comfort of the settlers) were sent over from England; the first shipments arrived in the fall of 1607 and the following spring. More came in during 1609-10.

Pocahontas, the beautiful Indian Princess, daughter of Powhatan, King of most of the neighboring tribes, was very helpful, bringing food almost daily, and showing many kindnesses to the whites. Several "forts" and fortifications were made at different points nearby. John Smith made explorations and drew a map. He also wrote a history of these early days in Virginia. The Indians taught the white men how to raise Indian corn and tobacco and many new methods to supplement the skill of the colonists in hunting wild game in the forests.

Pocahontas was baptized in the second church of Jamestown, and later married there by the Reverend Richard Buck, to John Rolfe. The wedding took place in the spring of 1614. Pocahontas, the Lady Rebecca, went on a visit to England with her husband and son. They were ready to return to Virginia when she fell sick and died, in 1617, at Gravesend.

The Government at Jamestown at first was in the hands of a President of the Council, or a Governor, or Deputy Governor, or Acting Governor, who, with the Council, ruled the colony. Added to this governing body, in 1619 the House of Burgesses was established; its members were representatives of the people.

The first House of Burgesses met on July 30, 1619, in the church "Quire," the third church at Jamestown. This was the first lawmaking body of representative government ever to meet on American soil.

In 1619 plans were adopted for the establishment of the first university in America. It was to be at the town of Henrico (at Farrar's Island) in Henrico County, and was called Henrico University and College. The ten thousand acres set aside for the university extended along the James to the Falls.

In 1619 arrangements were made for the "coming of the maids," who were "educated," well-brought-up young women coming to Virginia, where they would live with reputable families, well chaperoned, until they could be wooed and won by suitable husbands. The prospective husbands promised to give so and so many pounds of tobacco to pay the passage of their brides. It is estimated that two hundred of these "maids" came over to Jamestown.

A Dutch vessel arrived at Jamestown soon after this, bringing a cargo of Negroes to be used as servants by the colonists. This was the beginning of slavery in North America.

In 1622 the Great Massacre occurred. The town of Henrico and the beginnings of the university were wiped out. At almost every plantation some people were killed. The Indian Chanco's disclosure of the plot to Mr. Pace at Mt. Pleasant saved many.

In 1676, because of the indifference of Governor Berkeley to the safety of the colonists, in the face of continuing Indian attacks and depredations, a large number of the people arose under the leadership of Nathaniel Bacon II, of Curles in Henrico. This bitter difference between the two factions was called "Bacon's Rebellion." The devout adherents of freedom under Bacon burned their own homes and subsequently the whole of Jamestown, and defied the Governor openly; they also routed the Indians. After Bacon's death (of exposure and malaria) his followers suffered sad reprisals at the hands of the old Governor. In fact, the matter reached such proportions that His Majesty the King sent over a Commission to investigate and set things straight. The Commission consisted of Sir John Berry, Col. Herbert Jeffreys and Col. Francis Moryson. Sir John, the Admiral of a small fleet, brought several vessels, and was escorted by His Majesty's "red coats," in case they were needed. The members of the Commission were not only sympathetic and conciliatory, but they helped to effect peace. Governor Berkeley returned to England, and Col. Herbert Jeffreys became Governor.

Tobacco raising became a growing industry in Virginia, and furthered the settlement of more and more plantations. Glass works were established adjacent to Jamestown. The colony grew little by little in spite of various setbacks.

The last State House (the fourth) at Jamestown was burned in 1698. In April, 1699 Williamsburg became the new capital.

After Jamestown was burned during Bacon's Rebellion in 1676, it was never completely rebuilt. Then, after the removal of the capital to Williamsburg, Jamestown gradually became more and more deserted. Today the entire island belongs to the United States Government, with the exception of the twenty-two and one-half acres belonging to the Association for the Preservation of Virginia Antiquities. At Jamestown there are the Memorial Church and the old tower, the Relic House, and the Yeardley House used as a dwelling. There are many monuments and memorials, each with its own inscription. The churchyard has many historical tombs.

Williamsburg had its beginnings in 1632, when Dr. John Pott patented twelve hundred acres of land on the higher ground halfway between the James and the York. He invited settlers, and had palisades built between Queen's Creek, which flowed into the York, and Archer's Hope Creek, which flowed into the James. This settlement being high and dry (though with plenty of water from the nearby creeks and the deep wells), was a more healthful place than Jamestown. It grew, and people there seemed happy and prosperous. It was called Middle Plantation. In 1693 the long-planned college for the colony was established at Middle Plantation. It was named the College of William and Mary, in honor of their Royal Majesties.

It was at the meeting of the General Assembly in 1699, in Middle Plantation, that the town's name was changed to "the city of Williamsburg," and authorization made for "the building of the Capitol," which was erected between 1701 and 1705.

Two hundred and twenty acres were surveyed for the city of Williamsburg by Theodorick Bland. The first trustees for the city were Governor Nicholson, Edmund Jennings, Philip Ludwell, Esquire, Thomas Ballard, Lewis Burwell, Philip Ludwell, Jr., John Page, Henry Tyler, James Whaley, and Benjamin Harrison, Jr.

The first plan contemplated laying out the streets in the form of a W and an M in honor of Their Majesties, but this plan was somewhat difficult to put into execution, so the "old horse path," three quarters of a mile long, became the principal avenue and was called the Duke of Gloucester Street, and Governor Francis Nicholson named the streets on each side, Francis Street and Nicholson Street for "His Honor"—himself.

Named by Governor Nicholson for King William III, Williamsburg was chartered a city in 1722. The new city and the plantations up and down river grew in population and in wealth; in development of education and culture. Many brilliant men and women made Williamsburg a business, professional, educational, political and social center. As they became more educated and consulted with one another, the men of the region began to think and speak of liberty, and thought of casting off the yoke of the Mother Country. The flame of independence flared and spread, and, even as Jamestown had become the Cradle of the Nation, so Williamsburg became the Cradle of the Republic. The stirring events of the early days of the Revolution were centered in Williamsburg. Momentous crises were met here daily.

Williamsburg remained the capital of Virginia until 1779, when the seat of the government was moved to Richmond.

There was one institution, besides the College of William and Mary, however, that had had its beginning here, and which remained here, and tragically enough, it has grown and expanded. It is the Eastern State Hospital, the first hospital in the world that was operated entirely for the care of the insane. Many experiments, much study and vast improvement in the treatment of the mentally ill have been developed at Eastern State. Many cases, which in former years would have been deemed hopeless, today are "hopeful" cases. Already some such cases are fully recovered, and have again taken their places in society.

All the wars seriously affected Williamsburg, and she took part in all of them.

After the capital was moved to Richmond, however, Williamsburg receded into a state of semi-obscurity, until the late Reverend W. A. R. Goodwin, D.D., in 1927 envisioned a colonial city restored. He confided his dream to Mr. John D. Rockefeller. Mr. Rockefeller became interested. He said if such a project of restoration were to be undertaken at all, it must be carried out fully. The job was begun promptly, after Mr. Rockefeller had decided to undertake it, and has been continued to the present day. In all its phases the Restoration has accomplished miracles.

144

MEMORIAL CHURCH

ON May 11, 1907, The Memorial Church at Jamestown was presented by the Society of Colonial Dames of America in the State of Virginia to the Association for the Preservation of Virginia Antiquities.

On the walls of this shrine are tablets to the memory of: "Adventurers in England and the Ancient Plantation in Virginia"; the Jamestown Colonial Governors, and Presidents of the Council officially residents at Jamestown, 1607-1698; Pocahontas; Captain John Smith; Daniel Gookin; George Sandys; John Rolfe; William Claiborne; Thomas West; and Chanco.

This shrine was built on the site of three of the five previous churches which succeeded each other and served the spiritual needs of the colonists of Virginia from 1607 to 1758. Here still can be found traces of the foundations of three of those old buildings. Each of these sanctuaries has its respective distinction. The first wooden church was very crude, but it was built in 1607, and was the *first* church. The second wooden structure, built in 1608, was called the Lord Delaware Church, and it was the scene, in 1614, of the marriage of Pocahontas and John Rolfe. The third church, built 1617-1619, was called the Argall Church, and it housed the meeting of the first House of Burgesses, which was the first lawmaking body of representative government in America. The fourth church was of brick. It was built 1639-1647, and burned during Bacon's Rebellion.

The fifth church, the last serving the colonists at Jamestown, was brick, a reconstruction of the fourth church. It was built between 1676 and 1686, and served the colonists for almost sixty years after the seat of government was moved to Williamsburg. It was abandoned in 1758.

Its tower remains, and still stands, today, perhaps one of the best-known and most revered relics in this country.

It is just in front of Memorial Church.

FOUNDATION OF THE OLD STATE HOUSE

THE first State House, built at Jamestown in 1642, was burned in or about the year 1656. The second one burned down about 1660. The third State House, built or bought after the fire of 1660, was burned at the time of Bacon's Rebellion, 1676. This was replaced by one built on the same foundations by Colonel Ludwell in 1686. After the fire which destroyed this, the fourth State House at Jamestown, in 1698, the seat of government was moved to Williamsburg in the spring of 1699.

After Samuel H. Yonge built the protective sea wall in 1903, he made excavations at the site of the State House, unearthing the foundations, also a row of four other foundations. Besides the State House, which was seventy by twenty feet with walls two feet thick, there were the three Ludwell houses and the Country House, all forty by forty.

145

RUINS OF THE JAQUELIN AMBLER HOUSE

THE year after the massacre of 1622 Sir Francis Wyatt received a grant for land in "New Towne," that part of "James Citty" which was planned by Governor Wyatt and surveyed by William Claiborne. The property passed to William Sherwood and then to John Page, later to Edward Jaquelin.

Mr. Jaquelin's daughter, Elizabeth, was married to Richard Ambler, of Yorktown. In 1782 John Ambler, Elizabeth's grandson, inherited Jamestown Island.

The Jaquelin-Ambler house has been burned and rebuilt several times. Nothing remains now except the ruins, but from the foundations we can determine the dimensions. The mansion was 57 x 40 feet, with foundation walls thirty inches thick and partition walls eighteen inches thick.

GREEN SPRING

GREEN SPRING, about two miles north of Jamestown, was Governor Berkeley's country home. The Berkeleys entertained many visitors at Green Spring, and the place was noted as a home where gayety and beauty and happiness reigned.

However, Green Spring had its grim moments, too. Nathaniel Bacon established headquarters here after Berkeley fled across the York. Later, after Bacon's death, Governor Berkeley summoned the Assembly of 1677, which met here, to repeal all "Bacon's Laws" enacted by the Assembly of 1676. It was also from Green Spring that death warrants went out for some of the noblest and bravest of Virginia's colonists because of their participation in the Rebellion—Colonel James Crews, Giles Bland, William Drummond, and many others.

Berkeley refused hospitality at Green Spring to the Commissioners, Sir John Berry, Colonel Herbert Jeffrey and Colonel Francis Moryson, whom the King had sent over to investigate the trouble, and to try to make peace between Governor Berkeley and the colonists. They stayed at Swann's Point across the river. Sir William Berkeley went to England to throw himself on the mercy of the King. He fell ill there and died shortly afterward.

Lady Berkeley married Philip Ludwell, and they lived at Green Spring, which he inherited at her death. For many years the plantation remained in the Ludwell and Lee families by inheritance.

The original house was not as large as the later Ludwell-Lee mansion here, which burned during the Civil War. Excavations were made in 1928, showing the foundation of the original Berkeley house which once stood here.

POWHATAN

THREE miles west of Williamsburg is Powhatan, the big old brick home of the Egglestons. In 1635 Richard Eggleston arrived from England. He became a member

146

of the House of Burgesses, and in 1643 was granted by the Crown eleven hundred seventy-three acres of land near the Powhatan swamp. In the center of the swamp Chief Powhatan constructed a formidable fort, in the early days of Jamestown, and it is said to be in good condition still today. Across the swamp from Powhatan is the site of Green Spring.

The mansion at Powhatan is 54 x 34 feet, and is of brick laid in Flemish bond; the house is three stories high. The two immense chimneys are sixty feet high and are triangular in shape. There is a full basement with hand hewn beams overhead which are more than a foot square. The rooms have ceilings twelve feet high, and the brick walls are twenty-six inches thick in the basement, twenty-two inches in the first floor level, and eighteen inches in the second floor level. Oyster shell, which makes very durable mortar, was used in building the walls.

The continuous line of ownership, owing to loss of records, would be hard to establish. Mrs. Emily Blayton Major, who is a great-granddaughter-in-law of Dr. and Mrs. William Martin, says the Martins owned and lived at Powhatan during the Civil War. The Federals under McClellan took possession of the mansion, and while the soldiers were milling around, Mrs. Martin calmly packed a cartload of her belongings and "drove away to a place of safety." McClellan's men fired the house, which was badly damaged.

After the war the neighbors helped Dr. Martin repair the damage. Hand-rived cypress shingles, from trees in the swamp, were used for the roof, but the third story with the dormer windows was not rebuilt at that time. Dr. Martin must have owned the place a little over sixty years. He died near the turn of the century.

The plantation after that changed hands two or three times, but in 1903 Mr. Edward M. Slauson, from Iowa, bought the property. He repaired it during the next two or three years, but in the 1940's, under the direction of expert mechanics and qualified architects, a complete job of restoration was effected. The interior was made perfect, the roof was raised and the dormers set in, restoring the third story. The grounds were landscaped.

CARTER'S GROVE

WHEN Elizabeth Carter, daughter of Robert ("King") Carter, of Corotoman, was married to Nathaniel Burwell, of Carter's Creek, in 1690, her father gave her as a wedding gift a vast tract of land on the James, about five miles below Williamsburg.

The down-river wing of the mansion was built the year of the marriage, and the other wing, five to ten years later. Nathaniel Burwell died in 1721. His son, Carter Burwell, built the main building at Carter's Grove within the next ten years. The glazed blue and red bricks were burned on the plantation, and the wood for paneling, sills, floors, casings, etc., was cut on the place.

David Minitree, of England, was the architect for the house. His fee was one hundred fifteen pounds. He not only designed the building but also superintended its construction, which was carried out by slave labor. The entire cost of the house was

Carter's Grove, a magnificent Georgian colonial mansion, built by "King"
Carter's grandson, Carter Burwell, in 1751.

five hundred pounds. The construction work was started in June and the house was completed in September.

One remarkable thing about Carter's Grove is that the pilasters and the pediments of the front doors are made of brick instead of stone or wood.

Carter's Grove is considered one of the most perfect examples of Georgian architecture in America. Many people are convinced that it is the most beautiful house in America. The wings are perfectly balanced, and the six chimneys and the array of windows on both fronts make it an impressive structure. The center building is three stories high above the basement, and passages and wings are one and a half stories high. The first floor level has six windows on each front, the second has seven on each front, and the third is lighted by five dormers on each front and two dormers set in each end of the hipped roof. The passages have three dormers each on each front, and the wings the same. The floor level of the passages and wings is below that of the main building. Two massive chimneys rise from the apexes of the main roof, and each wing has a chimney at each end. Modillions and dentils decorate the handsome cornice. The pine paneling throughout the house is superb; authorities declare that there is none superior to it in America.

The house at Carter's Grove is two hundred feet long, and the walls are ivy-grown. The trees on the grounds are locusts, cedars, and poplars, and are of magnificent size.

It was in the drawing room at Carter's Grove that George Washington proposed to Mary Cary—and she refused him. There is an interesting story to the effect that years later Mary Cary watched the triumphant Continental Army enter Williamsburg after the Yorktown surrender. When she beheld her rejected suitor heading so much glory, she was overcome with chagrin and fainted in her husband's arms.

In the same drawing room at Carter's Grove Thomas Jefferson offered his hand to the "fair Belinda," Rebecca Burwell. He, too, was rejected.

During the Revolution Tarleton's men left sabre gashes in the balustrade of the stairs.

After Carter's Grove passed from the Burwell family, it changed ownership several times. It was owned by Dr. Edwin Booth for many years. It was restored by Percival Bisland in 1908. In 1927 Mr. and Mrs. Archibald McCrae acquired the property. Under their ownership the gardens were restored and the house has been redecorated. Now it is more beautiful than ever.

THE THOMAS ROLFE HOUSE

ACROSS the river from Jamestown, about two and a half miles from Scotland Wharf in Surry County, is the Thomas Rolfe House. A hundred and fifty acres was the "guift" to John Rolfe from the "Indyan King," Powhatan, who was his father-in-law. Here Thomas Warren, a member of the first House of Burgesses, built a neat little red brick house in 1652 for Thomas Rolfe, grandson of Powhatan. Rolfe had returned to Virginia in 1635 from England. He engaged in raising tobacco. He married Jane Poythress and had one daughter, Jane Rolfe.

The Rolfe house is fifty feet long and has massive end chimneys. A story and a half in height, the house has a full basement, three dormer windows set in the roof and two good-sized rooms downstairs and two upstairs, with a stair hall on each floor. Closets flank the fireplaces in all four rooms. The paneling, the balusters, the arched cupboards and pilasters, all have a remarkably simple beauty.

John Smith had built what is called "Smiths Fort" along Gray's Creek, facing Jamestown. Its earthworks on a high slope back of the Rolfe House, are still discernible. There is an underground passage running from the Rolfe house to the Fort.

In 1928 Mr. John D. Rockefeller, Jr., purchased the property and presented it to the Association for the Preservation of Virginia Antiquities. Beginning in 1934 a thorough and complete reclamation and restoration began, carried out under the supervision of the Committee of the Thomas Rolfe Branch of the Association for the Preservation of Virginia Antiquities and the Williamsburg Restoration. The Garden

Thomas Rolfe House, in Surry County, home of Pocahontas' son, Thomas Rolfe.

Club of Virginia has restored and replanted the garden. The Rolfe House is open to the public.

BACON'S CASTLE

THE Jacobean brick mansion known as Bacon's Castle, in Surry County, was built in 1655 by Arthur Allen, who came to America in 1649. It has unique curvilinear gables, cluster chimneys, steep roof, and walls two feet thick. The bricks are laid in Flemish bond, and there is austere dignity in the old structure. The design of the house is cruciform, unlike any other houses in America, except Christ's Cross (Criss Cross) in New Kent County, and the now vanished house at Malvern Hill, in Henrico County. Bacon's Castle has an entrance tower at the front and stair tower at the back. The paneling, doors, mantels, wainscot and oaken beams in the ceiling all bespeak the restrained simplicity of the period in which the structure was erected. There is a

150

Tudor dungeon and an attic with port holes for guns. A wing and porches have been added.

The estate has an unusually interesting growth of magnolias, cedars, lindens and elms.

The place was originally called Allen's Brick House, but during Bacon's Rebellion it was seized by a group of Bacon's followers under Major William Rookings, Lieutenant Robert Burgess and Captain Arthur Long, and fortifications were thrown up. Ever since, this house has been called Bacon's Castle.

After the Rebellion Governor Berkeley meted out cruel punishment to the leaders as well as to the seventy men who held the fort. Rookings was sentenced to hang, but died in prison.

Major Arthur Allen, son of the immigrant, inherited the estate of his father in 1670, and in turn left it to his son, Arthur Allen, in 1710. James Allen next inherited the property, and his sister, Katherine, who was married to Benjamin Cocke, was the fifth owner. After the Cockes there was a succession of owners, among whom were the

Bacon's Castle, in Surry County, built about 1653, was a rebel stronghold during Bacon's Rebellion.

Hankins family, the Berrymans and the Briggs. After William A. Warren acquired the property he gave it as a wedding gift to his son, Charles W. Warren, who married Miss Pegram. It has remained in their family for more than a century.

There are a legend and a ghost story connected with Bacon's Castle:

Tradition says that Arthur Allen, instead of being the English commoner records show him to have been, was actually a Prince of the House of Hanover who loved the same girl his twin brother loved. When he found that the lady returned the love of his brother rather than his own, he stabbed the successful suitor, came to Virginia under an assumed name, built Bacon's Castle, married, and raised a family.

The ghost story has been told many times. In fact, the ghost has been seen by many people. Not, however, by anyone we personally interviewed. But we have spoken with people who insist that they have talked with people who have heard of people who have seen the ghost. At any rate, the ghost's existence is stoutly vouched for in the vicinity.

It appears as a ball of fire, or a halo of light, and moves about on certain nights, during a certain phase of the moon, and at certain times of the year. It appears in or near the ruined garden at the Castle, and passes on to the burial ground at the ruins of Old Lawne's Creek Church, where secret meetings used to be held in the interest of liberty and the pursuit of happiness long before those beautiful words were penned by America's great patriot, Thomas Jefferson.

CHIPPOKES

A survey of land consisting of sixteen hundred acres, on the south side of the James, in what is now Surry County, was granted in two sections. The first section, or eight hundred acres, was granted to Captain William Powell, who came to Virginia in 1611, served in the first House of Burgesses, and was massacred by the Indians in 1622. His son, George, inherited the plantation and leased three hundred acres to Stephen Webb in 1642. Stephen Webb promised to build on the land "one good and sufficient framed house, under pinned with bricks, containing forty-five feet in length, and twenty feet in breadth, with two chimneys and glased windows to the same."

The price mentioned is "forty pounds" of current English money. The land which bordered on "Chipoakes Creeke," was to be held by the Webbs during the life of Stephen Webb, his wife, Dame Clare, and their step "sonne," Robert Webb. The rent to be paid later was one capon on the feast day of St. Thomas the Apostle, "if the same be lawfully demanded."

After the death of George Powell, the Chippokes property reverted to the Crown, and when Berkeley was Governor he was granted not only the half of the above-mentioned survey, the eight hundred acres not included in the grant to Powell, but he also received a grant for the Powell acreage. After his death Lady Berkeley and her third husband, Philip Ludwell, spent much time here. The property remained in the Ludwell family many years, during which time the house was much enlarged.

It is a clapboard house, with four huge end chimneys; an English basement;

dormers on both sides of the roof; front and back porches with high steps; mortised windows, and beaded weatherboards.

Chippokes (spelled six different ways) has belonged to several different families since passing from the Ludwell-Paradise family. Mr. Albert Carroll Jones owned the property, and built a brick mansion nearby in the middle nineteenth century. Since then it was for many years the home of Mr. and Mrs. Victor W. Stewart.

At Chippokes there are some handsome box, fine crêpe myrtles, large old mulberry trees and junipers.

FOUR MILE TREE

ON the south side of the James, in Surry County just across the river from Jamestown, is Four Mile Tree. This point originally marked the western corporate limits of Jamestown.

John Burrows married the widow of the Reverend Richard Buck, the clergyman who officiated at the marriage of Pocahontas and John Rolfe. In 1624 Burrows patented one hundred fifty acres at Four Mile Tree, but he called the place Burrows Hill. Mr. Burrows (before or during 1628) sold the land to one John Smith, who changed the name to Smith's Mount. The one hundred fifty acres later became the property of Captain Henry Browne, who in 1637 patented twenty-two hundred fifty acres, and soon after acquired nine hundred acres more. Part of this total acreage had been included in the Richard Pace Grant, dated 1620, of six hundred acres known as Pace's Paines. About the middle of the seventeenth century Colonel George Jordan purchased part of the large Four Mile Tree plantation. He was Attorney General of Virginia in 1670. His wife's tombstone in the orchard at Four Mile Tree is the oldest tombstone in Virginia with a legible inscription. The inscription reads:

> Here lyeth buried the body of Aylce Myles daughter of John Myles of Branton neer Herreford Gent: and late wife of Mr. George Jordan in Virginia, who departed this life the 7th of January 1650.

> Reader, her dust is here inclosed
> Who was of witt and grace composed.
> Her life was Vertuoue during health
> But Highly Glorious in her death.

Colonel Jordan requested that he be buried beside his wife "in Major Browne's orchard."

Four Mile Tree remained in the Browne family until the end of the nineteenth century. This family was prominent socially and in public life.

During the War of 1812 the British landed at Four Mile Tree. The captain of the Surry Militia, by hard riding, brought his company from Old Southwark Church and met and defeated the British at the plantation.

During the Civil War Mr. Algernon Graves lived at Four Mile Tree. He was Commonwealth's Attorney for the county, so probably felt some responsibility for the conditions existing at Jamestown at the time. The island was being used as a refuge by many runaway slaves. In going to investigate, Mr. Graves took with him in a boat his own little boy, his friend, Mr. Shriver, and a dependable Negro, Gilbert Wooten.

When they arrived at the island, the Negroes, resentful of this intrusion, met them as they got off the boat, took them to the bridge, lined them up and shot all of them. The three whites died instantly. Wooten, the Negro, who had been shot in the abdomen, pretended to be dead; later, after calling to each of his white friends and finding all dead, he escaped to the marsh, thence to the boat, and crossed the river back to Surry.

Four Mile Tree was fired upon from gun boats during the Civil War. One shell burst inside the house.

The mansion is a story and a half high, has a gambrel roof and five Dutch dormers across the front and the back of the roof. The four huge end chimneys rise high above the roof. There is a high basement and small front porch, and near the gate are the old-fashioned horse blocks from which it was customary for ladies to mount their horses.

The interior of Four Mile Tree is particularly interesting. In one room Dutch cupboards flank the reeded mantel, and the stairway is very lovely with its delicately turned balusters. The wainscot of square panels, the woodwork, the locks, hinges and fireplaces are also all old, which contributes to the house's atmosphere of charming antiquity.

EASTOVER

THE beautiful site of Eastover was part of the original grant of twenty-two hundred fifty acres to Henry Browne, of Four Mile Tree, in 1637. It was later (1657) bought from Browne by George Jordan. It is Colonel Jordan's wife, Aylce, who has the distinction of having the oldest tombstone with legible inscription in Virginia. Her grave is at Four Mile Tree.

The Eastover house is built in three parts, the center part, the oldest section, is a two-story clapboard structure, with decorated cornices at the roof and at second story level. It probably dates from the seventeenth century. The wings were added later, in all likelihood during the ownership of Charles Harrison, son of Benjamin Harrison, of Berkeley. This would mean that they were built before 1785.

The estate of Eastover now includes twenty-five hundred acres, some of which was land patented by Colonel John Flood in 1638. This large estate, varying in acreage from time to time, has been in the possession of many owners. Robert Watkins bought it from Charles Harrison in 1785. John A. Selden, Jr., inherited Eastover in 1843. After that, for some time, it was called Selden's and Selden Hall. It was also known as Goodman's and White's.

The view from Eastover is beautiful beyond description. The mansion is built on a high location, which slopes to wooded ravines on the east and west, while beyond the north front is the river, just below a one-hundred-foot incline, about one hundred fifty

Eastover, on the James.

feet from the house. The mouth of the Chickahominy is directly opposite. James River is very wide here; and the view extends for two or three miles up and down a broad expanse of water. Glimpses of neighboring mansions and gardens are caught between the woodlands, and the shore from Jamestown to Brandon is visible.

Eastover has a small formal box garden, many nice trees and shrubs, and a lovely lawn. There are dependencies, including a story-and-a-half clapboard house with dormer windows.

Mr. and Mrs. Albert Henry Ochsner acquired the plantation some years ago, and they have done a good deal of restoring and improving of the building and grounds.

THE OLD EPISCOPAL GLEBE

THE land on which the Glebe house, in Southwark Parish, was built in (or before) 1724, was willed to the parish by Captain Francis Clements, who died in 1721. The house is of brick, with a chimney at each end, and a Dutch roof sloping down back

155

and front to the second floor level, with Dutch dormers set in. For nearly a hundred and fifty years now, the Glebe has been privately owned, and during the years it has been restored, added to, and transformed into a very attractive farmhouse.

At the time the Glebe was built the Reverend John Cargill was rector of Southwark Parish. He is thought to have been the house's first occupant, and wrote the much quoted letter, to the Bishop of London, during his ministry at Southwark Parish, in which are described the conditions in the churches, and the plight of the families of ministers of Virginia. His letter, in part, reads:

> I have been here sixteen years. My parish is twenty miles in width and one hundred in length being a frontier parish. It has three hundred and ninety four families. The School for Indians is on the borders of my Parish. There are one church and two chapels, and seventy or eighty communicants. My tobacco now sells for five shillings per hundred. My salary from thirty to forty pounds. My Glebe is in a very bad condition and the Parish will not repair it, so I must look elsewhere. No school, no library in the Parish. What books I have are of my own purchase. Your Lordship will very naturally be lead to believe that I labor under difficulties for want of Books, when you observe that my salary is such a poor allowance for the maintenance of my family. If your Lordship would please to find out in your wisdom some way to extricate me from these difficulties and thereby enable me to be more serviceable in my functions, it shall with the most grateful sense of obligation be ever acknowledged by him who now craves the blessing and is in all duty—Your Lordships most obedient son and servant—John Cargill.

MOUNT PLEASANT

THIS old brick mansion, painted white, with massive walls, laid in Flemish bond, and great chimneys, was built in 1750. It has ten rooms and a basement. The house was at one time destroyed by a fire, but was rebuilt within the sturdy old walls.

Part of the land in the Mount Pleasant plantation was included in the grant of six hundred acres to Richard Pace and his wife, Isabella, in 1620, and was known as Pace's Paines.

On the night before Good Friday, March 22, 1622, two Indians who lived with the Paces were "lying in the House of Pace." Chanco, who was treated as a son by Pace, and had become a Christian, was urged by his brother to rise up and "to kill Pace, as he should doe Perry, which was his friend being so commanded from their King" (Opechancanough).

But Chanco, deciding he could not kill the kind friend who had done so much for him, disclosed the horrible plot to Pace. Pace locked up his home and while it was still night hurried in his boat to Jamestown to inform the Governor of what the Indians planned. Word was sent out immediately to the different settlements, warning all the colonists who could be reached and many of them were accordingly saved. Chanco has ever since been a beloved hero in Virginia.

156

The site of the house is on a high hill, from which there is a magnificent view of the river and surrounding country. There are fine old trees and box at Mount Pleasant.

The Coke family, which for many years made Mount Pleasant its home, has given the State distinguished citizens in every generation, and Coke descendants in other mansions of Virginia have continued this fine record.

Some years ago the Franz Von Schillings bought Mount Pleasant and have done a beautiful job of restoring the house and garden.

PLEASANT POINT

ACROSS the river from Jamestown is Pleasant Point, the old home of the Edwards family. William Edwards was granted, by patent, in September 1657, this plantation of "490 acres of Land, marsh & swamp, be it more or less, on the south side of James river"—etc. William Edwards was Clerk of the Council, and of Surry County. He left the place to his son, William Edwards II.

Mount Pleasant, where, in 1622, an Indian plot to massacre the settlers was discovered.

The situation of Pleasant Point is one of great beauty. The elevation on which it stands is terraced in wide steps descending almost to the river's edge; the view is entrancing. The huge gnarled mulberry trees, and the old crêpe myrtles, as well as the ancient pecan trees and old boxwood, bear mute witness to the antiquity of this fine old house.

The dependencies are interesting, especially a smokehouse and one of the kitchens.

The house itself is of early American or Colonial architecture, with emphasis on "early," for it is one of the oldest houses in Surry County. There are end chimneys and a small front porch. The ends of the house are of brick, but the front and back are of clapboard painted white. Three dormer windows are set in each side of the roof, and there are also gable windows. The windows have twelve panes to the sash. The original hinges and locks are still used throughout the house. There is an English basement, with stone floor, large fireplace, and hand-hewn beams. The staircase is handsome, with delicately turned balusters, and a fine handrail. The mantels are hand-carved, and the floorboards are eight inches wide.

During the Civil War there was a Confederate signal station near Pleasant Point, which operated directly to Hog Island by means of flags by day and turpentine lamps by night. The messages would then be relayed to Richmond every hour.

The wharf at Pleasant Point was a busy place in the old days; planters from nearby plantations in Surry and other counties used it for shipping and receiving.

Pleasant Point remained in the possession of the Edwards family until 1812. Since then it has had a succession of owners. While the estate was in the possession of Willis Morrison, he made a collection of interesting relics unearthed about the place. During Mr. Willis Bohannon's ownership the house was restored. Pleasant Point now belongs to Mr. Robert M. Hazelwood.

SWANN'S POINT

EARLY records show that Francis Chapman owned acreage at Swann's Point in the 1620's. His father-in-law, William Perry, "Gent," had possession or "tenure and occupation," in 1628, and by 1632 the property was called "Perryes Poynt." It was represented jointly with Smythes Mount in the House of Burgesses by Mr. John Smyth.

In 1635 William Swann patented twelve hundred acres here, the patent being given in consideration of his transporting twenty-four persons into the colony. Col. Thomas Swann, the son of William Swann, re-patented the same land when his father's patent had lapsed.

It was this Colonel Swann who was a member of the Council and entertained the King's Commissioners, Sir John Berry, (Admiral of the fleet which they brought over,) Colonel Herbert Jeffreys (who succeeded Sir William Berkeley as Governor of Virginia,) and Colonel Francis Moryson. The Commissioners were conciliatory, and their attitude at this time no doubt postponed the coming of the Revolution for many decades. It was Colonel Swann's kindness to these men that no doubt saved his neck. He had been in sympathy with Bacon, and was excluded from the Council,

Front of Pleasant Point, facing the James.

Parlor at Pleasant Point.

and "excepted from the Kings pardon" by Berkeley—but was forgiven by His Majesty on account of his hospitality and courtesy to his Commissioners. Colonel Thomas Swann's son, Samuel, married the daughter of William Drummond, who was hanged for participating in Bacon's Rebellion.

At Swann's Point is an old burial ground where, according to the records, as many as thirteen people of the Swann family are buried. They are William Swann, and his wife Judith, the father and mother of Colonel Thomas Swann, the Colonel, himself, at his father's feet, and the daughter-in-law who was Miss Drummond, "at Swann's Point at her own Mother's feet." Colonel Swann's tombstone, the only one in this cemetery, bears his coat of arms.

Colonel Thomas Swann was married five times. No doubt the five wives are buried here also "in a field near the river."

Major Samuel Swann emigrated to North Carolina, where he became Speaker of the General Assembly of that state.

The view from Swann's Point extends for miles on both sides of the river. The trees and gardens are fine and luxuriant, for the soil seems adapted to the growth of good specimens. The grounds are landscaped all the way to the river, and, the estate, while impressively ancient, is well preserved and well kept. There are two thousand acres in the plantation.

The mansion itself, one of the handsomest on the river, is modern. It is of clapboard construction, with two-story portico on the front, and has beautiful woodwork throughout.

Swann's Point was owned for some years by the Strotz family, of Chicago. After that it was for some years the country home of Senator and Mrs. Garland Gray, of Waverly. It now belongs to Mr. Robert M. Hazelwood of Toano.

WAKEFIELD

WAKEFIELD, in Surry County, on the James (not to be confused with Wakefield, birthplace of George Washington), is the oldest of the many Harrison homes in Virginia. Benjamin Harrison I acquired large acreage here in 1635. His various distinguished descendants have been Burgesses and Speakers in the House of Burgesses, and among them were a Signer of the Declaration of Independence, a Governor of Virginia, a General in the Revolution, a Secretary of the King's Council, an Auditor General, a Treasurer, and two Presidents of the United States.

Benedict Arnold burned Wakefield during the Revolution.

In the 1940's the J. Roland Rookes, of Richmond, bought Wakefield, and after much study of foundations and inventories, built a home there which might justifiably be called a restoration of the original house. He also enlarged the gardens. The original bricks were used for walks in the gardens.

This house of Wakefield, which borders on the river and has such a lovely setting, and which has been restored with such studious good taste, has a special appeal not only through its beauty, but also through its memories, and its rich historic past.

Swann's Point.

*Hall and dining room
at Swann's Point.*

CLAREMONT

CLAREMONT on the James, in Surry County, Virginia, is a replica of Claremont in Surrey, England, where Queen Victoria was born.

The first colonists visited the site of Claremont on May 5, 1607, which was before the settlement at Jamestown. At that time it was the seat of the Quioughcohanock Indians, who performed a rather special type of ceremonial. Captain John Smith describes these ceremonials, or celebrations, in his early Virginia History.

Arthur Allen patented a vast tract of land here in 1649, but it is not known just when the house was built. The same Arthur Allen built Bacon's Castle in 1655, and it is almost certain that it was he who built Claremont. The Allens held Claremont for more than two centuries, until the 1880's, and were a distinguished clan. John was a member of the House of Delegates, 1704-1788, and 1791, of the convention of 1788, and the Privy Council in 1799. Col. William Allen was Commander of the 71st Virginia Regiment in the War of 1812.

Major William Allen, of Confederate fame, changed his name from Orgain to Allen in order to inherit the property of his uncle, William Allen. Nevertheless, the major was a descendant of Arthur Allen on his mother's side. He was said to have been the largest landowner and the largest slaveholder in Virginia.

Major Allen had a railroad at Claremont, the rails of which were used to plate the ironclad *Merrimac*. He organized, uniformed and equipped a company of heavy artillery at his personal expense.

Claremont has been visited by many distinguished people. Edward VII, when he was Prince of Wales, was a guest here. Edgar Allan Poe, who lived in Richmond, is said to have visited at Claremont.

Part of the seventeenth-century house is left, but it was rebuilt and added to in 1717. From time to time changes and additions have been made. In this century the late General and Mrs. William Horner Cocke purchased the estate from Mr. and Mrs. Meredith A. Johnston and restored the lovely old house and the garden.

The house is of brick, and is T-shaped and a story and a half high, and has an English basement, dormer windows and clipped gables. The chimneys are interesting and numerous, rising high above the roof. The cornices are decorated with applied dentils. The one entrance has a porch in the Classic Greek Revival style. The door at the other entrance has a pedimented head.

The interior is sumptuously decorated. The two halls open into each other, and the drawing room and library flank the entrance hall. The staircase is unusually handsome, with balustrade and newels on both sides of the first four steps, which extend out in the hall. Door heads and frames are elaborate. All the mantels are decoratively carved and the floors are of very wide boards.

There is a large dining room adjoining the center hall, but the original dining room or banquet hall, is in the basement. It is 19 x 25 feet.

The dependencies, consisting of weaving house, bakehouse, large smokehouse, small smokehouse, and the office, are all very old. The office is a small four-story building.

The trees, the most prominent of which are lindens and magnolias, are impressively large and ancient. There are roses, dwarf box, bulbs and shrubs of various kinds in the garden, besides a profusion of perennial and annual flowers.

The view, like that from other river houses, is wonderful. Jamestown Island, Brandon and other estates are in sight, and the broad expanse of the river at the mouth of the Chickahominy stretches out in the distance for two or three miles.

In recent years Claremont has been the home of Mr. and Mrs. Ronald Balcom. It is now the property of Mr. and Mrs. James Walton Carter.

RICH NECK

IN 1685 a grant of twenty-two hundred fifty acres in Lawne's Creek Parish, on the College Creek of the Sunken Marsh, was received by Robert Ruffin son of William Ruffin, of the Isle of Wight. This home of the Ruffins is called Rich Neck, and the present house must have been built early in the eighteenth century.

The old brick mansion is large and impressive, and has miraculously escaped the hazards of fire and war. There are many windows, very tall chimneys (two at each end) and a high English basement. The porch is high, and is supported by four round brick columns. The doors bear the Cross and Bible. All the woodwork, including the lovely mantels with fluted pilasters, seem to be originals.

The burial ground is nearby.

Since Rich Neck passed from the Ruffin family, it has been owned by (among others) Mr. Walker Pegram Warren.

MONTPELIER

THE unique old house called Montpelier in Surry is the second house at the site, and is built on land inherited by Benjamin Harrison II in 1657 from his father, Benjamin Harrison I, who received a grant of land here from the King in 1632.

Montpelier (which had the same name as James Madison's more famous residence in Orange County) is located on the Cabin Point Road, which in olden days was a main thoroughfare to and from the Cabin Point Wharf. Much cotton and tobacco was shipped from this wharf, and all commodities used by the colonists of this community were received there.

The foundation of the first house is still discernible, and findings from excavations seem to prove the earlier house was burned.

The present house was built in 1724. It is a story and a half high with dormer windows and gable windows. Here we find chimneys that are twenty feet wide at the base, and have a small door and a small window; there is also a small passageway leading from one room to another. The floors are tongue-and-grooved by hand. The

163

mantels are beautifully hand-carved and reeded, and the original H and L hinges are still on doors and window blinds.

Commodore Harrison H. Cocke, who was an officer in the United States Navy, and later in the Confederate Navy, lived at Montpelier at one time.

For many years now Mr. Robert Lachmond has been owner of the old place.

OTHER HOUSES OF THIS AREA

THERE are many other interesting old homes in this area, some of which deserve mention.

Near Williamsburg, to the west, The Forest now long vanished, was the home of John Wayles, whose daughters were married to Thomas Jefferson and Francis Eppes, Jr., respectively. Belle Farm, on Indian Springs Road, in Williamsburg, was formerly a home in Gloucester. It was torn down and rebuilt on its present site, and is the home of Mr. and Mrs. John L. Lewis. It is described in the first book in this series.*

In Surry, originally a part of James City County, are located the following: Walnut Valley, The Baugh Home, The Taylor Home, Dripping Spring, Blackwater, Paris Holt Farm, Oak View Farm, The Thomas Rogers Home, The Pretlow Home, The Burt Home in Surry, The Miles Ellis Home, The Anchorage, Melville, Cedar Ridge, The Spratley Home, The King Home, Oakland, Cedar Ridge, The Wilson Home, Laurel Spring, The Maynard Home, and The Derring House.

THE WREN BUILDING

THE College of William and Mary in Williamsburg was founded in 1693.

Dr. James Blair went to England in 1691 for the committee on the establishment of a college in the Virginia Colony. He returned in 1693 with a royal charter and a liberal royal endowment. This money was added to the funds which had been carried over from the early seventeenth-century University of Henrico. Nicholas Ferrar, Sr., of London, had contributed in his will the amount of three hundred pounds for the University at Henrico at Farrar's Island, this sum being the first money ever donated to a school of higher learning in the United States. It went into the coffers of William and Mary College. Nicholas Ferrar, Sr., was the father of Nicholas Ferrar, Jr., the scholar and saint of Little Gidding. Mr. Ferrar, Sr., had three other sons: John, a businessman who owned a fleet of ships and several warehouses in London, Richard, a barrister of London, and William, also a barrister of London, who, however, came to Virginia and settled at Farrar's Island in Henrico. (He spelled his name with an "a" instead of an "e.")

For years William and Mary College donated forty-five pounds annually to help support "the infant College of Harvard, in Massachusetts," and forty-five pounds annually "to help propagate the gospel in New England." The new college was named for Their Majesties King William and Queen Mary of England.

* *Old Virginia Houses: the Mobjack Bay County*

The Wren Building, William and Mary College, in Williamsburg, said to have been built from designs by the famous English architect, Sir Christopher Wren. In the foreground is a statue of Lord Botetourt, most beloved Virginia governor.

Chapel in the Wren Building.

Dr. James Blair became the first president of the college. The Reverend William Stith was also an early president.

Located at the west end of Duke of Gloucester Street, in Williamsburg, the main entrance gates of William and Mary face down that street and are between Richmond Road and Jamestown Road. Intersecting this point also, is Boundary Street. Thus the gates are the focal point for five forks of constant traffic. Consisting today of many beautiful modern buildings, spreading back over several blocks of the fine old campus, William and Mary College still stems from, still uses, and more important yet, still takes more pride than ever in the beautiful old Wren Building, the original building that for many years, with the President's House and Brafferton House, was William and Mary College. The Wren Building is the oldest college building still standing in America.

Erected in the last years of the seventeenth century, by 1700 the building was completed, and classes were held there by the Reverend James Blair, who taught

166

Philosophy, Theology, Mathematics, etc. "Grammar classes" were presided over by Mungo Ingles, who was "Grammar Master." That was a broad subject, which included various phases of English Literature, rhetoric and composition, Greek and Latin classics, and even some history. The College soon introduced other subjects.

From the first the Wren Building was also used as a dormitory.

The name of the "Wren Building" was given in honor of the eminent English architect, Sir Christopher Wren, to whom is attributed the credit of designing the lovely old brick structure.

The Reverend Hugh Jones, Professor of Mathematics in 1722, is quoted as saying: "The Building is beautiful and commodious, being first modeled by Sir Christopher Wren, and adapted to the nature of the Country by the Gentlemen there."

The statue of the beloved Lord Botetourt, who had lived as though his motto were "to do Justice, to love mercy, and to walk humbly with thy God," is in front of the Wren Building.

The original structure was erected under the supervision of Thomas Hadley, who was a native of England. Henry Cary II, of Ampthill, directed the building of the southern wing which contained the old chapel. It was completed in 1732. There are several vaults and a grave in the crypt of the chapel. Here rest the remains of Lord Botetourt; of Sir John Randolph; Peyton Randolph and Betty, his wife; John Randolph, Attorney General; Bishop James Madison and his wife; Chancellor Thomas Nelson; and an unknown student.

During the Revolution the French army had officers' quarters here, and the Wren Building was also used as a hospital. During the Civil War the Federals occupied the College of William and Mary.

During the early days of the college George Wythe, the first professor of law in the United States, taught here. Thomas Jefferson, John Marshall, and many other famous Americans were educated at William and Mary.

The Wren Building has been burned down three times, and rebuilt as often, within the same walls. In 1929, through the generosity of Mr. John D. Rockefeller, it was beautifully restored, and made fireproof.

Tablets on the walls list the many priorities of the old college. They are as follows:

PRIORITIES
OF THE COLLEGE OF WILLIAM AND MARY.

Chartered February 8, 1693, by King William and Queen Mary.
Main Building designed by Sir Christopher Wren.

First College in the United States in its antecedents, which go back to the College proposed at Henrico (1619). Second to Harvard University in actual operation.

First American College to receive its charter from the Crown under the Seal of the Privy Council, 1693. Hence it was known as their Majesties' Royal College of William and Mary.

First and ONLY American College to receive a Coat-of-Arms from the College of Heralds, 1694.

First College in the United States to have a full Faculty, consisting of a President, six Professors, usher, and writing master, 1729.

First College to confer medallic prizes: the gold medals donated by Lord Botetourt in 1771.

First College to establish an inter-collegiate fraternity, the Phi Beta Kappa, December 5, 1776.

First College to have the Elective System of study, 1779.

First College to have the Honor System, 1779.

First College to become a University, 1779.

First College to have a school of Modern Languages, 1779.

First College to have a school of Municipal and Constitutional Law, 1779.

First College to teach Political Economy, 1784.

First College to have a School of Modern History, 1803.

> Presented by the Colonial Capital Branch of
> The Association for the
> Preservation of Virginia Antiquities,
> 1914.

THE PRESIDENT'S HOUSE

UPON entering the gates of William and Mary College, the President's House is on the right hand, the Wren Building is straight ahead, and Brafferton House is on the left.

The President's House was built in 1732 by Henry Cary II, of Ampthill. It is a lovely example of Georgian architecture. Although somewhat larger than the Brafferton House (see below), the two buildings balance each other in the plan of the early campus, and resemble each other strikingly.

This three-story brick house has a hipped roof with dormers on all four sides, and two great chimneys rising from the apexes. The projecting cornice is heavy and is decorated with applied dentils, and there is a slightly projecting belt course of brick at the second floor level. The door heads have handsome heavy pediments.

The house was burned during the Revolution (while occupied by the French) and was restored at the personal expense of the King of France. All presidents of the college have made this their home during their respective administrations.

BRAFFERTON HALL

ONE of the three original or earliest buildings at the College of William and Mary, Brafferton Hall, was designed on architectural lines similar to those of the President's House, though it is somewhat smaller. Built by Henry Cary of Ampthill in 1723, this three-story Georgian brick house, with towering chimneys, pedimented door head, pyramid steps and handsome cornice, was the seat of the first permanent Indian school in America.

The Earl of Burlington in his will left four thousand pounds for "pious and charitable uses." The money was invested in the Brafferton estate, in England. Through

The President's House, William and Mary College.

(below) Brafferton Hall, William and Mary College.

the influence of the Reverend James Blair, and through the benevolence of the Honorable Robert Boyle, nephew and executor of the estate of the Earl, the income from this money was paid for the Indian school until the Revolution. After that war Brafferton Hall was used as a dormitory and as an administration building. During the Civil War this and the other buildings were occupied by the Federals, who destroyed or carried away the fine paneling.

Mr. John D. Rockefeller, Jr., has beautifully restored Brafferton Hall and rebuilt the kitchen, which has since been used as an information bureau for the college.

BRUTON PARISH CHURCH

AT the center of Williamsburg, on Duke of Gloucester Street, Bruton Parish Church stands as a fine architectural reminder of the part played by religion in the daily life of colonial Virginia. Bruton Parish was formed in 1674 by merging two earlier parishes. The name was presumably derived from Bruton, County Somerset, England, from which several leading parishioners came, among them Thomas Ludwell, Secretary of Virginia. A new church was ordered built in 1677 on land given by Colonel John Page. Completed in 1683, this small brick church was large enough for a rural parish, but with the removal of the capital from Jamestown to Williamsburg, it soon became inadequate. In 1711-1715 the present church was erected and the General Assembly gave £200 toward the cost of providing space for official pews for the royal governor, councilors and burgesses. Bruton Church, therefore, was not only a parish church, but also the church of the court and government in Virginia.

The present church, completed in 1715, has been in continuous use ever since. Its interior was altered twice in the nineteenth century, but in the twentieth century a restoration on the lines of the original plan was made under the supervision of Dr. W. A. R. Goodwin, rector.

Bruton Parish Church has three sets of colonial communion silver, including the Jamestown silver of 1661. Its baptismal font was brought to Bruton from the last church at Jamestown, and a bell in the tower, given in 1761, is known as Virginia's Liberty Bell, for it rang out the news of the Declaration of Independence, of the surrender of Cornwallis at Yorktown, and the signing of the peace treaty in 1783. The west gallery is original. It was reserved for the use of the students of the College, whose initials, carved in the handrail, are still discernible.

In the church and churchyard are buried two colonial governors, a justice of the Supreme Court, and many others prominent in the church, state, and nation.

THE CAPITOL

THE Colonial Capitol at Williamsburg (built by Henry Cary I), the first State House to be so called in the colonies, was erected in 1701-1705, and stood at the other end of Duke of Gloucester Street from the College. It was a three-story brick, H-shaped building with dormer windows and a four-tiered tower, or cupola, rising from the

Bruton Parish Church, in Williamsburg, in the tower of which hangs Virginia's Liberty Bell.

Interior of Bruton Parish Church.

(above) Front view of the Capitol at Williamsburg. This is a magnificent reconstruction of the original first colonial capitol on the site.

ON FACING PAGE

(above) Chamber of the Burgesses, in the Capitol. The original speaker's chair is at the rear.

(below) The Chamber of the Governor's Council.

172

center of the roof. There were two huge circular bays, one on each side of the front, with conical roofs ascending to peaks. The first floor of these towers was lighted by round windows. The capitol grounds were surrounded by a handsome high brick wall. It was in the Capitol that the General Assembly and General Court met until the seat of government was moved to Richmond in 1779. The present building is a meticulously accurate reconstruction of the original building.

The Association for the Preservation of Virginia Antiquities has recorded some of the important events that took place here, as follows:

THE OLD CAPITOL

Here Patrick Henry first kindled the flames of revolution by his resolutions and speech against the stamp act, May 29-30, 1765.

Here March 12, 1773, Dabney Carr offered, and the House of Burgesses of Virginia unanimously adopted, the resolutions to appoint a committee to correspond with similar committees in other colonies—the first step taken towards the union of the States.

Here May 15, 1776, the convention of Virginia, through resolutions drafted by Edmund Pendleton, offered by Thomas Nelson, Jr., advocated by Patrick Henry, unanimously called on Congress to declare the colonies free and independent States.

Here June 12, 1776, was adopted by the convention the immortal work of George Mason—the Declaration of Rights—and, on June 29, 1776, the first written constitution of a free and independent State ever framed.

THE GOVERNOR'S PALACE

THE Governor's Palace in Williamsburg, facing the long stretch of grass called the Palace Green, is one of the most beautiful and one of the most perfect buildings in the United States. It is the restoration of the Colonial Governor's Palace which was originally built during the first decade of the eighteenth century. It was authorized by the General Assembly in 1705, but it was several years before it was completed. Governor Alexander Spotswood and succeeding Colonial Governors, as well as Patrick Henry and Thomas Jefferson, State Governors, occupied the Palace.

The central building, 68 x 74 feet, is of brick, three stories high, with dormer windows on all four sides of the hipped roof. The four chimneys rise high above the roof, with a two-tiered cupola in the center, and a railing extending around from chimney to chimney forms a roof deck.

The two wings, each a commodious two-story house in itself, with huge end chimneys and dormer windows, flank the main center section, and the entire structure is protected, on the street side, by high brick walls with imposing gateposts.

Besides the Palace itself, there are many dependencies, such as the Office, Guardhouse, Kitchen, Smokehouse and Laundry.

The Green Garden at the Palace is a memorial to Revolutionary War dead buried here. There are ten gardens of different types, that beautify the grounds. The Fish Pond and the Canal are two of the various decorative features of the gardens.

174

The Governor's Palace, also a Williamsburg reconstruction.

(below) Another view of the Palace.

The Palace is built on land originally the grant of Henry Tyler, ancestor of President Tyler. The Palace Farm lay behind the Palace—that is, to the north.

The interior of the Palace is beautiful beyond description. The drawing room, parlors and music room are richly furnished in antiques of the eighteenth century. The woodwork and wall treatment are perfect.

During the Revolution and after, the Palace served as a hospital for wounded soldiers. It was burned soon after the war. The wings were used as private dwellings, but during the Civil War they, too, were burned. For many years a school stood on the Palace grounds. It was called the Mattey School, in memory of a little boy, Matthew (Mattey) Whaley, the only child of James and Mary Whaley, who died when he was nine years old. When preparations were being made for the reconstruction of the Palace and all its dependencies, the school was removed. Little Mattey's name is being perpetuated in the present-day Matthew Whaley School.

The Governor's Palace is visited by thousands of people from all over the country every year. Extensive research was made, plans and descriptions were studied, and inventory lists were consulted, before reconstruction was begun. Everyone seems to agree that the restoration of the Palace was accurate and exact.

THE ST. GEORGE TUCKER HOUSE

PROBABLY the most picturesque house in the beautiful city of Williamsburg, Virginia, is the St. George Tucker House. Of white clapboard, the house is built in five parts. The main section is two stories high, and has a small Queen Anne porch which gives access to the center hall. This section has huge end chimneys and one-and-a-half story wings, with steep roofs and dormer windows. There is a one-story passageway connecting the west wing with another one-and-a-half-story wing. This last section of the house has tiny gable windows up beside the enormous end chimney, also dormer windows, and a front entrance. All the windows have many small panes. The length of the whole building is one hundred twenty-eight feet. Oil paintings, antiques and heirlooms enhance the beauty of the paneling and woodwork of the interior.

The history of this property goes back to 1716, when William Levingston leased three half-acre lots for a period of five hundred years. The property was mortgaged to Archibald Blair; when the mortgage was forfeited, Blair got possession and, when he died, left it with all the improvements (theatre, dwelling, and kitchen—see below), to his son, John Blair. After the theatre had served its purpose for many years, and then had been used as Town Hall and Hustings Court House, it changed hands several times. In 1772 John Tazewell claimed the lease had not been transferable, because Levingston had not left any children. Governor Dunmore agreed with Tazewell, and in his official capacity as Governor, granted to Tazewell the three lots for three pounds of tobacco. Tazewell bought all rights and satisfied the claims of the various owners. He later sold the entire property to William Rowsay, who conveyed it to Edmund Randolph.

The St. George Tucker House, in Williamsburg, on the site of the first theatre in America.

St. George Tucker bought the land from Edmund Randolph on July 3, 1788, and built the house soon after. It is thought by some authorities that the old buildings were incorporated into the lovely later residence.

Mr. Tucker was a very prominent and distinguished gentleman of his day and age. He studied law under George Wythe, the first professor of law in America, and himself became the second professor of law at the College of William and Mary. He was the first professor of law to write a book of law, and has been called the American Blackstone.

St. George Tucker married Frances Bland Randolph and raised her son, John Randolph, of Roanoke. Many think the greatness of the latter was partly attributable to the teaching and example of his illustrious step-father.

Mr. Tucker's own son, Henry St. George Tucker, became president of the Virginia Supreme Court. Nathaniel Beverley Tucker, another son, taught at the College of William and Mary. A great-grandson of St. George Tucker, the Honorable George P. Coleman, and his family have lived for many years in the beautiful old home.

177

SITE OF THE FIRST THEATRE IN AMERICA

FACING the Palace Green, on the lawn of what is now the St. George Tucker House in Williamsburg, stood the first theatre in America. Built by William Levingston, a New Kent merchant, in 1716, the building was used as a theatre until 1745, although it must be confessed the show business did not flourish all that time.

As soon as Levingston had leased from the Trustees of the City of Williamsburg three half-acre lots for a period of five hundred years (see above), he engaged Charles Stagg and Mary Stagg, his wife, to conduct a theatre here. Stagg was a dancing teacher, and it is supposed that he and his wife were a dancing team. The theatre was kept open until Stagg's death in 1735-36.

A number of prominent citizens subscribed to a fund to "underwrite" the theatrical venture, but Levingston mortgaged the property with Archibald Blair as financier. At Blair's death his son, John Blair, became executor of his father's estate, and sold the right and title of the property (which consisted of the theatre, a dwelling house, a kitchen and a bowling green) to George Gilmer for one hundred fifty-five pounds. Gilmer sold the Play House to the city of Williamsburg for a "Town House," for fifty pounds. The "gentlemen subscribers" donated their equity to the City. The deed for the property called for "the ground on which the theatre was built with six feet around it." Repairs were made, and the building was used first as a "Common Hall," then as Hustings Court House, until 1770, when the James City County-Williamsburg Court House was built on Market Square Green.

Soon after this, the old theatre is thought to have been incorporated in the St. George Tucker House.

THE FIRST PRINTING OFFICE IN THE SOUTH

THE Virginia Gazette, the first newspaper to publish the entire Declaration of Independence, began publication in Williamsburg, Virginia, in 1736. William Parks, who was in the printing business in Annapolis, Maryland, moved to Williamsburg and set up the first printing office in the South in 1730. It was located on Duke of Gloucester Street on Lot No. 48, just east of the Apothecary Shop. It was Parks who established the Virginia Gazette—which continued to be published here until 1780, after which it was published in Richmond.

Besides publishing the Gazette, Mr. Parks did custom printing here. He printed two editions of Stith's History of Virginia, and The Laws of Virginia. For the latter the General Assembly paid him one hundred twenty pounds in 1732; two hundred pounds in 1738; and two hundred thirty pounds in 1744. After that they paid him an annual salary of two hundred eighty pounds until he died, which was in 1750.

Later on William Hunter did custom printing in this old first printing office.

After being used as a post office, also a bookshop, the historic little building burned down in 1896. The Printing Office has been reconstructed.

RALEIGH TAVERN

THE original Raleigh Tavern was built prior to 1735. It was used as an "Ordinary," later as a tavern and finally as a dwelling.

This clapboard two-story structure had four massive chimneys, and twelve picturesque dormer windows extending across the front, with seven along the side. This side wing extends back from the front section at right angles to the latter.

In 1742 the tavern was owned by John Blair, who sold it to a company which employed Henry Wetherburn to operate it. He lived in the Richard Bland House, which was nearby, and kept the tavern for years. There was a long succession of owners over a period of years. These included John Dixon and Company, Alexander Finnie, John Chiswell and George Gilmer, William Trebell, Anthony Hay and James Barrett Southall.

Many famous guests visited the tavern, and patriotic meetings as well as social assemblies were held in it. Here, in the Apollo Room, some of the most brilliant men in American history met and discussed important matters. When Lord Dunmore dissolved the House of Burgesses, in 1774, to prevent enactment of further laws to promote the cause of liberty, it immediately reconvened in secret at the Raleigh Tavern. In the Apollo Room the Phi Beta Kappa Society was organized by students of William and Mary College.

The old building burned in 1859. After much study and research, Colonial Williamsburg, Incorporated, in 1930, erected a meticulously perfect reproduction of the famous original building. Following still extant inventories, the furniture and other appointments have been faithfully replaced.

ST. LUKE'S CHURCH

ST. LUKE'S CHURCH, in Isle of Wight County, for many years was called "Old Brick Church." It was built in 1632, and is massive Gothic in style like the ruins of the church tower at Jamestown. St. Luke's is the oldest brick Protestant church in America.

The windows are round-arched, and there are four on each side. The roof is very steep, and an imposing square tower stands in front of the nave of the church. The tower has a low, round-arched entrance, and above, in the second section of the tower, there are three round-arched windows. In the third and top section of the tower, the three round-arched openings are latticed, and not glassed in. The three stages of the tower are divided by string courses of brick.

The church was neglected from 1777 until 1821. Then in 1830 it was abandoned. In 1887 a great storm struck and partially wrecked the building. In 1890 restoration began. Today St. Luke's is as beautiful as it was when newly built.

(above) Raleigh Tavern, in Williamsburg, where the House of Burgesses convened in 1769, after Governor Dunmore had locked them out of the Capitol.

ON FACING PAGE

(above) Bar of the Raleigh Tavern. At the left is a vending box which, on insertion of a coin, dispensed tobacco.

(below) Dining room of the Raleigh Tavern.

180

Parlor in the Raleigh Tavern.

GEORGE WYTHE'S BIRTHPLACE

IN Elizabeth City County, a few miles north of Hampton, on Harris's Creek, is the small brick house in which was born, in 1726, George Wythe, one of Virginia's most illustrious sons. The house has a "shed room" or "lean-to," which has dormer windows.

George Wythe was not only the first professor of law in America, but he was also the first of the Virginia delegation in the Continental Congress to sign the Declaration of Independence. The beautiful and significant Virginia State seal, with its motto, "Sic Semper Tyrannis," was designed and inscribed by George Wythe.

THE OLDEST FREE SCHOOL IN AMERICA

IN a school building on Locust Street in Hampton is a brass tablet with the following inscription:

> Benjamin Sims, Founder of the First Free School in the American Colonies, 1634. Who devised two hundred acres of land on Poquoson River with the milk and increase of eight cows for the maintenance of a learned and honest man to keep upon the said grounds a free school.
>
> Thomas Eaton, Donor of five hundred acres of land on Back River with other properties for the support of a free school and able school master to educate and teach the children born within Elizabeth City County, 1659. The two schools were united on this site as the Hampton Academy by Act of Assembly, 1805.

POPLAR HALL

IN 1640, in a grant from the Crown, the Hoggard family gained possession of the site of Poplar Hall. Of this property there has never been a transfer. It has never been sold, only "willed" and inherited. Once in the remote country, on an eminence near the shore of Broad Creek, which is a tributary of Elizabeth River, Poplar Hall, though still on the same spot, now stands almost in the heart of Norfolk.

This fine old house of red brick is in the heavy, simple style of architecture, and has the old mellow look that seventeenth-century buildings invariably show. The end chimneys are thick and tall, and the small front porch gives access to the front door.

Standing two full stories above a basement, the front has a row of five windows at second-story level, these balancing the row of two windows, porch, and two more windows at the first-story level. The interior woodwork is lovely and attractive, but its simplicity is typical of the earlier houses.

Poplar Hall has some interesting dependencies. These, too, bear out the seventeenth-century feeling of the house. Members of the family think the house and the dependencies were built about 1645 to 1650.

The garden at Poplar Hall is very charming, the dominant feature being an enormous Persian lilac. The old plan of a large central square of flower-beds still prevails

(above) Belle Farm. This old home was moved from Gloucester County and rebuilt at Williamsburg. The building materials were stored for a quarter of a century between the demolition and the reconstruction. (See Old Virginia Houses: The Mobjack Bay Country, *p. 149).*

ON FACING PAGE

(above) Hall at Belle Farm.

(below) Dining room at Belle Farm.

184

(above) *Parlor at Belle Farm.*

ON FACING PAGE

(above) *St. Luke's Church, Isle of Wight, oldest brick Protestant Church in America.*

(below) *St. Paul's Church, one of the few Norfolk buildings not entirely destroyed by the British during the Revolution.*

186

here, and the long narrow borders at the sides are continued, too. There are many old roses, the very names of which evoke nostalgic memories. The lily of the valley is of prodigious growth, and has become naturalized in almost tropical luxuriance. There are many other old-fashioned flowers here. One item of interest is a spirea that was planted on the day that Lee surrendered.

The name of the place, Poplar Hall, derived from the many fine, tall poplars growing on the estate. They were reputed to have been imported, but the poplars native to Virginia also grow to enormous height and girth. Be that as it may, the poplars are all gone from around Poplar Hall, and a grove of fine pecan trees has replaced them.

Fire has not touched Poplar Hall, and through all the wars Virginia has experienced, the old mansion has passed almost unscathed. However, in 1812, some of the closet doors upstairs were scarred by the British breaking the locks. Then also, during the same war, three privateers, belonging to the Hoggard family, which were being built at the river, were burned.

THE MYERS HOUSE

BUILT in 1791, the Myers House is perhaps the best example of later Georgian architecture in Norfolk. The builder, Moses Myers, was a wealthy merchant and a prominent ship owner. In 1828 President John Quincy Adams appointed him Collector of Customs for the port of Norfolk.

Five generations of the Myers family have lived in the Myers House, and they always made it a notable center of hospitality. Henry Clay was a guest here during the Presidential campaign of 1844. General Winfield Scott visited here in 1850. In April, 1907, Teddy Roosevelt, President of the United States, his cabinet members and the British Ambassador, James Bryce, and their wives, were entertained in the Myers House at the opening of the Jamestown Exposition.

There is a lovely display of art in the Myers House. A portrait of John Myers, by Thomas Sully, hangs over the fireplace in the parlor. Portraits of Mr. and Mrs. Moses Myers, by Gilbert Stuart, are in the dining room. The original Adam mantels remain in the library and parlor, and the house is furnished with fine family antiques.

On the outside, the building shows considerable resemblance to the Marshall House in Richmond, but it is somewhat more ornate. There is a white masonry belt around the wall at second floor level. The cornice has dentils, the tops of the windows have heavy, rather elaborate white masonry insets, and while the porches are not very large, they are quite formal in design. The chimneys are very massive.

The Myers House has been a museum for some years.

BROAD BAY MANOR

IN the beautiful farming area of Princess Anne County, we find charming Broad Bay Manor. The land was patented in 1636 by Thomas Allen. He is credited with building the gambrel-roofed house still standing here, which has inside chimneys and large fireplaces, one at each end. At the west end an outside stairway leads to the upper story. He also built a small steep-roofed building here.

The main mansion, of Georgian architecture, stands two stories and a half high with very high ceilings. It is of brick in Flemish bond, and has two inside chimneys in the north end. The stairway is lovely, and the windows are deeply recessed. This house was built by Lemuel Cornick I, soon after he acquired the property in 1770. It is linked to a more modern wing by a tiny, one-room, steep-roofed stucture, probably also built by Allen who was responsible for the gambrel-roofed house described above.

Fine old boxwoods grow on both fronts, one of which faces Broad Bay.

The Cornick family held possession of Broad Bay Manor from 1770 to 1854. Mr. and Mrs. John B. Dey purchased the property in 1916, and made many improvements and additions.

LAWSON HALL

ONLY the garden and the foundation, laid in 1688, of Lawson Hall can claim great antiquity. The garden is said to have been one of the first formal gardens in Virginia.

A crown grant was made to Thomas Lawson, in the early seventeenth century, for land not far from the present city of Norfolk, and near Lynnhaven Bay. Col. Anthony Lawson lived at Lawson Hall during the Revolution. He was captured by Lord Dunmore, personally, during his (Dunmore's) depredations in the vicinity of Norfolk.

The original house was destroyed by fire near the turn of the century. The present mansion, larger and more commodious than the original, was built by Mr. C. F. Hodgman, who showed good taste and fine feeling in carrying out a partial restoration, at any rate, when building the later house.

The magnificent oaks, laurels and beeches at Lawson Hall are among the finest trees of Virginia. The garden, beginning at the terrace, is bordered with boxtrees.

When Mr. Hodgman gave the boxwood at Lawson Hall its first clipping in many years, although the clipping hardly showed, nevertheless, so great was the mass of the boxwood that the branches cut away weighed thirteen hundred pounds.

ADAM THOROUGHGOOD HOUSE

THE beautiful country around the Lynnhaven Farm House, known as the Adam Thoroughgood House, is a fitting setting for this ancient home.

In 1621 Adam Thoroughgood came to Virginia from Lynn, in Norfolk County, England. He first settled at Kecoughtan, now Hampton, and was prominent in the life of the Colony. He was a member of the King's Council, under Governor John

Adam Thoroughgood House, near Norfolk, the oldest brick house in America.

190

Harvey. Thoroughgood later settled in the Lynnhaven region, building a rude type of wooden home there. His wife was Sarah Offley, of England.

In 1635 a grant of 5,350 acres of land was received by young Thoroughgood, the grant stating that the lands were given him "at especiall recommendation of him from their Lordships and others of His Ma'ties most Hon'ble Privie Counsell of the State of Virginia and also due for the importation of one hundred and five persons." Among these "imported" persons was Augustine Warner, who settled in Gloucester County and became an ancestor of George Washington, Robert Edward Lee and Queen Elizabeth II of England.

The house, built of sun-baked, straw-bound bricks, has stood for more than three centuries. The house is forty-eight feet long and twenty-one feet wide. It has huge T-shaped end chimneys, a steep roof with dormer windows, fan-shaped steps at both fronts, a hall running straight through the house, and fireplaces in every room. The walls are thick and the pine paneling in the interior is beautiful in its simplicity.

Miss Grace Keeler (whose father, Judge Keeler, bought Old Lynnhaven Farm early in this century) has made an effective and fitting restoration of the house, and has refurnished it in early American antiques very similar to those used by the Thoroughgoods in the seventeenth century. In selecting these items Miss Keeler was guided by Madame Thoroughgood's inventory.

Mr. Roscoe Thrasher is a more recent owner of the Adam Thoroughgood House.

An inscription placed by the Norfolk Branch of the Association for the Preservation of Virginia Antiquities reads:

> The House of Captain Adam Thoroughgood. Built by him between 1636 and 1640. Believed to be the oldest dwelling now standing in Virginia.

PART FIVE

YORKTOWN, YORK AND NEW KENT COUNTIES

THE area of land comprising the counties of York and New Kent, and Yorktown, was first visited by Englishmen in 1607. Orapax, in what is now New Kent, was where John Smith saved his own life by showing the Indians his puzzling pocket-compass. On his first map Smith notes the locale of present-day Yorktown with the word "Kiskiack," because it was the territory inhabited by the Kiskiak Indians.

John Smith, in writing of his explorations in 1607, says: "Fourteene myles Northward from the river Powhatan is the river Pawmunke which is navigable for 60 or 70 myles, but with Catches and small Barkes 30 or 40 myles farther."

According to the authority of Sally Nelson Robins, who was born and raised near the York River, and who was National Historian for the Colonial Dames of America, the land up and down the York River and its tributaries, the Pamunkey and the Mattaponi to the north and the south, was in the very early days called Pamaunke Shire, just as the river was called Pamaunke. (The River was later the Charles, and finally became the York.)

Subsequently this territory is referred to as Yorke, York County, Charles River Shire, and Charles River County. (Of course all Virginia school children are taught Virginia history both in the fourth grade and again in the seventh grade. They, along with other students of Virginia history, learn that in 1634 this territory became officially, by act of the General Assembly, Charles River Shire and, in 1652, York County.)

New Kent became a county in 1654. The people of New Kent were closely associated with their neighbors in York County and Yorktown, and also with those in Charles City County, James City County and Williamsburg. They visited each other, exchanged ideas on architecture, crops and gardening—and discussed fashions, furniture and families.

New Kent was a county of fine homes, and from two of them came the wives of two Presidents of the United States, Martha Custis Washington and Letitia Christian, first wife of John Tyler. From still another New Kent home came an ancestor of the two Harrisons, Presidents of the United States.

Bounded on the north by the Pamunkey River and on the south by the Chickahominy, New Kent got its name from Kent Island in the northern waters of the Chesapeake, so tradition says, and was so named in honor of William Claiborne, who came to Virginia when he was exiled from his home on Kent Island by Lord Baltimore of Maryland.

The broad, fairly level land bordering on the rivers, both in New Kent and York, offered many fine plantation and manor sites; these sites were eagerly taken up by settlers from other areas.

In 1620 a French engineer named Nicholas Martieu (Martiau) came to America to build forts. He changed his nationality by special proclamation of the King of England, and received a grant for sixteen hundred acres of land, which included the land on which Yorktown now stands. His name in the patent was spelled "Martian," though his correspondence showed that he continued to sign his name "Martiau." But he is listed in his official posts as "Martian." Besides being the owner of the land at the Yorktown site and the builder of the fort at Yorke, two miles below the Yorktown site, Nicholas Martian had the distinction of being the earliest ancestor of George Washington, and also of General Thomas Nelson, in America.

It is interesting to note that Martian was the person who in 1635 organized the general opposition to Governor John Harvey, which resulted in Harvey's being thrust from the office of Governor.

On the monument erected to his memory at Yorktown in 1931 by the Huguenot Society of Pennsylvania in cooperation with the National Federation of Huguenot Societies and the Yorktown Sesquicentennial Commission, his name is spelled in the French manner, Nicholas Martiau.

In 1691 Yorktown was established on the Martian land and lots were sold to the settlers by his grandson, Benjamin Read, who was the son of Colonel George Read and Martiau's daughter, Elizabeth.

Yorktown has a beautiful location. It is a tranquil, serene old town and seems to have forgotten that it once was the stage on which a great historic drama was enacted.

CRISS CROSS

IN the Library of Congress in Washington there are scale drawings of Criss Cross, which was built in 1690. A unique 17th-century brick house, this old home possesses some of the austere characteristics of Bacon's Castle, and also of vanished Malvern Hill.

Speaking of central halls in 17th-century Virginia, Thomas Waterman says in

194

Mansions of Virginia, "Altered examples that now possess partitioned-off central halls are Bacon's Castle, The Thoroughgood House and Criss Cross, in New Kent County." Mr. Waterman speaks of the fine-timbered ceiling, and goes on to say "—the ceiling to the porch room has a transverse girder, into which small floor joists are framed all chamfered with low relief mouldings."

Originally entirely of brick, sometime during the 18th century a wooden wing was added. The house is in the shape of a cross—hence the name—and there is a porch chamber; also a door carved with massive crosses. There is some fine paneling in the house. The name Criss Cross is a corruption of the words Christ's Cross. This was the colonial home of the Terrell and the Burton families and was also owned for a time by the Pomfreys.

There remain at Criss Cross some of the trees of the fine grove that at one time surrounded the house. Also remnants of the fine old English boxwood are still to be seen.

Criss Cross is situated about four miles from New Kent Courthouse and twenty-five miles from Richmond.

THE WHITE HOUSE

JOHN CUSTIS, the fourth of his name in America, bought the White House, a mansion on the Pamunkey River in New Kent County, and gave it to his son, Daniel Parke Custis, for Daniel's bride, when Daniel and Martha Dandridge were married in 1749. The young husband died in a few years, leaving Martha a very wealthy young widow with two children, John Parke Custis and Martha Parke Custis.

In May, 1758, General Washington was introduced to Mrs. Custis at Poplar Grove, the home of the Chamberlaynes, on the Pamunkey. They were married at the White House the following January, and made this their first home there. It was from this White House on the Pamunkey that the White House in Washington got its name.

John Parke Custis inherited the White House, but he died in 1781, so the place passed to his son, George Washington Parke Custis, whom George Washington adopted. When George Washington Parke Custis died he left the White House to his grandson, William Henry Fitzhugh Lee, who was General Robert E. Lee's second son. Mrs. Robert E. Lee came to stay with her daughter-in-law, Charlotte Wickham Lee, in 1861. The husbands of both were in the war, and Arlington, the Lee Mansion, across the Potomac from Washington, was too near enemy territory.

In 1862, when McClellan and his army were approaching the vicinity of the White House, on the march up the peninsula, the two Mrs. Lees left to go over into Hanover, to take refuge in the Ruffin home, Marlbourne, but before going Mrs. Robert E. Lee wrote the following note, and left it on the front door: "Northern soldiers who profess to reverence Washington, forbear to desecrate the home of his first married life, the property of his wife, now owned by her descendants."

Criss Cross (short for Christ's Cross), a 17th-century house built in the shape of a cross.

An answer was placed under the note: "Lady, a Northern Officer has protected your property in sight of the enemy, and at the request of your overseer."

Although there was an encampment here, and supplies were stored on the place, General McClellan did protect the White House. However, after McClellan's defeat at Gaines Mill on the 27th of June, 1862, in the confusion that followed, the White House was burned.

HAMPSTEAD

ONE of the handsomest mansions in Virginia is Hampstead, situated on a high bluff overlooking the Pamunkey River in New Kent County. It is on the site of the original house which was the colonial home of the Webb family. Various members of that clan were prominent in the public and social life of the colony. George Webb was Treasurer of Virginia for many years.

The present house was built in 1820 by Colonel Conrad Webb for his bride, the former Miss Osborne, of New England.

In the family burying ground near the house are several gravestones of fine marble. They bear inscriptions in memory of various members of the Webb family.

The mansion is of brick and stands two full stories above an English basement. The chimneys tower high above the roof, and the double cornice is probably more handsomely decorated than any in Virginia. The house has lavish masonry trim, and the identical porticoes at either front are in the elaborate Federal style; each has four imposing columns supporting the second-story roofs.

The large rooms, the fine woodwork, the pine floors of wide boards reputed to have been made from old ship's masts, together with the beautiful spiral staircase, make the interior as fine as any we have found in Virginia.

Surrounding Hampstead are plantings made in colonial times supplemented by more recent plantings. There are original-growth forest trees, fine crêpe myrtles, and one of the largest magnolia trees in the state. Much English box remains in the fine old terraced gardens which were spread out between the house and the river. They were at one time the most elaborate terraced gardens in the state. There are many interesting dependencies at Hampstead.

After the Webb regime, Colonel W. W. Gordon, of the famous Stone Wall Brigade, for many years owned Hampstead and made it his home. Mrs. William J. Wallace is the present owner of this truly elegant Virginia home.

CUMBERLAND FARM

ON the Pamunkey River in New Kent County the 17th-century home of the Littlepage family stands on an eminence overlooking the river. It is called Cumberland Farm, and is now the home of Colonel and Mrs. Benjamin H. Brinton.

The original house was of framed construction, on a basement of brick laid in

Hampstead, in New Kent County, overlooking the Pamunkey River, was built in 1820. In the burying ground here are gravestones of the Webb family, original owners of the plantation.

198

Another view of Hampstead.

Famous spiral stairway at Hampstead.

Drawing room at Hampstead.

Dining room at Hampstead.

English bond. This part of the house is large, and two full stories high, with a handsome two-story pillared portico on the front. Two large two-story wings of brick have been added in recent years, making the mansion very large and imposing. The entrance hall has a fireplace at each end, a medieval feature that is almost unique in Virginia. When the house was restored the original flooring and stairway were retained, but antique paneling from a century-old house was used for the dadoes in the hall.

Recent plantings have been made at Cumberland Farm, and the restoration of the gardens has added to the beauty of the old place.

After the Littlepage ownership the Chamberlaynes and the Fauntleroys owned and occupied Cumberland Farm. In more recent years it was owned by Mr. William Forbes from whom it was purchased by Colonel and Mrs. Brinton.

During the Civil War a large encampment of Federal troops occupied the extensive plain near the house. The Cumberland Landing was in use for many years.

CHESTNUT GROVE

SITUATED on the Pamunkey River, in a fine location, stood Chestnut Grove, home of Col. John Dandridge. Col. Dandridge's daughters spent their childhood and girlhood at Chestnut Grove. Martha was married the first time, to Daniel Parke Custis, a young man of considerable wealth, and went to live at the White House, also on the Pamunkey River. Later, after Martha became a widow, she met George Washington at Poplar Grove, home of the Chamberlaynes, on the Pamunkey River, in New Kent County. They fell in love and were married within six months.

Early in the 19th-century Chestnut Grove was purchased by Colonel R. P. Cook, who made it his home. For some years after his death the house was occupied by Mr. and Mrs. O. M. Chandler; she was Col. Cook's granddaughter. At the time the house was burned in 1926, Chestnut Grove was the property of a great-granddaughter of Col. Cook, Miss Ione Smith.

ELTHAM

THIS palatial Georgian house was built on the site of Matchot, an Indian village. It was situated on the Pamunkey River just opposite West Point. This, considered one of the finest colonial homes in Virginia, was the seat of the distinguished Bassett family.

Burwell Bassett of the fourth generation of Bassetts in America, was born in 1734 and died in 1793. He married Anna Maria Dandridge, daughter of Colonel John Dandridge, and sister of Martha Washington. From Burwell Bassett and his wife descended the two Harrison Presidents of the United States.

The Bassetts and the Washingtons had close social ties. Washington frequently visited Eltham. He was there at the time of the death of his step-son, John Parke

Cumberland Farm, in New Kent County.

Custis, who died at Eltham in November 1781. He had been a soldier at Yorktown.

The central part of the house was three stories high, and the flanking wings two stories.

In later years Eltham was the home of the distinguished Lacy family of New Kent. The mansion was burned in 1875.

PROVIDENCE FORGE

THE name of the old mansion, Providence Forge (on U. S. Route 60), derived from a forge built nearby in 1770. The mansion, of frame construction, erected in 1770-71, was two stories high, with a full basement and a pair of linked chimneys at each end, with five dormers extending across the roof on the front and on the back.

During the Revolution, Tarleton's raiders destroyed the iron works, and Cornwallis occupied Providence Forge mansion. It was here, too, that Lafayette camped in the summer of 1781.

Providence Forge has belonged to several families. For many years it was the home of Major Edward Christian and his heirs. In 1863 it was purchased by Robert G. Farley; then in 1912 Dr. George Potts acquired the estate, making his home there for many years. He was a most remarkable man, was dubbed the "high priest of Masonry," and was still holding office at the advanced age of ninety. After Dr. Potts' death in 1937, the property passed to Dr. Ashton Harwood. He lived there until 1947, when the State Highway Commission, building the four-lane highway between Richmond and Norfolk, decided that the Providence Forge house stood right across the path of the proposed thoroughfare. The mansion accordingly was marked for demolition, but finally Mrs. Virginia Braithwaite Houghwout bought it and had it moved, piece by piece, to Williamsburg, rebuilt it there, redecorated it and furnished it. Now it stands in the restored city in all its original beauty, but bears a new name, Providence Hall.

OTHER HOMES OF NEW KENT COUNTY

THERE were many other important colonial homes in New Kent, some of which have survived. A few of them are:

Poplar Grove, home of the Chamberlaynes, where George Washington met his future wife.

Spring Hill, the plantation of Richard Graves, who had there a famous race course; later a Sherman home, then a Bradley home;

Savage's Farm, the home of the distinguished Major Thomas Massie;

Mount Prospect, or Prospect Hill, a Macon home;

Grove Hill, the home of William Lacy;

Windsor Shades, an Osborne home, later the property of the Christians;

Foster's Castle, home of Bromleys, later, the Gregorys;

Rockahock, near the Chickahominy, a Custis home;

Orapax, a Christian home, later a Turner home;

Dunreath Abbey, a Vaiden home;

Orchard Grove, formerly a Lacy home, then a home of the Vaidens;

The Holmes Farm first belonged to the Holmes family, later to the Watkins family and the Colter family.

CHISCHIACKE
(Old Lee House)

THE tiny old brick house, often called the Lee House, was in early years known as Chischiacke or Kiskiack (spelled about eight ways) and was the very first home of the Lees in America. This substantial, attractive little old house must have been cozy and comfortable back in those early days, with its two huge chimneys, its fireplaces, its dormer windows, gable windows and low-ceilinged, second-story rooms. There was also a small front porch.

It was built by Henry Lee, not a great many years after he came to Virginia, some time after 1633. His patent was for two hundred and fifty acres. Richard Lee, presumably Henry's brother, came to Virginia from Shropshire, England, as did Henry, and in the late 1640's acquired land on the other side of the Rappahannock. He settled there and became the ancestor of many distinguished descendants.

Henry Lee's descendants lived at Chischiacke until the fire of 1915, which destroyed the interior; but the walls were left intact. In 1920 William Warren Harrison Lee, of the ninth generation, sold the old brick house to the Government of the United States. It now stands within the grounds of the Navy Mine Depot at Yorktown.

BELLFIELD

CAPTAIN JOHN WEST, one of the four West brothers who came to Virginia early in the seventeenth century, received a grant of land from the Royal Council "in the right of his son being the first born Christian at Chischiack." That was in 1632, and two thousand acres of the land were on the York River. The place was called Bellfield, and was sold by John West to Edward Digges in 1650. The Wests moved to West Point, and there continued the West tradition of service to the colony.

Edward Digges, son of Sir Dudley Digges, came to Virginia from Chilham, in England. Edward's father was important in the service of King Charles I, and was also a member of the London Company. In 1655 Edward Digges became Governor of Virginia, serving under Cromwell. He is probably best remembered in connection with his attempt to establish the silk industry in Virginia. The old, gnarled mulberry trees scattered through the Yorktown area, as well as those around Williamsburg and Jamestown, are survivors of this experiment.

Edward Digges turned out to be a good governor during his term in office. He is also remembered for his interest in, and development of, the tobacco trade. He had

204

Chischiacke, in Yorktown, was built by Henry Lee in the first half of the 17th century. It is the ancestral Lee home.

a trade-mark (E.D.) for his tobacco, and it always sold well in England, as well as in other countries. The plantation was called The E. D. Plantation, and became Bellfield in the 18th century. Edward Digges, after serving as Governor of Virginia, became Auditor General, and a member of the King's Council.

Ringfield, also on the York, was the next plantation to Bellfield. It was the home of the Rings.

Bellfield must have been quite a fine mansion. Excavations show the foundations were forty-seven by thirty-four feet, with walls twenty-eight inches thick. An inventory listing slaves, furniture, etc., made in 1692, describes the house as having "hall parlor, yellow passage, yellow roome, large roome against ye yellow roome, ye back rooms against ye large room, the red room, the garretts, the back roome, the sellar and the kitching."

The estate remained in the possession of the Digges family until 1787, when it was sold by William Digges, Jr., to William Waller. It was later owned by the Reverend Sarvant Jones.

The house has long since vanished, and the land of Bellfield, as well as the neighboring field, now belong to the United States Government and is part of the Colonial National Historic Park, while Ringfield belongs to the Navy Mine Depot.

SHEILD HOUSE

THE oldest house in Yorktown now belongs to Judge Conway Sheild. Long in the possession of his family, members of which were historically important, the name, Sheild House, is, of course, most appropriate. Just across Nelson Street, a quaint, charming rural road, is York Hall, the Nelson House. The Sheilds and Nelsons are closely connected by intermarriage.

The Sheild House was built in the 1690's by Thomas Sessions. It remained in his family for a few years, then passed through many hands. It was occupied by the Federals at the time of the Civil War, serving as headquarters for General Negley, who was with General McClellan when the latter invaded and occupied parts of the Peninsula, in 1862.

The house is two stories high above a full basement; the second story is lighted by dormer as well as gable windows. There are five dormers on the front. The end chimneys are huge and towering; the gables are clipped; the small-paned windows have outside blinds. All this, with the vine-covered, substantial old brick walls, the small front porch and the hedges with gate posts, combine to make one of the most picturesque homes in all Tidewater Virginia.

The interior is interesting and beautiful, and still has the original woodwork. The front door is remarkably large. There is a marble hearth in one of the rooms. The staircase goes up at the back, being approached through an arch from the large center hall. The paneled doors have H and L hinges.

The Sheild House has been visited by many distinguished people, including at least five Presidents of the United States.

Sheild House, in Yorktown.

Grace Church, in Yorktown. When the British occupied Yorktown during the Revolution, the church was used as a magazine for ammunition, and it was burned by them in 1814, during the War of 1812.

THE OLD CUSTOM HOUSE

AT Main and Read Streets in Yorktown stands the oldest custom house in America. It is a substantial two-story brick building with a hipped roof, a tall thick chimney, and a decorative cornice. There is a belt course around the wall at second floor level. The doors and windows are slightly arched, and there are wooden window blinds and eighteen panes of glass to the window.

In the eighteenth century all ships taking cargo from Virginia to Northern cities or England had to clear through the Yorktown Custom House. Richard Ambler, who married Elizabeth Jaquelin, of Jamestown, was Collector of Ports, and it was he who built the Old Custom House.

Here was a center where news items from abroad, from the north, from ships and reports about pirate attacks were discussed. Many true and many legendary stories which were told first in the Old Custom House, have been repeated for several generations among families living in Virginia's old homes.

The Old Custom House is now the quarters of the Comte de Grasse Chapter, Daughters of the American Revolution.

An inscription on the wall reads:

Early Colonial Custom House
Built 1706
Yorktown
Was Made A Port Of Entry At
General Assembly Of The Colony And Dominion
Of Virginia, Begun At The Capitol In The City
Of Williamsburg The Twenty-Third Day Of October
1705 In The Fourth Year Of The Reign Of Her
MAJESTY QUEEN ANNE
THE COMTE DE GRASSE CHAPTER
The National Society Of The
DAUGHTERS OF THE AMERICAN REVOLUTION INC.
Purchased This Custom House 1924
BOARD OF MANAGEMENT
At The Time Of Purchase
MRS. EMMA LEAKE CHENOWETH, Regent
Mrs. Elizabeth Fox Madison
Mrs. Nannie Cooke Curtis
Mrs. Lula Wade Renforth
Mrs. Nettie Richardson Clements
Mrs. Lillie Hudgins Walthall
Mrs. Margaret Crooks Smith
Restored By
MRS. LETITIA PATE EVANS
Member Of The Comte De Grasse Chapter
1929   1930
Dedicated to Perpetuate
The Memory And Spirit Of The Men and Women
Who Achieved American Independence

The Cole Digges House, in Yorktown, dates from 1705. At the end of the street is the Old Custom House, built in 1706, the oldest custom house in America.

210

COLE DIGGES HOUSE

ON lot number 42 on Main Street in Yorktown, across the way from the Old Custom House, is the story-and-a-half brick Cole Digges House, built in the early American style of architecture. It has a steep, slanting roof, dormer windows, huge chimneys and small-paned windows; a dormer-windowed L extends back from one end. The pine paneling of the high ceilings is most attractive.

The house was built by John Martin in 1705, and sold by him to Cole Digges on January 18, 1713. The lot had previously been owned by John Seaborne, then by Thomas Pate, and later by Joan Lawson.

The Digges family retained possession of the old house until April 19, 1784, when it was sold for 175 pounds to David Jamison (or Jameson) who ten years later sold it at the same price to George Goosley. The latter kept it for five years, when he sold it at a profit of seventy-five pounds to John Southgate. After that the property was inherited by various heirs. In 1925 the house was restored by Mrs. Carroll Paul, of Marquette, Michigan.

Cole Digges's son, Dudley Digges, was born in the Cole Digges House. He was named for his great-grandfather, Sir Dudley Digges, Master of the Rolls in the reign of Charles I. Dudley Digges was prominent in the Revolutionary period. He, with ten others, Thomas Jefferson, Patrick Henry, Peyton Randolph, Benjamin Harrison, Dabney Carr, Edmund Pendleton, Archibald Cary, Richard Bland, Robert Nicholas and Richard Henry Lee, made up the Virginia Committee of Correspondence which first suggested the convening of a representative body to discuss a proposal that the colonies unite in resisting British oppression. The outcome of this suggestion was the first Continental Congress in Philadelphia, in 1774. Dudley Digges later served as Lieutenant Governor of Virginia with Governor Thomas Nelson, Jr. During that time he resided in Williamsburg, and was an associate and close friend of Patrick Henry.

WEST HOUSE

IN 1706 Miles and Emanuel Wills built what is now known as the West House on a lot purchased from the trustees of Yorktown. It is a typical colonial house of frame construction, with center hall, two rooms to the right and two to the left of the hall and corner fireplaces in each room upstairs and down. Thus the two huge towering chimneys serve all eight rooms. The staircase, in the rear of the hall, has a nice balustrade. The paneling, moulding and beading of the interior decorations are typical, but in exquisite taste. The second floor of the house is lighted by gable and dormer windows, and the modillions on the cornice add a decorative touch. The small front porch is in Greek Revival style, so must have been added at a later date.

During the Revolution this old residence was used as quarters by some of the British officers. When the French and Americans were, by General Nelson's orders,

The West House, in Yorktown.

212

firing on the Nelson House to dislodge Cornwallis, who had headquarters there, they fired three cannonballs into the walls of the West House. It stood diagonally across the street from the Nelson House.

Major John R. West, who married Elizabeth Nelson, a granddaughter of General Nelson, bought the property from Mrs. Nicholas, who was Dudley Digges's daughter, in 1821. It was from John R. West that the West House got its name. Later owners were W. H. Sheild and William Nelson, Jr.

Old gnarled mulberry trees grow in front of the West House.

OLD YORKTOWNE HOTEL
(or The Philip Lightfoot House)

THE Philip Lightfoot House, in Yorktown, at one time called the Old Yorktowne Hotel, is of brick with dormer windows, a steep slanting roof and huge end chimneys. The chimneys have breaks and slopes, then higher up, breaks and slopes again, and are in attractive proportion to the gables, the many-paned, arched windows, and the sloping roof with its modillioned cornice. The interior, with mantels and other woodwork, is very attractive. There is a dormered wing extending to the back at right angles to the main building.

Situated directly opposite Grace Church, on the corner of Main and Grace Streets, the Lightfoot House has been a silent witness of all the historic events that have taken place in the old town. Elizabeth Powers bought the lot in 1707, and her sole heir, Joseph Mountfoot, in 1716, sold the house and lot to Philip Lightfoot, the year Elizabeth Powers died. Philip Lightfoot and his wife, Mary Walner, lived here until 1783, when they sold to John Moss of Richmond.

During the residence of the Lightfoots, Yorktown built up, the Revolutionary War was fought, the British Armies, under Cornwallis, arrived, then the French, under Comte de Grasse and Lafayette, and the Colonials under Washington came and besieged the British. Cornwallis's surrender was effected and independence was won.

John Moss built a store on half of the lot, and so for a time possession of the lot was divided, the store was kept by John Moss, of Yorktown, and the house was occupied by Peyton Southall. Later the two halves were joined together again. But in 1885 they were once more divided and have remained so ever since.

At the time of the Civil War the Lightfoot House, considerably enlarged by the addition of a wooden wing, was used as a hospital. Later the building became a hotel.

In the 1930's, under Dr. B. Floyd Flickinger's superintendency, the National Park Service restored the Lightfoot House to its original form and condition. There are several dependencies.

FOUNDATION OF SECRETARY NELSON'S HOUSE

NO treatise about Yorktown, either historical, architectural or devoted to annals of domestic life, would be complete without mention of the foundations of Secretary

The Old Yorktowne Hotel (Philip Lightfoot House) dates from 1710. It served as a hospital during the Civil War.

214

Nelson's house, which now belong to the Association for the Preservation of Virginia Antiquities. These foundations mark the location of one of the early houses of Yorktown, the home of Thomas Nelson, who was Secretary of the Colony of Virginia. He was the son of Thomas Nelson, the immigrant, known as "Scotch Tom." Secretary Nelson was the brother of William Nelson, of the still extant Nelson House (see below), who served as President of the Council and was the father of the famous General Thomas Nelson, Governor of Virginia and Revolutionary patriot.

The foundation walls of Secretary Nelson's House measure forty-five and a half feet in width and fifty-seven and a half feet in length, and are two feet thick. Tradition says it was a more commodious house than the Nelson House, now known as York Hall. Located near the intersection of Main Street and Hampton Road, the fine old home became the first headquarters of Cornwallis in Yorktown. Secretary Nelson was permitted to leave Yorktown under a flag of truce on the eleventh day of October in 1781. This was the beginning of the occupation of Yorktown by the British, and of the strategic siege which soon began and continued until that day of destiny, the 19th of October, 1781.

Early during the siege Secretary Nelson's home and the home which his father, "Scotch Tom," had built nearby and lived in until his death in 1745, were both demolished. Lord Cornwallis now moved his headquarters to the Nelson House.

YORK HALL
(The Nelson House)

AT Main Street and Nelson Street (formerly Pearl Street), in Yorktown, stands York Hall, or the Nelson House, as it was formerly called. This, one of the finest examples of Georgian architecture in Virginia, is a famous shrine, and is visited by thousands every year.

Built of rich red brick embellished with fine masonry trim in white stone, the mansion is three stories high, over a full basement. The third floor is lighted by dormer windows and gable windows. The first and second story windows have twenty-four panes of glass each, and they are surmounted by slight arch forms, with a decorative keystone above each window. A handsome double cornice belts the building at third floor level, following the roof below the dormer windows, and stretching across the walls at the ends of the buildings, below the third story windows. A corresponding cornice follows the gable-ends of the roof, thus forming a triangle of modillioned cornice at each end of the building.

The large, heavy, paneled doors are flanked by magnificent casings and surmounted by rich, broken-arch-with-pineapple door heads. Two enormous chimneys tower high above the roof.

The staircase, in the central hall, is one of the handsomest that we have seen. The mantels, the paneling, the doors and all the woodwork at York Hall are rich and fine.

The grounds of the mansion are enclosed by a tall, thick brick wall, and the

York Hall (the Nelson House), in Yorktown, was the home of General Thomas Nelson of Revolutionary fame.

216

The garden of York Hall.

217

Dining room at York Hall.

218

garden is very extensive. It is laid out in formal design, and profusely planted with box, various shrubs, trees, and many fine flowers.

The Nelson House was built about 1740, by William Nelson, President of the Council. Some say that "Scotch Tom," his father, built it. He lived until 1745, and owned the land on which this house was built; but most authorities agree that William Nelson was the builder. No doubt the father, an old gentleman living very nearby, was consulted, and probably watched the progress of the work daily. Tradition says that William Nelson brought his infant son, Thomas (the future General) to the building and guiding his hand, helped him lay a brick in the wall of the new mansion which was to be his own future home.

During the siege of Yorktown the Nelson House was the second headquarters of General Cornwallis. General Nelson's family had been moved to Hanover County for safety, but General Nelson, General of the Virginia Militia, was in Yorktown with Washington and Lafayette. Noticing that the gunners, in trying to dislodge Cornwallis, avoided directly hitting the Nelson House, General Nelson at once offered a reward to the cannoneer in Lafayette's battery who made the first direct hit. Soon several cannon balls crashed through the walls of the fine old house. Today two of them are still imbedded in the wall to the east. General Nelson spent his entire fortune for the cause of his country.

General Thomas Nelson was educated in England. He married Miss Grymes, and the couple were very prominent in social and official life in Virginia. Of their eleven children, seven married into the Page family, and many distinguished descendants live in Virginia today.

Six generations of Nelsons, among whom are General Thomas Nelson, his Uncle Thomas Nelson, his father William Nelson, and his grandfather Thomas Nelson ("Scotch Tom"), lie buried in the church yard at Grace Church in Yorktown.

Soon after the turn of the present century Mr. Joseph Bryan of Richmond bought the Nelson House from the Nelson family. Later it was bought by Captain George Preston Blow, and today it is the home of his son, Mr. George Blow and Mrs. Blow and their family.

THE MOORE HOUSE

IN 1631 Sir John Harvey received a grant of land on the York River a little below the present site of Yorktown. He called the place Yorke. Here later developed what was called York Village, or Churchfield, where the old York Church stood, and where the county seat for York County was located until almost the end of the 17th century.

Temple Farm was a part of this Harvey grant, and was later owned by George Ludlow. His land joined the tract belonging to Nicholas Martian (Martiau) (see above). Ludlow became prominent in the colony, was a member of the Council, and was on friendly terms with his neighbors, Henry Lee, the West family, Captain Felgate and others.

Col. Thomas Ludlow, a nephew of George, was the next owner of the land on

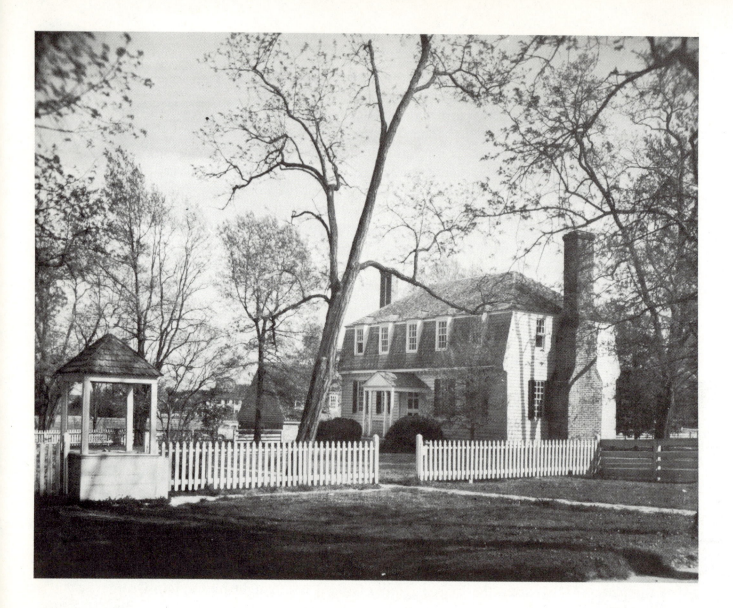

The Moore House, Yorktown, in which the preliminary negotiations for the surrender of Cornwallis were held.

Dining room in the Moore House.

Parlor in the Moore House. In this room, on October 18, 1781, the terms of capitulation were arranged for the surrender which was finally to establish the independence of the United States.

which later the Moore House was built. Thomas's widow married the Reverend Peter Temple, from whom the name Temple Farm was derived. Lawrence Smith purchased the property from the Temples, and his two sons, John and Lawrence, were the next owners. Lawrence II's son, Robert, inherited the property and sold it to Augustine Moore, husband of his sister Lucy. It was Moore who built the house which bears his name.

Legend says General Spotswood was connected with the Temple Farm, and that his tomb was there—that Moore was the husband of Spotswood's daughter, Katherine —but this legend has in greatest part been conclusively proved to be without foundation in fact.

The Moore House is of frame construction, two stories high, with a hipped roof and clipped dormers in the second story. The windows of the first floor have eighteen panes to the window, and window blinds. The chimneys are heavy, graduated and T-shaped. They tower high over the roof. The walls of the second floor, front and rear, slant back slightly from the second floor level to the roof, making necessary dormer windows, and giving a semi-gambreled-roof effect. There is a slightly over-hanging effect at the second floor level, where the slanting part of the second-floor wall joins the straight wall of the lower story. This overhang is embellished with a decorative cornice. The front porch is small and rather formal, and is approached by high steps. The house has a full basement. The interior of the Moore House is attractive, and has fine woodwork. The central hall gives access to all first floor rooms.

The restoration of this fine old colonial building was made in the nineteen thirties, soon after the sesquicentennial at Yorktown in 1931, which was attended by more than two hundred thousand people, a large percentage of whom visited the historic old house. At that time it was a more or less mongrel conglomeration of mended, added-to and rebuilt sections; it had been hastily "fixed-up" for the celebration of the Yorktown Centennial in 1881, the idea then being just to repair the serious damage the house had suffered during the Civil War. But there had been no thought of a complete restoration.

Mr. John D. Rockefeller, Jr., however, bought the historic house one year previous to the sesquicentennial of 1931, and presented it to the United States Government, so it could become a part of the Colonial National Historic Park. When the treasury of the sesquicentennial committee showed a substantial balance, it was decided to make a proper restoration of the structure. The wings were removed, a thorough study was made, and a beautiful and perfect restoration effected.

The chief historic significance of the Moore House, which makes it a national shrine, consists in the fact that within the walls of this building, the home of Augustine and Lucy Moore, on October 18, 1781, commissioners met to draft the Articles of Capitulation for the British army. They met, and after heated discussions, completed their work in the northwest room on the first floor. Representing Lord Cornwallis, the British commander, were Lieutenant-Colonel Thomas Dundas and Major Alexander Ross, while General Washington and Count Rochambeau, the latter commanding the French forces, were represented by Lieutenant-Colonel John Laurent and Colonel Vicomte de Noailles. The actual Articles of Capitulation were signed by the commanders of the opposed forces on October 19th. The surrender took place the afternoon of the 19th.

This document, which set forth the terms and conditions for the surrender of the British forces at Yorktown, is one of the most important in our entire history. The Declaration of Independence embodied a passionate hope, desire and determination; the Capitulation at Yorktown transformed this hope, desire and determination into historic fact.

The United States of America was now a free and independent country!

BIBLIOGRAPHY

Virginia, A Guide to the Old Dominion. Compiled by Workers of the Writers' Program of the Work Projects Administration in the State of Virginia. New York, 1940. Oxford University Press.

Andrews, Matthew Page. *Virginia, The Old Dominion.* Richmond, 1949. The Dietz Press.

Brock, Henry Irving. *Colonial Churches in Virginia.* Richmond, 1930. The Dale Press.

Burton, Right Reverend L. W. *Annals of Henrico Parish.* Richmond, 1904. Published by The Trustees of St. John's Church.

Byrd, William, of Westover. *Another Secret Diary.* Edited by Maude Woodfin, decoded by Marion Tingling. Richmond, 1942. The Dietz Press.

Byrd, William, of Westover. *Secret Diary.* Edited by Louis Wright and Marion Tingling. Richmond, 1941. The Dietz Press.

Chamberlayne, C. G. *The Vestry Book of Petsworth Parish, Gloucester County, Virginia.* 1677-1793. Transcribed, Annotated and Indexed by C. G. Chamberlayne. Richmond, 1933. The Library Board.

Chandler, J. A. C. *Makers of Virginia History.* New York, 1904. Published by Silver Burdett and Company.

Chandler, Joseph Everett. *The Colonial Architecture of Maryland, Pennsylvania and Virginia.* Boston, 1892. Bates, Kimball & Guild.

Christian, Frances Archer & Massie, Susanne Williams, Editors. *Homes and Gardens in Old Virginia.* Revised Edition. Richmond, 1950. Garrett and Massie, Inc.

Coffin, Lewis A., Jr. & Holden, Arthur C. *Brick Architecture of the Colonial Period in Maryland & Virginia.* New York, 1919. Architectural Book Publishing Company, Inc.

Colonial Churches of Virginia. Richmond, 1908. The Southern Churchman Company.

Cooke, John Esten. *Virginia, A Story of the People.* Cambridge, Mass., 1883. Published by The Riverside Press.

Cox, Edwin P. *A Brief Outline of Some Salient Facts Relative to the History of Chesterfield County, Virginia.* Chesterfield Court House, 1936. Published by the Home Demonstration Club Advisory Board.

Crozier, William Armstrong. *Virginia Heraldica, Being a Register of Virginia Gentry Entitled to Court Armor, with Genealogical Notes of the Families.* New York, 1909. The Genealogical Society.

Davis, Deering. *Annapolis Houses, 1700-1775.* 1947. Architectural Book Publishing Company, Inc.

Davis, Deering, with Dorsey, Stephen P. and Hall, Ralph Cole. Special Article by Nancy McClelland. *Alexandria Houses.* 1946. Architectural Book Publishing Company, Inc.

Davis, Deering with Dorsey, Stephen P. and Hall, Ralph Cole. *Georgetown Houses of the Federal Period, Washington, D. C. 1780-1830.* 1944. Architectural Book Publishing Company, Inc.

Dawson, Warrington. *Les Français Morts Pour L'Indépendence Américaine de Septembre 1781 à Août 1782 à la Reconstruction Historique de Williamsburg Bose des Armées de Rochambeau en Virginie.* Paris, 1931. Editions de L'Oeuvre Latine.

Department of Agriculture and Immigration of the State of Virginia, George W. Koiner, Commissioner. *A Handbook of Virginia.* Richmond, 1909. Everett Waddey Company, Printers.

Dodson, E. Griffith. *The Capitol at Richmond.* Richmond, 1938. Published by Author.

Dowdey, Clifford. *The Land They Fought For.* Garden City, 1955. Published by Doubleday and Company.

Eberlein, Harold Donaldson. *The Architecture of Colonial America.* Boston, 1915. Little, Brown & Company.

Elliott, Charles Wyllys. *The Book of American Interiors.* Boston, 1876. James R. Osgood & Company.

Forman, Henry Chandlee. *The Architecture of the Old South, The Medieval Style, 1585-1850.* Cambridge, Mass., 1948. Harvard University Press.

Forman, Henry Chandlee. *Jamestown and St. Mary's, Buried Cities of Romance.* Baltimore, 1938. The Johns Hopkins Press.

Frary, I. T. *Early American Doorways.* Richmond, 1937. Garrett and Massie.

Frary, I. T. *Thomas Jefferson, Architect and Builder,* Third Edition. Richmond, 1950. Garrett and Massie.

Freeman, Douglas Southall. *George Washington.* New York and London, 1948. Charles Scribner's Sons.

Freeman, Douglas Southall. *R. E. Lee.* New York and London, 1934. Charles Scribner's Sons.

French, Leigh, Jr. *Colonial Interiors.* New York, 1923. William Helburn, Inc.

Gibbs, James. *Rules for Drawing the Several Parts of Architecture.* London, 1732. Printed by Bowyer for the Author.

Glasgow, Ellen Anderson Gohlson. *The Freeman and Other Poems.* New York, 1902. Published by Doubleday Page and Company.

Gloucester County, Virginia. *Educational Survey Report.* Richmond, 1928. State Board of Education.

Goodwyn, Retherfoord. *A Brief History of and Guide to Jamestown, Williamsburg and Yorktown.* Richmond, 1930. Published by Cottrell and Cooke.

Grant, Walter E., Chairman Board of Supervisors. *Henrico County, Virginia*. Richmond, 1893. Published by Whittet & Shepperson.

Gwathmey, John H. *Historical Register of Virginians in the Revolution, Soldiers, Sailors, Marines, 1775-1783*. Richmond, 1938. The Dietz Press.

Gwathmey, John H. *Legends of Virginia Courthouses*. Richmond, 1933. The Dietz Press.

Gwathmey, John H. *Legends of Virginia Lawyers*. Richmond, 1934. The Dietz Press.

Gwathmey, John H. *Twelve Virginia Counties*. Richmond, 1937. The Dietz Press.

Hamlin, Talbot. *Greek Revival Architecture in America*. London, New York, Toronto, 1944. Oxford University Press.

Hardesty's Historical and Geographical Encyclopedia. Special Virginia Edition. New York, Richmond, Chicago, Toledo, 1885. Published by same.

Hergesheimer, Joseph. *Balisand*. New York, 1924. Alfred A. Knopf.

Historic American Buildings Survey. Washington, 1941. National Park Service.

Historical Records Survey and Work Projects Administration. Inventory of County Archives of Virginia, Prince George County, Virginia Conservation Commission. Richmond, 1941. Published by the Historical Records Survey of Virginia.

Howe, Henry. *Historical Collections of Virginia*. Charleston, S. C., 1849. Published by W. R. Babcock.

Howells, John Mead. *Lost Examples of Colonial Architecture*. New York, 1931. William Helburn, Inc.

Huntley, Elizabeth Valentine. *Peninsula Pilgrimage*. Richmond, 1941. The Press of Whittet & Shepperson.

Jackson, Joseph. *American Colonial Architecture*. Philadelphia, 1924. David McKay Company.

Jett, Dora Chinn. *In Tidewater Virginia*. Richmond, 1924. Published by Whittet and Shepperson.

Johnston, Frances Benjamin and Waterman, Thomas Tileston. *The Early Architecture of North Carolina*. Chapel Hill, 1941-1947. University of North Carolina Press.

Johnston, George Ben, M.D. *Some Medical Men of Mark from Virginia*. Richmond, 1905. Reprinted from the *Old Dominion Journal of Medicine and Surgery*.

Joyner, Maude Atkins. *Story of Historic Sites and People of Chesterfield County, Virginia*. Chester, 1950. Privately printed by Home Demonstration Club of Chester.

Kellam, Sadie Scottand and Kellam, Hope. *Old Houses in Princess Anne, Virginia*. Portsmouth, 1931. Printed by Printcraft Press, Inc.

Kibler, J. Luther. *Colonial Virginia Shrines*. Richmond, 1936. Published by Garrett and Massie, Inc.

Kibler, J. Luther. *The Cradle of the Nation*. Richmond, 1931. Published by Garrett and Massie, Inc.

Kibler, J. Luther. *Historic Virginia Landmarks*. Richmond, 1929. Published by Garrett and Massie, Inc.

Kocher, A. Lawrence and Dearstyne, Howard. *Shadows in Silver*. New York, 1951. Published by Charles Scribner's Sons.

Lancaster, Robert A., Jr. *Historic Virginia Homes and Churches*. Philadelphia and London, 1915. J. B. Lippincott Company.

Land, Robert Hunt. *Henrico and Its College*. Reprinted from William and Mary College Quarterly, Volume 18, Number 4, October, 1938.

Langley, B. *City and Country Builder's and Workman's Treasury of Designs*. London, 1745. Published by S. Harding.

Lee, Mrs. Marguerite du Pont. *Virginia Ghosts and Others*. Richmond, 1932. The William Byrd Press, Inc.

Legg, Carrie Mason. Unpublished Manuscript. Elmington.

Library of Congress. *Colonial Churches in the Original Colony of Virginia*. Washington, D. C. U. S. Government Printing Office.

Lutz, Francis Earle. *Chesterfield, an Old Virginia County*. Richmond, 1954. Published by the William Byrd Press, Inc.

Mann, Etta Donnan. *Four Years in the Governor's Mansion of Virginia*. Richmond, 1937. Published by The Dietz Press.

Mason, George Carrington, Transcriber and Editor. *Colonial Vestry Book of Lynnhaven Parish, Princess Anne County, Virginia. 1723-1786*. Newport News, Virginia, 1949. Published by Editor.

Mason, Polly Cary. *Records of Colonial Gloucester County, Virginia*, Volume I. Compiled by Polly Cary Mason. Newport News, Virginia, 1946. Mrs. George C. Mason. Post Office Box 720.

Massie, Susanne Williams and Christian, Frances Archer, Editors. *Homes and Gardens of Virginia*. With an Introduction by Douglas S. Freeman. Richmond, 1931. Garrett and Massie, Inc.

Maxwell, William. *The Virginia Historical Register and Literary Advisor*. Richmond, 1848. Published by McFarland and Ferguson.

Meade, William, bp. 1789-1862. *Old Churches, Ministers and Families of Virginia*. Philadelphia, 1872. J. B. Lippincott & Company. Reprinted, Lippincott, 1931. Two volumes with Wise Index. First published 1857. Second edition 1861.

Moore, Virginia. *Virginia Is a State of Mind*. New York, 1942. E. P. Dutton and Company, Inc.

Mumford, Lewis. *The South in Architecture*. New York, 1941. Harcourt, Brace & Company.

Nixon, Old. *History of Virginia*. London, 1708. Printed for John Nicholson at The King's Arms in Little Britain.

Nutting, Wallace. *Virginia Beautiful*. Framingham, Massachusetts, 1930. Old America Company.

O'Neill, John P., Compiler and Editor. *Historic American Buildings Survey*. Washington, 1938. Printed by the United States Government Printing Office.

Osborne, J. A. *Williamsburg in Colonial Times*. Richmond, 1930. Dietz Printing Co.

Paxton, Annabel. *Washington Doorways*. Richmond, 1940. The Dietz Press.

Peckard, Dr. P. *Life of Nicholas Ferrar*. London, 1852.

Poe, Edgar Allan. *The Poetical Works*. New York, 1859. Published by Redfield.

Rawson, Marion Nicholl. *Sing, Old House*. New York, 1934. E. P. Dutton & Company, Inc.

Rhodes, Mary Lou. *Landmarks of Richmond*. Richmond, 1938. Published by Garrett and Massie.

Robins, Sally Nelson. *Love Stories of Famous Virginians*. Richmond, 1923. Published by the Dietz Printing Co.

Robinson, Ethel Fay, and Robinson, Thomas P. *Houses in America*. New York, 1936. The Viking Press.

Rothery, Agnes. *Houses Virginians Have Loved*. New York, 1954. Rinehart Company, Inc.

Rothery, Agnes. *New Roads in Old Virginia*. Revised Edition. Boston and New York, 1937. Houghton Mifflin Company.

Rothery, Agnes. *Virginia the New Dominion*. New York, London, 1940. D. Appleton-Century Company.

Sale, Edith Tunis. *Boxwood and Terraced Gardens of Virginia*. Richmond, 1925. The William Byrd Press, Inc.

Sale, Edith Tunis. *Colonial Interiors, Second Series*. New York, 1930. William Helburn, Inc.

Sale, Edith Tunis, Editor. *Historic Gardens of Virginia*. Compiled by the James River Garden Club Committee; Edith Tunis Sale, Laura C. Martin Wheelwright, Juanita Massie Patterson, Lila L. Williams, Caroline Coleman Duke. Foreword by Mary Johnston. Richmond, 1925. The William Byrd Press, Inc.

Sale, Mrs. Edith Dabney (Tunis). *Interiors of Virginia Houses of Colonial Times*. Richmond, 1927. The William Byrd Press, Inc.

Sale, Edith Tunis. *Manors of Virginia in Colonial Times*. Philadelphia and London, 1909. J. B. Lippincott Company.

Scott, Mary Wingfield, *Houses of Old Richmond*. Richmond, 1941. Valentine Museum.

Scott, Mary Wingfield. *Old Richmond Neighborhoods*. Richmond, 1950. Published by the author.

Smith, Mrs. Sydney. *Old Yorktown and Its History*. Yorktown, 1920. Published by the Author.

Society of Colonial Dames of America in the State of Virginia. List of Members. Richmond, 1913. Mitchell and Hotchkiss.

Spencer, F. Blair. *Jamestown, Williamsburg and Yorktown*. Published by the Author 1907. Privately Printed.

Squires, W. H. T. *An Anthology of Virginia and Virginians*. A Volume of Manuscripts Presented to the State Library of Virginia.

Squires, W. H. T. *The Days of Yester-Year in Colony and Commonwealth*. Portsmouth, Virginia, 1928. Printcraft Press, Inc.

Squires, W. H. T. *Through Centuries Three*. A Short History of the People of Virginia. Portsmouth, Virginia, 1929. Printcraft Press, Inc.

Stanard, Mary Newton. *Colonial Virginia, Its People and Customs*. Philadelphia and London, 1917. J. B. Lippincott Company.

Stanard, Mary Newton. *Richmond, Its People and Its Story*. Philadelphia and London, 1923. Published by J. B. Lippincott Company.

Stanard, Mary Newton. *The Story of Virginia's First Century*. Philadelphia and London, 1928. J. B. Lippincott Company.

Stanard, W. G. *The Capitol of Virginia and the Confederate States*. Richmond, 1894. Published by James E. Goode.

Stanard, W. G. *Some Emigrants to Virginia*. Richmond, 1911. Published by The Bell Book and Stationery Company.

Stanard, William G. and Stanard, Mary Newton. *The Colonial Virginia Register*. Albany, 1902. Joel Munsell's Sons, Publishers.

Stark, Marion L. *The First Plantation; A History of Hampton and Elizabeth City County, Virginia*. Hampton, 1936. Published by Houston Printing and Publishing House.

Stevens, John Austin. *Yorktown Centennial Handbook*. New York, 1881. Published by C. R. Coffin & Rogers.

Stevens, William Oliver. *Old Williamsburg and Her Neighbors.* New York, 1939. Published by Dodd Mead and Company.

Sturgis, Russell. *How to Judge Architecture.* New York, 1903. Baker and Taylor.

Tate, Leland B. *The Virginia Guide, The Land of the Life Worth Living.* A Manual of Information About Virginia. Lebanon, Virginia, 1929. Leland B. Tate.

Tuthill, William B. *Interiors and Interior Details.* New York, 1882. William T. Comstock, Architectural Publisher.

Tyler, Lyon Gardiner. *History of Virginia.* Chicago and New York, 1924. The American Historical Society.

Verrill, A. Hyatt. *Romantic and Historic Virginia.* New York, 1935. Dodd Mead & Company.

Virginia Highway Historical Markers. Strasburg, Virginia, 1930. Shenandoah Publishing House, Inc.

Wallis, Frank E. *How to Know Architecture.* New York, 1910; 1914. Harper & Brothers, Publishers.

Waterman, Thomas Tileston. *The Dwellings of Colonial America.* Chapel Hill, 1950. The University of North Carolina Press.

Waterman, Thomas Tileston. *The Mansions of Virginia, 1706-1776.* Chapel Hill. 1945. The University of North Carolina Press.

Waterman, Thomas Tileston. *Thomas Jefferson, His Early Works in Architecture.* August 1943 number of *Gazette des Beaux-Arts.*

Waterman, Thomas Tileston and Barrows, John A. *Domestic Colonial Architecture of Tidewater Virginia.* New York-London, 1932. Charles Scribner's Sons.

White, Benjamin Day. *Gleanings in the History of Princess Anne County.* 1924. Privately printed by the Author.

Williams, Henry Lionel and Williams, Ottalie K. *Old American Houses and How to Restore Them.* Garden City, New York, 1946. Doubleday & Company, Inc.

Wilstach, Paul. *Tidewater Virginia.* Indianapolis, 1929. The Bobbs-Merrill Company.

Writers' Project. *A Guide to Prince George and Hopewell.* Hopewell, 1939. The Board of Supervisors of Prince George County, The City Council of Hopewell and the Hopewell Chamber of Commerce.

PERIODICALS

Calendar of Virginia State Papers.
Henings Statues of Virginia.
Lower Norfolk County Virginia Antiquary.
Tyler's Historical and Genealogical Quarterly.
Virginia Historical Register.
Virginia Magazine of History and Biography.
William and Mary Quarterly Historical Magazine—First Series.
William and Mary Quarterly Historical Magazine—Second Series.

CURRENT PUBLICATIONS

Commonwealth Magazine.
Virginia and the Virginia County.

NEWSPAPERS

Baltimore Sun.
New York Times.
Richmond News Leader.
Richmond Times Dispatch.